Mrs Miles's Diary

The Wartime Journal of a Housewife on the Home Front

Constance Miles

Edited by S. V. Partington

SIMON & SCHUSTER

London · New York · Sydney · Toronto · New Delhi

A CBS COMPANY

First published in Great Britain by Simon & Schuster UK Ltd, 2013
A CBS COMPANY
In association with Imperial War Museums

1 3 5 7 9 10 8 6 4 2

Simon & Schuster UK Ltd
1st Floor
222 Gray's Inn Road
London WC1X 8HB

www.simonandschuster.co.uk

Simon & Schuster Australia, Sydney
Simon & Schuster India, New Delhi

A CIP catalogue record for this book
is available from the British Library

ISBN: 978-1-47112-558-4
ebook ISBN: 978-1-47112-559-1

Typeset by M Rules
Printed and bound by CPI Group (UK) Ltd, Croydon, CR0 4YY

Editor's Note

Constance Miles wrote her diary as a series of journals, eleven in all, each of which covered three or four months of the thirty-seven for which she kept a record. She had her own typewriter but, no doubt for the sake of speed, she wrote mostly in longhand, sending each journal out to be typed up in the village and later bound. Her handwriting was not easy to read, and the original typescript includes a number of mistranscriptions which she subsequently crossed through and amended in pen. Some she misssed: her friend Bey Hyde, for example, is spelled 'Bay' throughout at least one of the later journals, and Eudo Andrews appears several times as Endo. The niece of old Mr Stevens is sometimes called Miss Stevens and sometimes Miss Scott. These, together with a couple of geographical errors and some muddled dates, have been corrected for this edition rather than reproduced verbatim.

For much of the diary she referred to people by their initials. Thus her friends Bey and Barbara and her son Basil all appear at various times as 'B', and 'Mrs R' can be either Mrs Rapson or Mrs Rayne. As a general rule, where the person is known from the context I have named them in full to avoid confusion; or their identity, if less certain, has been suggested in footnotes.

In some cases, however, it has not been possible to establish who the intial stands for.

Forty pages of the original diary are missing, and what happened to them is not known. The typed pages are numbered in pencil, and page 535, which concludes the entry for 18 May 1940, belongs to the journal labelled by Connie '3A: 3 March – 20 May 1940', while page 536 continues with the entry for 1 July and is marked, in type, in the top right-hand corner 'B41'. We know that at one point she sent the journals to her stepmother in Lumsden, Aberdeenshire, for safekeeping: it may be that these particular pages were lost in transit.

The full diary runs to more than 1,800 pages of typescript and falls not far short of half a million words, which meant that far more material had to be cut than could possibly be included in this book. Much of what Connie recorded, however, consisted of newspaper articles or extracts from other accounts published during the course of the war. For copyright as well as editorial reasons it was a straightforward decision to exclude most of these and concentrate on her own words and impressions, allowing her wonderful and distinctive voice to shine through.

However much we know about the Second World War, there is no substitute for reading about it in the words of those who lived through it. I live not far from Connie's home village and know the district she writes about well, yet I Iearned a great deal from her diaries that was new to me, not only about the war on her Surrey doorstep but in its wider context.

I am immensely grateful to Mary Wetherell, daughter of Connie's younger son Basil, for access to her family photographs and to some of her family papers, including a memoir by Connie's sister Mildred of her mother (Connie's stepmother) and another about Mildred herself, along with some of Basil's own wartime correspondence. Most helpful of all were the family memoirs that Connie wrote for her sons, which provided invaluable insight into her husband, Elystan (Robin) and into the Miles family, whose history is less in the public domain than that of Connie's father William Robertson Nicoll, but is no less interesting.

Spending several months in Connie's company through her diary, it is impossible not to feel that I have got to know her. I only wish I could have met her, in order to have got to know this amazing woman better.

Contents

Introduction

The small Surrey village of Shere nestles comfortably under the shoulder of the North Downs, midway between the towns of Guildford and Dorking. Nearby are the well-known beauty spots of Newlands Corner, where in 1926 Agatha Christie's car was found abandoned, sparking a week-long police hunt for the missing writer, and the Silent Pool, where legend has it a woodcutter's daughter once drew the attention of the future King John.

To the west is the neighbouring village of Albury with its red-brick barley-twist chimneys, where the seventeenth-century diarist John Evelyn laid out the grounds and gardens of Albury Park. Eastward lie Gomshall and Abinger Hammer, where in 1909 the landmark clock on which Jack the Blacksmith strikes the hours was erected to commemorate the ancient iron industry of the Weald. South of Shere is Peaslake, and beyond that the heather and pines of the Surrey Hills; a district which, until the railways brought the Victorians to colonise its secluded slopes and valleys, was once a wild and lawless place, the haunt of smugglers and thieves.

Shere itself sits prettily on the Tillingbourne river, its main street still lined with shops, its houses an eclectic mix of old half-timbered cottages and newer, more substantial stone-fronted villas. It seems an unlikely setting for a Second World War journal, let alone one which so vividly captures the daily struggles and hardships of living through the war years as does the diary of Constance Miles.

When we think today of the home front in wartime Britain, we tend to call to mind images of bombed-out buildings in our major cities – London, Coventry, Glasgow, Swansea – or of stoical crowds sheltering in tube stations. But what Constance Miles (known to her family and friends throughout her life as Connie) does so powerfully in the journal she kept between August 1939 and April 1943 is to show us that even in this relatively rural corner of the prosperous south-east, the impact of the war on ordinary people going about their daily lives could be both relentless and devastating.

In any event, Shere was not so remote from the war as one might suppose. Surrey had long been designated a reception area for evacuees from London, and by the end of 1940 the population of the parish had effectively doubled, stretching both the ability of the village and its surrounding farms to accommodate the influx and the ability of its inhabitants to cope. Not only children but entire offices and even government departments were relocated to the countryside; and later in the war, once the air raids had begun in earnest, many of those whose London homes had been destroyed or who were fleeing the bombardment of the south coast ports sought refuge in Surrey's towns and villages.

Not that Surrey was safe from air attack, either. It lay beneath the flight path of the Luftwaffe raids on London, and not infrequently, random bombs fell, jettisoned by aircraft seeking to lighten their load and make their escape. Between the end of August and the end of November 1940, Connie records a long succession of nights disturbed by the constant drone of hundreds of planes overhead, and by the sound of detonations too close for comfort.

On the night of Sunday 8 December, several incendiary bombs landed on the village, and Connie remarks on the many small fires that resulted. One fell on the family home of her daily help, whose account is both graphic and grimly comic: 'Went through the roof, quite a small 'ole, slanted across to James's bedroom, then made a bigger 'ole and ... went through the scullery below.'

Not all the bombs dropped on Surrey were incidental, although Connie quotes a German airman whose plane was brought down over Dorking in September 1940 as saying, 'we had no intention of bombing Dorking. We did not know where we were.' From 10 July until 31 October the Battle of Britain was fought in the skies above the south-east, as the Luftwaffe sought to disable the RAF. Airfields at Kenley and Croydon in the east of the county were targets, the latter being bombed on 15 August by planes which had been aiming for the former, with sixty-two civilian deaths. The Hawker Hurricane, the most successful RAF fighter aircraft of the war, was manufactured in Kingston upon Thames, then still very much part of Surrey, and assembled in the Hawker sheds at Brooklands, Weybridge. Wellington bombers were also designed and built at the Vickers Armstrong works at Brooklands, and on 4 September, after the Luftwaffe turned their attentions from airfields to aircraft factories, eighty-three people were killed and 419 injured in a raid on the Brooklands complex – the worst single incident of the Battle of Britain up to that time.

Between June and October 1944, some 9,500 V-1 flying bombs – the infamous doodlebugs – fell on London and south-east England, before their launch sites in France and Belgium were destroyed. In total, wartime casualties in Surrey were second only to those in Kent among the southern counties, and more than double those of Sussex or Essex.*

Troops were stationed all over the county. The army town of Aldershot lay on the other side of Guildford, just inside the Hampshire border, and at different times both Canadian and British soldiers were billeted at Netley Park, across the A25 from Shere. In the build-up to D-Day, thousands more Canadian troops were stationed in camps on the North Downs and on the Surrey commons, including Albury Heath, where General Montgomery addressed them before the Normandy invasion. Also in preparation for D-Day, the Dennis vehicle works at Guildford, six miles from Shere, manufactured Churchill tanks.

Closer to home, the GHQ Stop Line, the main line of defence against a German land invasion, ran along the escarpment directly above the village, and the surrounding countryside positively bristled with defensive installations. Surrey stood squarely between the south coast and London, and in the summer of 1940, following the withdrawal of British forces from Dunkirk and the Fall of France, with Germany in full control of the continental Channel ports, an array of tank traps and machine-gun emplacements were built along rivers and railway embankments, at crossings and bridges and overlooking the junctions of lanes and tracks: wherever they might impede or prevent the passage of German forces. The Surrey Defences Survey, begun in 1989, estimates that there are still some 2,000 such fortifications, the most visible being pillboxes and dragons' teeth, remaining in the county's woods and fields today.

On 15 July, having been out to look at one concrete

* Surrey County Council Special War Executive Report, 1945.

emplacement under construction, Connie writes, 'We are trying to take in that we are in a village where a line of defence (is it for London?) nearly cuts into us', commenting also that 'We shall, I suppose, look back, if we are spared, on this time with amazement.'

Connie decided to keep her diary before the war had fully begun, recording her opening entry on 24 August 1939, eight days before Germany invaded Poland and ten days before Britain and France declared war on 3 September. She broke off writing it in April 1941, resuming it in December of that year and maintaining it until 15 April 1943, when she gave it up for the second and final time.

In the covering note she sent to the Imperial War Museum in 1947, she describes herself both as a housewife and a professional journalist. She was a published author, who had earned enough from her writing to put her two sons, Harry and Basil, through public school. She wrote children's books under the pseudonym Marjory Royce, and, in her own name, articles and book reviews for a number of magazines. With her younger brother, Maurice, she wrote a novel, *Lord Richard in the Pantry*, which was later adapted as a stage play and was made into a film in 1930.

Writing was in her blood. She was born Isa Constance Nicoll in 1881 in Kelso, Scotland, although her family moved to Hampstead in London when she was three years old. Her father was William Robertson Nicoll, a Scottish churchman and noted founder of two successful periodicals: the nonconformist *British Weekly* and *The Bookman*, a literary magazine whose contributors under his editorship included such luminaries as W. B. Yeats, Edward Thomas, G. K. Chesterton, Arthur Ransome and Hillaire Belloc. He was literary advisor to the publishers

Hodder and Stoughton and knew many of their authors personally, amongst them Winston Churchill and J. M. Barrie. A staunch supporter of the Liberal party whose journalistic skills were particularly valued by Lloyd George, he was knighted in 1909 and made a Companion of Honour in 1921.

Her mother Isa (Isabel) Dunlop, whom her father adored, loved music, especially Beethoven, and was an excellent pianist. Connie was thirteen when Isa died and fifteen when her father remarried, after two years of what his friends described as somewhat chaotic domestic arrangements. His second wife was Catherine Pollard (known as Katie, even after she became Lady Catherine Nicoll), a talented artist and illustrator whose work was published in magazines and books. Connie's half-sister Mildred was born in 1898. Despite the sixteen years between them, she and Mildred were always close, as indeed she was to her stepmother, writing to her throughout her life and always calling her 'Mother'. It was in this heady atmosphere, in which literature and politics were always under discussion, that Connie grew up. While she attended schools in Hampstead from the age of seven, her father also encouraged his children to educate themselves by reading widely. This was a habit that never left her. Years later, her granddaughter, Mary Wetherell, recalls that her abiding memory is of Connie always having a book beside her, or in her hand. In her diary, apologising for quoting at length from a book which had nothing to do with the war, Connie writes: 'It may seem strange that I should copy this into a war diary, but I want it to be clear ... that I got through the war as I did simply because I had this secret life of reading.'

All three children inherited both their father's love of the written word and his formidable work ethic. Maurice became a psychologist whose books included a multi-volume commentary on the work of Gurdjieff and Ouspensky, which was considered for many years the authority on the subject. Mildred was an accomplished poet who wrote a series of articles for *Homes and Gardens* on family life in wartime, which subsequently grew into a novel, *Family Postbag*.

In 1909 Connie married Elystan Miles, an officer in the Royal Artillery, and threw herself into the life of a soldier's wife. Elystan served with distinction in the Great War, and was awarded the Military Cross for his actions at Ypres, where he commanded a Heavy Battery. Connie wrote in her family memoir that 'that war period was the high spot of his life'. However, he was not entirely happy in his army career, being too keen to suggest improvements which were not always well received (a trait which remained in his later life, as Connie's journal makes clear). In one report his superiors wrote: 'this young officer is too fond of having new ideas'. And having attained the rank of major, he dreaded further promotion because, in Connie's words, 'a colonel had to be so much in his office, and Elystan hated paperwork.'

He resigned his commission in 1920 and, with a timely legacy 'from stormy Aunt Minnie', he bought Plas Meon in Soberton, Hampshire, and set up a chicken farm. An outdoorsman by nature, he loved to be physically active and disliked spending time in towns, seldom accompanying Connie on her trips to London.

In 1928 they moved to Shere, a village which Connie had known from childhood visits with her parents. They settled at Springfield, an imposing house set high above a sunken lane on the south side of the village, where Elystan kept himself busy with gardening and building, and Connie supplemented his army pension with her writing. Although well connected, they were not wealthy: they divided the house into two, living in the

Connie as a young woman
Photograph courtesy of Mary Wetherell

Elystan as a young man
Photograph courtesy of Mary Wetherell

upstairs apartment and letting the downstairs to tenants to boost their income.

Harry had been born in 1912 and Basil in 1914. Harry followed his father into the regular army, serving with the Loyal Regiment (North Lancashires) until he was diagnosed with ankylosing spondylitis, a potentially disabling bone disease. Invalided out in 1940, he emigrated to what was then called Rhodesia, where Elystan's younger brother Bevis had a tobacco farm, and took no further active part in the war. Basil had not long qualified as a doctor when war broke out, and joined the Royal Army Medical Corps, serving first with the Royal Engineers and then with the Scots Greys in North Africa, where he was severely wounded on the first day of the Second Battle of El Alamein. The entries in which Connie writes about waiting for news of Basil, receiving conflicting messages and not knowing even if he was still alive are among the most immediate and moving in the diary. They grow increasingly brief and sporadic. At one point she says merely: 'I cannot write much about this', a reticence which, for someone who poured herself into her pages, itself speaks louder than words.

At times Connie questioned her motives for keeping her journal. She told herself that it was for Harry and Basil, but more than likely she wrote in the main because she felt driven to do so. No other reason explains why she wrote well over 400,000 words, of which the present book represents a fraction. Writing for her was not just a means of earning a living. Words were both her solace and her passion. Contemplating the destruction of Paternoster Row in what came to be called 'The Second Great Fire of London' on 29 December 1940, she grieved for the lost works of the publishing houses which had stood there as much as for the more tangible wreckage of bricks and mortar, writing: 'Five to six million books have perished. Oh, the brave, bright paper jackets, the lovely purple covers, the crisp, unopened pages, the quips and cranks, the love scenes and the thoughtful essays, the learned remarks, the verses and the valuable paragraphs, the pure new bindings in red and yellow, blue and mauve and olive green, the messages and signals to the human race that were embraced by the horrible flames!'

Her own writing style is impressionistic, moving swiftly from one scene or thought to another; but what impressions they are. Remarks made almost in passing linger indelibly in the memory. In the freezing winter of January 1940, with fuel for heating already in short supply, Elystan sits 'slowly knitting a khaki scarf with chilly fingers'. An anguished father whose son is reported missing in Singapore 'strides about the countryside for hours to try and forget it'. In the village canteen, 'at one table sits the Squire's sister, very determined and ruthless under a blue hat, who kisses no-one, but does kiss her clever old black poodle.' On a crowded railway train, a soldier switches his wireless set on, and the passengers are transported by the story of Grimalkin read out on *Children's Hour* – only, being British, no one will admit to listening in.

She has a gift for the sharp poetic phrase. She summarises the state of the nation in April 1941 as 'the necessary machinery of a million households cracking'. Trying to forget the war for a moment in the glorious autumn of Netley Woods, she writes, 'Walked with Basil to look at the beautiful and death-struck year.' But she also has a fine ear for comic dialogue. On a bus, apropos of food shortages, she overhears one woman saying, 'I had nothing in the house to give my husband yesterday, so he had vegetables. And do you know, in the evening, he was quite limp! Hadn't had his proper dinner, you see.'

*

Quite apart from her skill as a writer, the great value of her journal lies in her unusually wide acquaintance. Connie's is not the only voice we hear. Her network of correspondents sent a constant stream of letters from all over the country, which kept her – and keep us – informed of events outside the confines of Shere. Letters were vitally important, not just for contact but as a means of emotional support, and many are revealing as to their writers' states of mind.

She had friends or family in Canada, the USA, the Netherlands, France, in Africa and Singapore, so we also have snapshots of what was happening overseas. A refugee tells of a narrow escape from the Germans advancing on Paris. Letters from the USA reveal the deep divisions between those who felt that America was morally bound to join the war and those who believed that she should not. Before the war, Connie had friends in Germany, too, with whom Basil stayed while he was at medical school in Tübingen, near Stuttgart. Much as she loathed Hitler and all he stood for, she writes of her concern for the Von Brunn family, even though their son had joined the Hitler Youth.

She is accustomed to being on first-name terms with public figures. She lunches with Montgomery's sister; discusses Churchill with William Nicholson, celebrated painter; chats with the vice-president of the Stock Exchange, who happens to live nearby. But she is equally at home in the local workers' cottages, the ease with which she moves between these two very different worlds reflecting the makeup of rural Surrey in the 1940s, where the Stockbroker Belt and the old farmworkers' families whose roots on the land went back generations still lived side by side.

She read the newspapers daily and listened avidly to the radio, quoting Churchill's speeches one moment and German propaganda broadcasts the next, reporting news from Finland or Greece as much as from the home front, recording a kaleidoscope of views and reactions from the highest decision makers to – literally – the man or woman in the street.

Two voices in particular add their own distinctive character to the diary. One is that of Elystan, whose wonderfully pithy and caustic remarks punctuate it for all the world like a kind of one-man Greek chorus. The other is that of May Browne, later May Sinclair, Connie's closest friend, whose several roles as a shopkeeper, an ATS instructor and a manager at the BBC make her a kind of Everywoman whose comments Connie valued above almost anyone else's.

When Connie began her journal, Britain had been making preparations for the outbreak of war for some time. Regulations and training concerning Air Raid Precautions had been in force since 1937. Plans to evacuate London children to rural enclaves were first put in place in September 1938, and local volunteers, of whom Connie's downstairs tenant, Madge Davidson, was one, were actively engaged in finding billets. This was no easy task, since, as Connie succinctly explains: 'The women of England [were] depressed to death at the prospect of the shared kitchen and the children unknown.'

The promise of peace brokered by Prime Minister Neville Chamberlain in Munich in September 1938, which enabled Hitler to annexe the Czech Sudetenland unopposed, had already proved hollow when Germany occupied the rest of Czechoslovakia in March 1939. Several families in and around Shere were hosting Czech refugees who had fled the invasion, so the village was well informed about the threat of Nazi aggression.

Yet the sense of shock when war was declared is clear, as is the extent to which people were not in fact prepared. From its opening lines, the overwhelming impression we get from the first few entries in the journal is of confusion amplified by fear, and the sense that what people were dreading was not the prospect of war itself so much as the disruption it brought with it.

Certainly the popular image of everyone pulling together was not much in evidence during those first few months. The so-called Phoney War, in which neither side ventured a major land or air offensive while shipping losses mounted, lasted well into the spring of 1940. People were edgy, disquieted, waiting for something to happen and deeply unsure what was going on. Everyone had something to complain about, from the shop-keepers struggling to deal with the bureaucracy of rationing to the tensions between the evacuees and their hosts. ('Shan't we be glad to get out of this blinking house!' chant two small boys at one of Connie's friends.) On 3 October, Connie writes: 'What shall we be like at the end of the war? Poor, and ... quarrelling among ourselves.'

The German invasions of Norway and Denmark in April and the Netherlands and Belgium in May brought the Phoney War to an end. On 13 April, Connie writes that 'the war is now on our doorsteps'; and on 18 May, that she had 'never felt so acutely a sense of impending disaster'. Watching a cricket match on the village green, she warns: 'I sometimes think we deserve to lose this war. Boys of twenty-six are not yet called up. A look of infinite boredom breaks over many faces when Robin urges that trenches should be dug ...'*

Two months later, France had fallen, the air war had

* Connie refers to Elystan as Robin throughout the journal. This name seems to have been in common use between them, as there is a photograph of Elystan as a young man on the reverse of which is pencilled in Connie's writing: 'Elystan (Robin)'.

intensified and, with the Battle of Britain, the conflict began in earnest for those at home. On 10 September, three days after the start of the Blitz, she writes: 'Various men and women with suitcases appeared in the village today, trying for rooms. They have been bombed out of their homes.'

Gradually, the unthinkable becomes commonplace. The famous Blitz spirit comes to the fore as ordinary men and women are called upon to make extraordinary efforts, and step up to the plate. The fear of invasion, while Hitler abandoned his initial plans in September, did not diminish for many months. The government was still issuing instructions about what to do in such an event in March 1941, at which point Connie was keeping a backpack by the door in case they should have to leave home at a moment's notice. Food becomes a constant concern – the sheer grind of obtaining it, stretching out rations, never knowing from day to day what the shops might have in stock. The litany of losses grows longer, too, until almost everyone Connie knows has lost a son, a husband, a brother, a cousin, a friend.

But perhaps the most poignant and least familiar aspect of her account is the amount of peripheral suffering caused indirectly by the war: the loss not of homes or lives but of livelihoods, hopes and dreams. Tradesmen and craftsmen – the gardener, the chef, the piano tuner – lost work because their clients had moved to safer districts, or else no longer required or could not afford their services. Those whose premises were wrecked by bombs lost everything. Small businesses suffered terribly, owing to either lack of supplies, lack of customers or having all their staff called up; and sometimes, as with May Browne's shop, a combination of all three. Connie's hairdresser had put all her savings into her one shop and has to try and keep it solvent entirely alone, with no assistants. Another woman, who had built up a small successful school, finds herself homeless and jobless at forty-five, her life's work gone. There was no financial safety net or support for those who found themselves in such circumstances, other than friends or charity; or, for those who were totally destitute, poor relief.

Life was altered not just for individuals but for the country as a whole; and reading the journal one gets a real sense of the changes the war was bringing. Domestic service for middle-class families vanished almost overnight as women of working age were called up for war work, and many often elderly people found that they had to clean and cook for themselves for the first time. Young women took on many roles, from offices to factories, which had not been open to them before, prompting Connie to comment that 'girls are the gainers in this war'.

Wondering what sort of world the younger generation would inherit when it was over, she followed the debate that led eventually to the formation of the National Health Service and the welfare state. Towards the end of the journal, in March 1943, she recounts a conversation in which a mechanic says to Elystan that the changes must come, or there will be revolution; to which he replies that 'life in this country after the war will not be Paradise'. Connie herself was greatly in favour of universal health care, but was cautious enough to hope that the government would not promise 'all sorts of impossible things'.

Meantime, however, in April 1941, she was one of many who were struggling to meet the demands of increased income tax. Needing to economise, she decided that she could no longer afford to buy the paper she needed to keep the journal. On 18 April, the day after a long and particularly evocative entry in which she recorded a visit to London and the effects of the damage wrought by the Blitz, she put it aside.

*

During the eight months for which she was silent, the war became a conflict on a truly global scale. In June, Germany invaded Russia. By late autumn, Japan was threatening both British and US interests in south-east Asia, and on 8 December, following the Japanese bombing of Pearl Harbor, America entered the war.

Connie resumed her journal on 17 December 1941, writing: 'The news is, as I begin again, quite bad ... We are delighted with the Libyan and the Russian front, but anxious, very anxious, about Hong Kong and even more about Singapore.' But, she says, 'The spirit of the people, as I find it in my little circle (stretching from the north of Scotland to the west of England) is calm and patient and unmoved. Yes, the outlook is hopeful, in spite of everything.'

Soon, however, the tone is different, as almost immediately things grow grimmer, and two days later she writes that 'Christmas is indeed subdued. I never remember a Christmas so sombre, and with so slight an air of festivity.' On Christmas Day itself, hearing that Hong Kong was about to fall, she writes sadly of her great friends the Eustaces, 'Every penny they had was invested in Hong Kong and Shanghai. He is white-haired, but will have to find a job.'

The sense of endurance is palpable. On 3 January her friend Rachel writes, 'I'm afraid I don't even feel any delight in thousands of Germans being done in. We can only drift on, just snatching at passing happiness, and doing any kindness we can along the way.' On 23 February May Sinclair writes, 'Do you have a horrible feeling that nothing will ever be the same again? One will never just be quite pleased with life ... Just as you are going to enjoy it, a memory of this horror will come like a cloud over the sun. More and more I feel I'd like to go and live, afterwards, somewhere that doesn't remind me of post-war

England.' Connie herself wrote, also in February: 'I place it on record calmly and gravely that this stage of the war is the worst that we have gone through.'

It is easy to understand why they should have felt so pessimistic in 1942. The Germans were sweeping triumphantly across Russia. Rommel was pushing forward in the deserts of North Africa, where each hard-won Allied success was followed by a series of reverses. News from the Far East, where Japan was in the ascendent, was unremittingly bleak.

By Thursday, 2 July, 'one of the blackest days of the war', Connie was close to despair, writing: 'We have been making Crusader tanks, which are no use; we have not yet put a big anti-tank gun into production. Nor have we dive-bombers. The muddle seems ghastly. And our men are fighting what may be a decisive battle now in the Egyptian heat, under a sultry sky, out-gunned, out-tanked. I cannot think, taking it all in – the fall of Sebastopol, and the fact that we are fighting against heavy odds in Libya – that we can *ever* have so black a day again.'

But even at her lowest ebb, she never loses hope. On 18 July she writes that she is 'sick with fear ... really shivering with vague, sharp apprehension', and on 20 July that the news is 'appallingly serious about Russia. They are yielding town after town'. Then on 21 July, as though to rally herself, she writes firmly: 'I don't think I convey enough in these pages my belief that We Shall Win.'

Connie made no bones about how hard she and others found the war years. Yet, having stared at the prospect of defeat through those darkest months, she ends her diary on a more optimistic note. Two events in particular signified, in late 1942 and early 1943, that the balance of the war was tipping at last in the Allies' favour: the eventual victory at El Alamein, which changed the course of the conflict in North Africa, and the epic Russian defence of Stalingrad, which not only halted the German advance but broke their aura of invincibility.

Perhaps that was also why she stopped abruptly in April 1943, with no explanation other than that she did not want to stay in and write while the sun was shining. On some deep level, feeling more confident now of the future, she no longer felt the need to take refuge in her writing.

She was a harsh critic of her own work. Her difficulty was that she did not know what to include in her journal and what to leave out. She herself says, 'So much came my way.' Overwhelmed by the weight of the events she was recording, she did not have either the time or the inclination to edit what she wrote. Consequently, when she did read over her journal, she was disappointed with it, judging it too disjointed and too full of ephemera to stand the test of time. She could not see the value of it as we can now from a distance of seventy years, or recognise what gems it contains, illuminating the mood of wartime Britain as surely and as precisely as the searchlights that ranged to and fro across the skies.

Fortunately for those of us who now have the privilege of reading her diary, she chose despite her doubts to send it to the Imperial War Museum, adding to it a modest note in which she concludes: 'I guess that I have done enough and said enough to show what war days were in 1939, 40, 41, 42, 43.'

Indeed she has.

S. V. Partington, June 2013

List of Abbreviations

ARP	Air Raid Precautions
ATS	Auxiliary Territorial Service
CO	Commanding Officer
FANY	First Aid Nursing Yeomanry
HAC	Honourable Artillery Company
IRA	Irish Republican Army
LCC	London County Council
NAAFI	Navy, Army and Air Force Institutes
NCO	on-Commissioned Officer
RA	Royal Artillery
RAF	Royal Air Force
RAMC	Royal Army Medical Corps
RASC	Royal Army Service Corps
RE	Royal Engineers
VC	Victoria Cross
WAAF	Women's Auxiliary Air Force
WRNS	Women's Royal Naval Service (Wrens)
WVS	Women's Voluntary Service

Constance Miles, *circa* 1920
Photograph courtesy of Mary Wetherell

Springfield
Shere
nr Guildford

October 1947

This journal was kept by Constance Miles, wife of retired Major Elystan Miles, late RA, living in their own house, in the top of two flats, downstairs the Misses Davidsons, friends and tenants, who went off to Scotland for a time. Mrs Miles is a professional journalist; daughter of the famous editor the late Sir William Robertson Nicoll, who founded the *British Weekly* and *The Bookman* among other periodicals and was in close touch with many well known people of his time. Mrs Miles originally wrote the journal for the benefit of her two children, one of whom, Harry, lives in Rhodesia, invalided out of the Regular Army (Loyals), and Dr Basil Miles, medical officer in the war, of the Royal Engineers and eventually the Scots Greys, dangerously wounded at El Alamein, where the Greys were in the forefront of the battle. This copy of the journal is offered to the Imperial War Museum, with the reminder that the writer was aged fifty-eight, a housewife in a pretty Surrey village. May it be of some use some day!

PART ONE

August 1939 to April 1941

Elystan Miles (Robin) *circa* 1914
Photograph courtesy of Mary Wetherell

1939

Thursday, 24 August

Here I am, sitting alone in the library at 8.10 p.m. Robin is wandering about the garden; the dug-out is not finished. Today the news is very bad. 'We are,' says Mr Chamberlain, 'in imminent peril of war.' Nobody seems to be happy any more. It was rather dreadful to see the people at Woolworths struggling around the curtain hook counter to buy apparatus for their dark draperies. I bought various wrong things in haste, and also had great difficulty in getting some cold ham at the equally crowded grocers. It was thronged with worried women, trying at the last moment to lay in things.

Miss Sandworth, a fine old woman, tells me she has a class of thirty Czech refugees who are learning English. The men have all been helping with the hay harvest. Her friend Fred Pethick Lawrence has been trying to get the authorities to allow the Czechs to do a bit of work, and to slacken the regulations against it.*

The wireless has just said, speaking of football: 'Let us hope

* Frederick Pethick Lawrence, Labour MP and noted advocate of women's rights. He was Secretary of State for India and Burma from 1945–7, and was involved in negotiations for Indian independence. He lived in Peaslake, just south of Shere.

the crisis will pass, and the grand old game be more popular than ever.'

I feel there is no hope left – and that we are in for the most terrible years.

Basil is at Netley,* Harry at Singapore. What will become of them?

I have none of the happy conviction with which I went into the last war.

Saturday, 26 August

A hot, fearfully sunny day. The news is vague. Aeroplanes roar over. Bey Hyde comes in to ask me if she can put through a trunk call to Leamington Spa. She tells me she has lost her job through all this, at her fashionable town school. She must find another pensionable job.

I, lightly: 'Oh, you will join the Women Terriers?'†

Bey: 'One-and-six a day! No thanks.'‡

Later on in the bank a young cashier like a half-fledged sparrow advises a brand new customer: 'If we close at the outbreak of war, it is only for, say, a day.'

'I should like to cash some money. Ought I to do it today?' she asks.

I intervene to tell her that the moratorium before the last war was for four days and I advise her to get money now.

* The Royal Victoria Hospital at Netley, Southampton, a purpose-built military hospital constructed in the 1850s and demolished in 1966.

† 'Terriers' was short for the Territorial Army, the volunteer force of the British Army. Female volunteers in 1939 joined the Auxiliary Territorial Service (ATS), formed the previous year. Their pay, however, was only 66 per cent of that of male volunteers.

‡ One shilling and sixpence, or seven and a half pence in decimal currency. There were twenty shillings in a pound and twelve pence in a shilling.

The maid Nancy's wedding is postponed. Her Argyll and Sutherland[*] can't get leave from Fife. The wedding cake is finished and is iced, the pale blue dress ready. Poor Nancy.

Tuesday, 29 August

I have forgotten what it is like to read a book. I am glad to work and to think; think hard of how to go through each day.

Nancy's fiancé is guarding the Tay bridge. Her wedding cake, really a lovely one framed in sugar lilies, is being stored at the Guildford bakers till the wedding can take place.

Barbara[†] writes: 'I notice, talking to people here, that everyone seems very tired and sleepy in the daytime, and wakeful at night, and that seems to me to be the sort of natural adjustment in anticipation of things to come.'

She tells a story of an old maid in her village who was overheard talking to herself. 'Hitler thinks he'll get everything (stamps her foot) but he won't. I'll see he doesn't.'

Wednesday, 30 August

The little dark-eyed would-be bride is going about her work rather sadly today, with a wistful look. However, there seems a slightly hopeful pause in the Germans' onslaught. *Why does it not all begin*?

I hear that a certain lady here is offering dachshund puppies for nothing. There was quite a serious letter in *The Times*

* The Argyll and Sutherland Highlanders, a Scottish infantry regiment.

† The writer Barbara Euphan Todd, best known as the creator of the children's character Worzel Gummidge.

yesterday from a famous author, begging people not to be unkind to German dogs!

I feel so exhausted I can hardly write this, and it is hot again. I can see on the allotments little groups of men talking interminably about Adolf.

Ella McR. writes that 1,600 children from Glasgow are being evacuated there, and she is to have four girls. But nobody in these factory towns is thinking much about it. The women of England are depressed to death over the idea of the shared kitchen, and the children unknown. I saw Miss B. this morning, who confessed she had agreed to nothing more than two teachers in her little, comfy square house with its Chippendale chairs and soft pink carpets, and her old brown and white cups. She 'could never afford to get together such things again if the marauding mob broke them up', and seems to see a vision of lonely old age 'in a back attic room, if crowds come down and storm us'.

The sky is rosy, and pale brooding grey clouds are over Netley Park,* where the mansion is being got ready for the refugee babies and mothers.

Thursday, 31 August

Just heard that the evacuation of children is to begin tomorrow. Seventy are to arrive by buses here about 10.30. The evacuation notices are most inappropriately given out by BBC young men, who know little what despair enters the hearts of various women expecting the strangers and afraid to have them. Men just haven't the foggiest.

* No connection to Netley Hospital. Netley Park, now owned by the National Trust, is a small estate and country house on the slopes of the North Downs, just across the A25 from Shere.

The Ministry of Health produced a series of emotive appeals in English and Welsh newspapers, asking for people to take in evacuees.

Photograph © IWM PST15108

All hope of peace seems gone tonight. The Reserves are called up – every category. Only my old man remains, a trained soldier of many years service, peacefully smoking his pipe, and bricklaying his dugout.

We have shrunk into three rooms now, and the bedrooms are all ready for the refugees who with admirable *sangfroid* refrain from coming.

A cordial invitation to come down to Picket Post, where the hundred windows of the school have all dark blinds.* One longs for friends at this dreadful hour; dear friends to be close at hand.

Robin calls me. 'Come and listen!' I fly in, to hear a long set of Hitler's conditions and terms for Poland. The first is the unconditional surrendering of Danzig. We are surprised, and there is no explanation. Go to sleep feeling that this is unsatisfactory.

Friday, 1 September

The morning papers tell us that these terms were submitted to Poland very hurriedly, and without adequate time for the wretched country to cope with them. Robin strolls down the village at ten a.m. and returns to say that he hears that Germany has *begun* hostilities in Poland. I can hardly believe it. I sit at my writing-table trying to fill up income tax forms, and I accept the announcement with incredulity.

Later it dawns on me, and the first sensation is that of intense relief. Hitler must be shown that his policy is a menace. I think immediately of my sons, of Harry and Basil.

* Connie was a frequent visitor to Picket Post, a hamlet in the New Forest (now bisected by the A31) where her friend Muriel Andrews ran a boarding school for boys.

Harry (standing) and Basil as schoolboys
Photograph courtesy of Mary Wetherell

I write at 9.30 at night on the most fateful evening. We are blacked out, seriously and properly tonight, and it's very sultry, and hard to bear the closely-pulled curtains. The BBC is instructing Terriers to report immediately.

One hundred children arrived here at one, instead of ten a.m., and were duly sorted. Fancy, old Mrs C. takes ten in her large empty house at the top of the hill. The children are very popular – Nancy is delighted with three little brothers parked on her mother. They hailed a worm in the garden by a delighted and awed exclamation: 'Coo! See that snake!'

Saturday, 2 September

Madge this morning went to the school at nine and filled the Girl Guides' palliasses with straw from Netley barn, and motored round, distributing blankets to cottages that had not a supply. Then a consignment of mothers and babies arrived, and were carted about and dolloped quite correctly, according to plan.

This afternoon my boarders called from London to tell me that their Harley Street house is much disturbed, as all the specialists are getting attached to hospitals and will not be using their consulting rooms in the West End. One great man said he just couldn't pay his quarter's rent as his patients wouldn't pay up. I fear Joan will lose very heavily on this house of hers, which she has on lease from the Crown and pays for through specialists' rents.*

A peaceful hush lies over all England. It seems incredible that we should have to leave our gardens, full of the dying fires of red phlox and yellow rudbeckia, to listen to this string of injunctions from the BBC about lighting restrictions, conscription and so on.

* Connie's friend Joan Hoffman and her companion Mrs M. arrived in Shere on 4 September. Many people left London at this time for friends and relations in the country but returned when the threat of early air attack did not materialise.

Dr S. came to see Edie last night, and said: 'Oh, I've had a jolly day, finishing up with sacking the cook. I found that she had been calling the Austrian housemaid "You dirty German", so I said "You'll pack up your things NOW and go."'

Basil wrote that he could not get away from Netley, and asked us to send his gas mask.

Warsaw has been bombed *six* times today.

Sunday, 3 September. Outbreak of War

The Prime Minister, in the most delightfully English voice, told us just after eleven that we were at war.

It seems incredible! As I write, the sad day has gone by. The evening sun is glowing on the garden, and Edie's border shows her marigolds still beautifully fresh and golden. The low voices of the tenants, one of them the exhausted billeter, float up.* Robin is round at a cottage getting quarters for Hoffman's car. Our visitors arrive tomorrow. For how long?

Early this morning Madge reported that news had come from London that a great increase in the billeting lists was expected, and that compulsory billeting must begin at once. She asked me to go and watch over a tearful neighbour, an old widow, solitary in a large house, frightened of what might be coming to her.

Robin and I went in a hurry over to the loft; he said that ten soldiers might be billeted there comfortably. Who was to move the billiard table? 'Easily done,' was his calm reply.

How one longs for all this NOT to have happened at this

* Edie and Madge were the Misses Davidson, who rented the ground floor of Springfield House, which Connie and her husband had divided into upper and lower flats. Madge was the billeting officer, whose task was to organise homes for evacuees.

deceiving time of year! In no time the autumn winds will be howling and sobbing and moaning about, and we shall be darkening windows early. I wish this whole house were let to some reliable people, that the tenants were safe in Grantown, that Robin and I were safe in Rhynie, he tilling the land, and I with Mildred* and the twins, brushing up my knowledge in a calmer air.

Aeroplanes drone by all day long, all night long.

My neighbour, Mrs F., says a blazing light comes from my window. This is terrible! I thought it was perfectly screened. Robin is going round to gaze tonight. I have a baby bulb above my head, tiny, so that I can just read. I think it must be the moon on the glass.

The King spoke on the radio, curiously slow and sad and with much lack of vitality. Better far that the Queen had spoken.

I dread tomorrow, with all its guests and adjustments. How I wish I were near some friend I really love just now. The children from town are not coming till late, so the village hall is rapidly prepared. I go past, and see mattresses and blankets airing outside. Many Londonish figures go by pushing prams, and the cottagers are well pleased with their guests, and reckon to make money out of the eight-and-sixpence each. One of our greatest women authorities on Africa sits checking in allowances at the school. What this war is going to cost the country! Mothers get five shillings a week allowance and three shillings for each child, and free billets.

* Connie's younger half-sister, Mildred, lived in Lodge of Auchindoir, Rhynie, Aberdeenshire, with her husband Grange Kirkcaldy and their three children; Rosemary, sixteen at the outbreak of war, and thirteen-year-old twins, Pamela and Prudence.

Monday, 4 September

Today came news of a ship torpedoed going to Montreal. The *Athenia*.*

H. and M. arrived hot and tired about teatime. They had been up two hours last night owing to an air raid signal; it was a false alarm. No raids here yet, and the village is dreaming in quiet apparently. But inside Drydown House Mrs C. must be contending with her ten children. 'I took too much on, Mrs Miles,' said the gallant old lady, pounding up the long sunny hill today.

Sara writes that the billeting arrangements in Weymouth have been very faulty. Children alone were expected. As they sat assembling gas masks in the schoolroom, about one hundred mothers laden with children, infants and impedimenta were suddenly thrust upon them. In dark and rain they took them round, begging and imploring people to have them. Much misery.

Tuesday, 5 September

More about the dreadful sinking of the *Athenia* in the papers, and the survivors' own stories on the wireless. Women baling out water from the lifeboats with their shoes. Terrible!

Into Guildford, where a noticeable air of strain and excitement could be seen in the sad faces of the shoppers. Odd, in the library, to see that masses of the books on 'Will Hitler

* The SS *Athenia*, a passenger liner en route from Glasgow to Montreal, was torpedoed in error by the German submarine U-30. 112 of the 1418 passengers and crew were killed, among them 69 women and 19 children.

March?' are standing unread and unopened. That is all over now. But there is an ominous lull.

Where are our men going from Aldershot? The FANYs* are in great demand there, worked to death by the Army Service Corps, and proud to be so worked.

Helen's tiny London refugee, aged two, was in the car with her in Guildford today. She bought it some new underclothes, as its trousseau was infinitesimal. When her husband returned this evening, the babe picked up its new pantaloons and said in a tone of great self-complacency, 'Mine', and then, waving its vest, 'Mine'.

In Guildford, about a third of the people were carrying gas masks. Mrs F. at the Shetland Shop says her business has completely ceased.

Half our scheduled children have not arrived yet and probably never will. The mothers billeted at the Rectory want to use the Aga stove, and are driven out of the kitchen, so some have gone home.

Madge has gone night-driving – a rehearsal I suppose for ARP.† People are having their cars edged with white paint along the footboards and mudguards.

A hot, glorious night. There were silver wheels of spiders' webs on the mauve daisies and white roses this morning.

* The First Aid Nursing Yeomanry was a charitable volunteer organisation first set up in 1907, which had filled a vital role in the Great War driving ambulances and tending to the wounded. In 1938 the FANY Corps formed the Women's Transport Services, the motor transport arm of the Auxiliary Territorial Service, and it was as drivers that they were chiefly used in the Second World War.

† At the outbreak of war, there were already over 1.5 million Britons enrolled as wardens or other civil defence personnel concerned with Air Raid Precautions.

Wednesday, 6 September

Mrs M. (an alien)* went to the police station in Guildford to register, and was told that she must not go further than five miles from Shere without getting a permit EACH time from this office. As she had to have her photo taken, she can't go to London tomorrow to see a solicitor about her doctors in Harley Street leaving their practices.

Apples keep falling, rosy and green ones, and the London children are asked in to pick them up.

I went to buy some fish for dinner, and was told that there was none, so am opening a tin of tongue.

Greatly cheered and fortified by a letter from Harry, all kindness and sympathy for us.

After breakfast a sobbing sound rent the air, and we thought it was a warning of an air raid, but apparently it was an All Clear. The milkman explained that there had been two raids at Aldershot. I gather, however, that we shall not be told much by the authorities, who are studiously vague about it in tonight's report.

Mother writes inviting us to come to Scotland.† I *wish* I could, but it is not possible at present.

Friday, 8 September

The brother of a woman here rang up from Blackdown to say he was going to France tomorrow, and must see a relative

* Mrs M., Connie's London friend, came originally from Germany, and although she had lived in Britain for some time the outbreak of war meant that she became in the eyes of the law not only an alien but an enemy alien. Restrictions on individuals such as Mrs M. eased once they were assessed as posing no threat.

† Connie's stepmother, Lady Catherine Nicoll, known as Katie, lived at the Nicoll family home in Lumsden, Aberdeenshire.

before going. It is all over the village – very wrong of him to give it away.

We have sent for a petrol licensing book. Cars are not about Guildford now so much. The shelves of the local grocers are emptying fast. There seems no authentic news in the paper; it is to be a hush-hush war.

My guest (American) enquires blandly if I am not leading my normal life just now? If not, why not? With the whole of life darkened and apprehensive! But *she* has no sons – or ties.

The newspapers are almost all smaller today. I think the *British Weekly*[*] may die.

Saturday, 9 September

Fetched Basil at about three-thirty. A Queen's man[†] told Robin at the crowded station that they were off to France next day. Basil looked pale but smiling; it was just three weeks since we had left him at Netley, when no war had started and peace still brooded (though very uneasily) on Southampton Water.

Basil dislikes the red tape and bad organisation of the Army hospital – so many forms, such lack of co-ordination – yet he enjoys the work of his wards. He is very anxious now about his future, where he will go, where he will be sent – so long as he can get some work of a medical nature. Ambulances, field hospitals, trains and so on are all being assembled at Netley; many doctors gathering under canvas.

* The magazine founded by Connie's father, Sir William Robertson Nicoll, in 1886, to which she was a regular contributor.

† The Queen's Royal Regiment (West Surrey), the second most senior infantry regiment in the British Army.

The brilliant heat continues. 'There is nothing to look forward to, and nothing to talk about save war,' says Madge disconsolately.

Gosh, how nervous we all feel at this intolerable thing! The government has announced that they will prepare for a three-year war. I should say the nerves of our fliers would not stand it for so long as that.

'Do not listen to too much news,' says Basil. 'No evening paper for me.'

Monday, 11 September

Today I went to London by car with Joan, the loveliest drive in sunshine. As we came up to the top of Putney Hill I caught sight of the most attractive lot of silver balloons floating above London.* I was extremely struck by them, there were so many against the serene sky of September blue. It seemed all day, as I went about town, that they were on active guard, like silvery birds of friendliness.

At first we went to the police station in Battersea, which was so heavily sandbagged it was hard to squeeze into the doorway. There Joan tried to get a permit for her housekeeper to come back to London. In vain: regulations for the unnaturalised† are very stiff in this war.

The streets in London are distinctly better than they were, vastly relieved of traffic. No Lifeguards on duty in Whitehall. Charles I's statue not sandbagged, nor Eros in the Circus, nor David at Hyde Park Corner. On I went, under the silver

* Barrage balloons, designed to impede low-flying aircraft and hence to protect a potential target from aerial attack.

† Someone who is resident in Britain but not a British citizen.

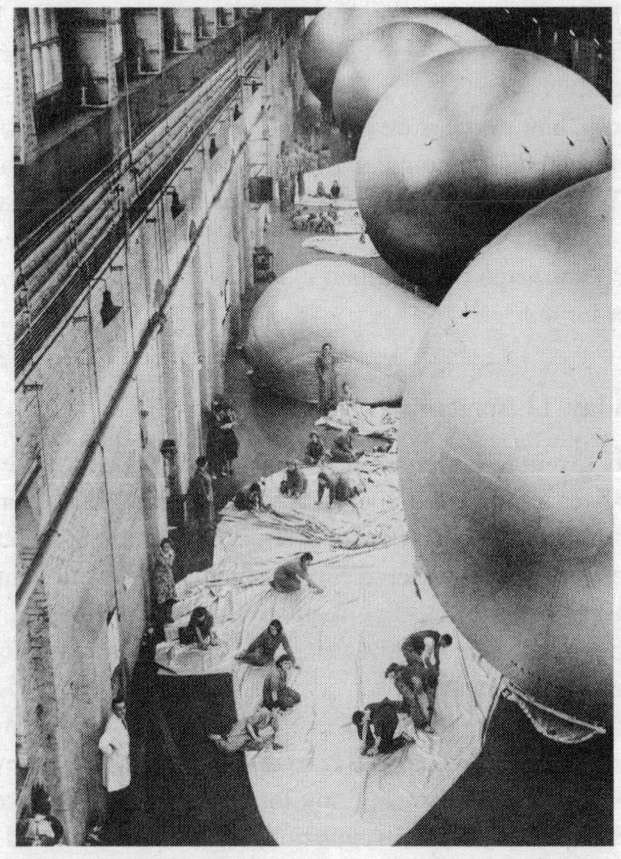

'Silvery birds of friendliness . . .' Barrage balloons being built at the Dunlop Balloon Factory, Manchester.
Photograph © IWM HU36241

balloons, to buy a winter coat which was got very easily at Swan and Edgars, which was almost empty. Strange to glance in at the great evening dress department, all pretty models, with not one soul buying.

Wednesday, 13 September

I felt this afternoon that I was at last resting a bit. Since the war started there has been no rest at all, only misery and agitation and struggling to make things go right.

The women of the village seem keen on NOT sending their billeted children to a canteen proposed by the ladies of Shere, where sixpenny dinners may be served.*

Thursday, 14 September

Went to tea with the Kennings; they have a little London school installed in their charming house. E., the artist, gives up her studio for children's beds and sleeps fitfully above it on her balcony. Jean, the musician, gives up her music room as a classroom. Mrs K. finds the catering for about sixteen people very difficult.

Joy Annett told me of driving unexpected mothers and children to cottages on Albury Heath, of the tears, and the reluctance to stay, and the horrified London glance round a tiny cottage room: 'Oh, I can never stop *here*.' Joy regards the dirty condition of the children as most reprehensible, and thinks we must mould the world afresh.

In the evening Mr Struben, the South African, calls. He has withdrawn his house from the market: he, at about seventy-five, 'cannot run away from England to my native land'. He is a warden and is short of ARP masks, and perplexed by the demands of visitors for them. It *is* a funny war: strange faces, people with their masks, often in very clumsy receptacles,

* Connie adds later in a handwritten footnote that this view altered completely once the canteen was open, to the extent that 'they might send their own children as well'.

walking about, the young women from town with prams looking very cross and worried.

Here is an extract from the evening paper about the terror going on every moment in Poland:

> Behind the front, farm after farm, village after village, is in flames. Where shops are still intact long lines of Poles stand before them waiting for food ... As the Army advances columns of Labour Service youths come up in the wake to repair roads and bridges. Hurriedly they impress all available labour, especially Jewish labour. Under their charge long rows of aged Jews with black beards and astrakhan hats are seen at work in the streets. Often they have no picks or shovels and have to dig with their bare hands.

Friday, 15 September

The permit has come, and my visitor Minna can go back to her loved cooking stove in Battersea! There are great packings; the beds are left here with pillows and six blankets.

Saturday, 16 September

Basil came. We had gone to Guildford, a changed place; many soldiers, many refugee families turning into Woolworths, which had made itself ugly like the rest with strips of brown paper over its windows to guard against the Grand Assault.

Some hospital units have gone to France from Netley already, and troops carried past Basil's window, on the broad river in the dark, without lights, slipping away from the land of comfort and home to the Unknown.

Sunday, 17 September

We think cars will become very cheap. All is so black at night, people won't go out, or pay the motor tax to keep a car so severely rationed.

Rang up May Browne.* She says she is getting on well at her FANY work: 'The officers are so civil to us all, they speak to me as if I were Queen of England.' She thinks the war will last two-and-a-half years for certain.

Russia has invaded Poland. What news!†

Tuesday, 19 September

Poland has collapsed, and the Soviet men are motoring across it freely, annexing it, I suppose, as they go. Jews are being executed in large numbers.

It's the second day of the canteen in our village: cold beef and hot suet pudding for the children – so many tiny, who all, in the most distressing manner, carry the gas masks that seem almost as big as they are. This sight moves me more than any other in 'Hitler's War'; and also the sight of Clive Modin moved me yesterday, the young man nervously drinking sherry, and explaining to me that he had always had Liberal principles and disliked so utterly and entirely the idea of going into the Army. He is twenty-five, volunteered, and is a Royal Fusilier – to his own amazement – and about to be trained in camp.

* May Browne was Connie's closest friend. Connie quotes her frequently, referring to her as May Browne or May B. (later May Sinclair or May S. after her marriage to John Sinclair) to distinguish her from Robin's sister May, or Mayo.

† Russia had signed a non-aggression pact with Germany in August 1939, and did not enter the war on the Allies' side until she herself was invaded by Hitler in June 1941. Two weeks and two days after Germany had invaded Poland from the west, Russia invaded from the east.

Even small children, such as these evacuees, learned to carry their gas masks with them everywhere.
Photograph © IWM D824

Wednesday, 20 September

Thrilled by stories of the bravery on the sinking aircraft carrier, *Courageous*, but how bad to lose over 500 lives!* Hitler says he will drop five bombs for every one of ours.

Bernard Shaw† writes an excellent letter on Russia invading Poland . . . he feels Hitler will quarrel with Stalin and lose all.

* HMS *Courageous* was sunk by German submarine U-29 off the coast of Ireland on 17 September while on anti-submarine patrol. She was the first Royal Navy warship to be lost in the Second World War.

† George Bernard Shaw, playwright, novelist, essayist and committed socialist, was known for his outspoken and cleverly argued commentaries on a wide range of issues.

Thursday, 21 September

Lovely letter from Harry in Singapore this morning, by air mail. I have replied by air – long may this way last!

Felt rather happier today, everything is quiet, and though there were some noticeably worried faces in Guildford, the shops were cheerful.

Robin gave me a waterproof case for my gas mask to sling over my reluctant shoulder.

Saturday, 23 September

The bank cashier is nearly done in by hours of acting as fireman, watchman at headquarters in Guildford, and by masses of work. Grocer harassed – will I mind having only one pound of sugar today, very short – Heinz things likely to go short too. 'All those books,' said the newsagent, pointing to the usual conglomeration of magazines and weeklies in gay covers on his counter, 'will stop at the end of the month. They will have to be ordered separately.' Our neighbours with the viola fields wonder what to do, as their flowers are now not ordered by London. So it goes on.

Monday, 25 September

Heard from Barbara this morning that she has been to London to meet several friends, all thrown out of work by this war and in a financial mess, specially authors. One is a famous children's writer.

Little dark-eyed Nancy is to go up to be married in Scotland to her Argyll and Sutherland Highlander who is to be there another few weeks. Her fare is paid for by her kind employers downstairs.

Joy Annett came, and I told her about the FANYs. She is very keen on joining up, and is to go to Aldershot tomorrow to try. You have to sign on for the duration of the war and to promise to go anywhere they send you. She is so brave, charming and pretty. I do wish her well.

Tuesday, 26 September

Mrs K. said on the phone that the West End is full of soldiers billeted: Cadogan Square is known as Barrack Square now, and it is not safe for a woman to walk there at night; the black-out is desperately difficult.

A lugubrious letter from Sara – no men to repair anything; broken glass stays broken glass.

Warsaw holds out but is being shot to pieces. German machine guns are even firing at the food queues. How lucky then are we to be here this fair afternoon of September going about our lawful occasions.

Thursday 28 September

When will the Germans attack London by air? Oh when? Many offices are returning there full of hope.

Went to see Miss B. in bed ill. Mrs Coppinger was there; her husband, a naval officer long retired, is minesweeping off Harwich. She confessed she cried over the Russian down pillows on her beds ruined by the little billeting children. The woman's husband, a painter from Fulham, came and stayed three days, smoking cigarettes in her drawing-room calmly, 'and never getting up while I was standing', cries the pretty, injured creature who had given her bathroom to the strangers.

The cottagers are only now discovering that there is no money in billeting and considerable unrest is reported.

I asked Robin last night why the Poles in Warsaw, now fallen, held out so long. He said 'Hate.'

Met Margaret Bray, who is a land girl and was milking cows at four-thirty in moonlight this morning. Her hostess, who is chairman of a Sudeten refugee committee* was rung up today to be informed that a) they wanted more pillow-cases, and b) some felt so miserable that they even contemplated suicide.

Friday, 29 September

The papers reveal what a vast CHAOS this war is, people underpaid, overpaid, people demanding, people wailing, people out of work and likely to be; poets, authors, journalists, artists, actors; household women in vast demand, all cooks bright as rubies and as rare, gardeners longed-for. Meanwhile the Misses Drew, old and undaunted ladies here, have bought a tiny new Peke, who rolls round reproachful eyes at them, and at all cats.

We have filled in National Registration cards,† and I have called myself a journalist.

* Since it was the Munich Agreement negotiated by Neville Chamberlain that had allowed Germany to annexe the Sudetenland unopposed, many people in Britain felt a particular obligation to help the Sudeten refugees.

† The National Registration Bill became law on 5 September. From May 1940, as fears of invasion grew, anyone over the age of sixteen had to carry their card at all times. Possession of a validated identity card was also required in order to obtain a ration book.

Sunday, 1 October

The second month of the War. Rang up May Browne to be told that her army of women soldiers at Aldershot were doing well. A good lot; but there are constantly casualties with girls finding the work too much, etc., so she thinks our friend Joy Annett may soon get in.

Monday, 2 October

Churchill made a capital speech on the wireless, finely phrased. He remarked that Hitler had started the war when he wished, but he will not finish it when he wishes. The Germans are to march through Warsaw in triumph. What a march through desolation and dead bodies! They say the city is such a ghastly ruin that even the German airmen reconnoitering above are white-faced and silent.

Tuesday, 3 October

Waited ages in the bank – and in the grocers. A man asking for a bottle of brandy was willing to pay the fantastic price asked – there is little left.

Illustrating American sympathy with us, here is a letter received from my best American friend at Nantucket:

'Both B. and I had bad emotional effects from that awful week of uncertainty. We sat with our ears glued to our wireless snatching at any straw which might mean that war was not upon you. We neither ate nor slept and when the final news came, we both caved in.'

Everywhere the pace of life slackens in the country. We are going to buy pony traps and horses, we are going to stay at home every evening and get to know our neighbours better. What shall we be like at the end of the war? Poor, and possibly quarrelling among ourselves.

Wednesday, 4 October

Yesterday evening listened to the German wireless in English. A good deal about the English and their queer insistence on war.

Tonight falls the first autumnal rain, bleak, ice-cold, and the ache for our men in France begins to be felt. Robin is telling me how he often lay out in his sleeping bag all night when they were moving, up at Ypres, 'but took no harm'.

Friday, 6 October

Madge found London much more lively than when I was up. A run on warm clothes. She could not get any vests at Lewis's, and the overall department was besieged by war workers, all very matey while trying them on.

As I write I hear that 'ten newsreel cinemas will keep open until ten o'clock in London now'.

I heard Hitler's speech at two o'clock. I was not in the least impressed; the only thing that really was of profound interest was his peevishness, and the absence of any exultation in his words. His gabbled offer of peace I feel we cannot entertain. I wonder if we shall put forward any counter-proposals.*

* The main thrust of Hitler's speech to the Reichstag on 6 October was to justify the invasion of Poland, while denying that Germany posed a threat to Denmark, Holland, or Belgium, or other countries which might have reason to be nervous of German intentions. He also maintained he had no desire for war with France or Britain.

Saturday, 7 October

How terrible this pause is. Hitler's speech has made everybody very miserable. A shadow moves nearer. Old Mr Struben is actually roofing in his rafters with a layer of corrugated iron, as a protection against bombs.

Sunday, 8 October

Basil came yesterday, from Netley. He thinks his orders will arrive this week, owing to a note he had from the War Office.

May B. spoke of the marching away of the troops. Hundreds have left Aldershot. The strange thing is that they don't march away with song and band, waving of flags and hands, flowers flung at them or tears shed. Not a bit of it! Quietly they slog down the ugly streets of this most hideous of towns, and the maidens in khaki, thick in the streets, often turn to look in at the shop windows, even before the boys have swung past. No excitement. Nothing inspired. May observes the lack of vitality common in the new generation, fed on the wireless and cinema.

Monday, 9 October

A day of rain and pessimism.

I hear Captain C., well known in the village as a shabbily-dressed retired naval man, is now at work again on the North Sea, and very dashing and young in his uniform ... a resurrection.*

* Probably Captain Coppinger, judging from the entry for 28 September. In a handwritten note Connie adds: 'Later, he was killed.'

Tuesday, 10 October

As we go to sleep, of a night, in this peaceful, beautiful red-roofed village, more wanderers are about in Europe, homeless, threatened, cold, and full of terror. Children and old people, babies and young wives alone, without a refuge. Women who loved their pretty things at home as much as I do, and the evening stroll in the summer dusk with their dear ones. The imagination boggles before the picture, shrinks away from the tears, the perplexity, the obstacles and the poverty. Thousands are starving in Warsaw. Heil Hitler!

Wednesday, 11 October

Now all Europe is wondering about the fate of Finland. Fearful regret that one has not been to these Northern countries now threatened, to see them when they were yet happy and free and full of a fine independence.

Friday, 13 October

Lunched with General Montgomery's sister. He is in command of our Third Corps, just going out to France. She said her brother had foretold accurately how things would go, so far; especially he had forseen the friendship 'twixt Germany and Russia.

Saturday, 14 October

The gas ration card has arrived, and is too wonderful and mysterious, reminding me of some of the sealed sacred books of the East, whose meaning none – even the wisest – can decipher. Madge says she can understand it, but when I ask if she can tell the difference between her meter and ours in the cellar, she quails. I shall leave it all alone, wear a coat when I can instead of lighting my fire, and have a few extra colds. The kitchen cooking cannot in any way be controlled, at a distance.

Sunday, 15 October

It poured and poured with rain. The Sunday papers were full of a curious optimism, and seem to take for granted that Hitler's game is up. It seems stupid to me. It has scarcely begun.

Nobody can understand what will happen re Russia v. Finland.* The Kings Gustav, of Sweden, Christian of Denmark and Haakon of Norway call a meeting. Their thrones must seem to them to be trembling and shaking. I hope they will wear their lovely jewelled crowns, while they still may.

Monday, 16 October

Have just heard that there has been an attempted air raid on Edinburgh.†

A not-too-young lady with scarlet lips, pale face and ugly trousers has called to ask Madge if a house-to-house collection

* Fears concerning Stalin's expansionist ambitions were confirmed when Russia invaded Finland on 30 November.

† The first air raid of the war, on the Royal Naval base at Rosyth, on the Firth of Forth. There were no British casualties, but two German airmen were shot down and killed. They were buried in Edinburgh with full military honours, a consideration which was not to last as the war intensified.

could be made of onions and carrots, to help a refugee nursing home at Shalford. Even *one* carrot from each household would help!

Ernest Brown, Minister of Labour*, un-eloquent usually, talks on the wireless about calling up the new conscripts. *England expects* ... *Scotland expects* ... *Wales expects* ... we hear.

Thursday, 19 October

Muff the Puss is now exalted when he gets a herring and is dropping all his fancy ways. The butcher tells Robin that he only gets twenty per cent of his usual ration of imported meat.

Friday, 20 October

To the cinema: a tragic film with a tragic end, Bette Davis in *Dark Victory*. Very fine, and singular. There was news. Photos of our Tommies behind the lines, grinning under Glengarry caps at the camera, just as bright as we want to feel they are.

Madge runs upstairs to tell us there will be no gas or electricity ration after all, so that will make a great difference to the good spirits of our winter.

Sunday, 22 October

The sixth week of Hitler's War.

Basil could not get back from Netley, telephoning to say he

* Ernest Brown held the post of Minister of Labour under both Stanley Baldwin and Neville Chamberlain, and was succeeded by Ernest Bevin in 1940.

must stay by a very sick patient, to whom he was giving blood transfusions. He said that a convoy of 180 soldiers had arrived from France, the very first. Not wounded, but ill.

May B. and John Sinclair came. J. S. had noticed a tiny procession of King's College Choir boys going in to evensong in the chapel, in their top hats, Eton jackets, and alas, gas masks slung on! It struck him as horrible.

Went to the ten o'clock service. Virginia Shrapnell-Smith came in, and said of her brother Tommy, who crashed fatally last week in an aeroplane, 'He very much enjoyed the party while it lasted.'

Monday, 23 October

Saw two little London boys today in the lane. They said they liked Peaslake village better than Fulham. I showed them some coloured leaves I had picked for a vase. 'Our lady picks them like that for her vases,' they said. They then told me that they had crossed the tree trunk that spread across the path from two high banks. And one in the river. They were keenly interested when I said I used as a child to put paper boats in the Tillingbourne, hoping they would sail safely to the sea, by the Wey and the Thames. They didn't know the Tillingbourne water went into the sea. They had just had roast beef at the canteen, and apples and rice.

Tuesday, 24 October

To tea three people. Mrs H. spoke of interviewing some of the evacuated mothers here. 'Poor things, they stand in the street and cry, and say their homes will never be the same again, and what have they to do with this village?'

Talked with May B. on the phone. She spoke of the excessive demand, freshly in, of income tax on her small income. About one hundred and seventy pounds on four hundred! She says it just can't be paid. All over the country these demands must be ignored, especially in retrospection. A mistake has been made by the Exchequer; the tax will paralyse trade, paralyse individuals, and create more unemployment. May thinks that the government is doing all sorts of foolish things in its attempt to appear prepared this time. Why could not the evacuation, for instance, have been purely voluntary? Why pool all butter, bacon, fats and so on, and charge so little per pound that the poor trader will be forced out of existence, by making hardly any profit? May is busy with the eternal anti-gas arrangements at Aldershot, organising decontamination squads, etc.

Wednesday, 25 October

Ribbentrop's speech is a mass of nonsense.*

Thursday, 26 October

Christmas things, rather half-heartedly displayed in the shops, give one a queer feeling. 'This war may last thirty years if it is not going to have any big offensive' was the remark I heard, passing from one man to the other in the High Street.

* Joachim von Ribbentrop, German Foreign Minister from 1938 until the end of the war. He was hanged for war crimes in 1946 after the Nuremberg Trials.

Friday, 27 October

Two letters came in by evening post from Harry. Splendid. I wrote him two letters today which was half-a-crown well and truly spent.*

Madge tells me that Colonel B., only fifty-four, is chafing to be employed, but nothing doing.

Barbara writes that specialists are finding that no-one in England is being ill in wartime. On the other hand, my own doctor tells me he is never finished till nine-thirty, so when the wounded do come, and there are lots of anaesthetics to be given, he will have no time to breathe. Barbara says that when rationing comes in 'with its immense muddles', she means to register with one butcher, and her husband with another, and the dogs with another!

We are now having Radio Paris broadcasts; they are charming, and much better mannered than ours. We heard a delightful description of Orleans in wartime the other day, speaking of streets I know and love, where the black-out seems as entire as here, by the broad, swiftly-flowing Loire.

Saturday, 28 October

North-easter, and rain. Will the Germans go through Belgium? That is the question of today.

At Blenheim Palace, where Malvern School is billeted now (at the cost of £5,000 in alterations†), the boys may not use ink, in case they spoil anything.

* A crown was a five-shilling coin in pre-decimal currency, and half-a-crown was two shillings and sixpence.

† Approximately £240,000 today.

Monday, 30 October

Rather terrible stories filter through of muddle in Army hospitals in Woolwich, of officers lying shivering without hot water bottles, and so on, and there is a great scarcity in the Army of gum boots, which, however, the noble ARP at home are being supplied with.

No Sunlight soap in the shop today. The butcher says all fat will be taken off his meat soon by the government.

The German propaganda reports us as very hard up for food, and says potatoes will be rationed here soon.

No FANY woman has yet been sent abroad. No need, in this tremendous lull.

Travelled in the train with a woman who said that when the children in Guildford were billeted, they were all set down on the edge of the pavements, a long forlorn row, then pushed into the houses, often compulsorily. She accepted two little boys, though she had rooms booked in a hotel in Cornwall for a holiday. This she quietly gave up.

On the BBC tonight the repetition of the famous play *Lost Horizon* was peculiarly appropriate to our times.* The dread that everything fragile and beautiful will be lost. I passed the Tate Gallery today, and forgot for a moment that it had been emptied of treasures. It is a close secret, jealously guarded, as to where the Blakes and the Monets lie today.†

* Filmed by Frank Capra in 1937 and later adapted by the BBC as a radio play, the 1933 novel *Lost Horizon* by James Hilton imagines an isolated valley in Tibet known as Shangri-La, where the wisdom of the world is preserved in time of crisis.

† Paintings from the Tate and other galleries were removed and stored for safety in the tunnels of Manod Quarry in north Wales, which had been specially adapted for the purpose.

Thursday, 2 November

Went to the Hospital League today.* Mrs Wilmott, the mother of a local boy who went down in the *Royal Oak*† came in, a large woman in black. When she had paid her subscription, and gone, my fellow worker told me that she had paid a visit of condolence to that poor mother after the dreadful news. Mrs Wilmott had said: 'Well, if I had known he would be drowned, I would never have let him join the Navy!'

As I write, at 9.25, before the fire, Sir Ernest Swinton is talking to us on the BBC of the touchy proposition of forcing the Siegfried Line. Neither side is likely to atttack, Swinton says. Time is on our side, thank God.‡

Nancy's brother is on twenty-four hours leave from Gibraltar. He was on a sloop, one of forty, forming a convoy to protect passenger ships and trading ships of every sort. He says he was not in dry clothes once through the eight days they took to zig-zag through the German mines.

Sunday, 5 November

To tea Marna and John Hopgood, both emancipated through the war. John (aged eighteen) is quite a man now, walking

* Before the formation of the National Health Service in 1948, numerous local voluntary organisations operated subscription schemes to ensure the welfare of hospital patients and provide for their daily needs. These were the basis of what would later become the League of Friends.

† The battleship HMS *Royal Oak* was torpedoed by German submarine U-47 while at anchor in the harbour of Scapa Flow in the Orkney Islands on 14 October 1939. Of her 1208 officers and men, 833 were killed.

‡ Major General Sir Ernest Swinton, KB, CBE, DSO was a war correspondent and military writer who, during his active service, had helped to develop the first tanks. The Siegfried Line was a system of defensive fortifications and tank traps constructed along the full length of Germany's western borders during the 1930s.

about London; his lawyer's office is in the West End. Marna is sharing a bed with a Guildford stationer's daughter at Woking, billeted with a policeman's wife in a bungalow. She is a Woman Terrier Clerk, and fills in forms all day long. The government pays the woman one pound each for the girls; they don't expect tea for that, but breakfast, and midday meal and a night snack. She washes their sheets; the girls supply bath towels. Marna is cheerful: it is all new; she goes to shilling hops, dances Boomps-a-daisy with the soldiery, and is very gay. I think of her mother over in France, probably uselessly worrying over these two, who are roving free.

Monday, 6 November

A letter from Canada. Beryl writes that the country is solidly behind England, troops drilling at the top of their street, and looking very dashing. She writes: 'They parade past our window at eight-thirty, and cause mild heart-flutters.'

I copy this out of the papers today from the advertisements, showing the need for men:

> Wanted: milling setters, universal millers, vertical millers, internal and universal grinders, thread millers and borers, tool shapers, surface grinders, slotters and rate fixers.

Wednesday, 8 November

Went to Guildford to see the house taken over by the Town Council for child evacuees who could fit in nowhere else. The desolation of the place inside is unutterable, no floor covering of any kind, bare boards of a poor wood, a steep dismal staircase, of course bare, with marks of former carpets. Dreadful black-grey blankets on the camp beds, and only one sheet on each. Everything gloomy, uncared for, big windows dirty – and in short, a scandal for rich Guildford.

I planted six iris bulbs, very small, but I hope they will yield bright purple flowers. I got them for a penny a dozen at Woolworths, who are today reducing all their bulbs.

The silver birch in the front garden does look graceful and wonderful. There are high winds at night now, and everyone wonders when the Germans will begin their offensive; huge beams of searchlights ray out across our darkened heaths and lanes.

Thursday, 9 November

'The sooner we are all dead the better,' said poor Mrs Murray to me just now, 'what with the world in such a state, and all our best young men likely to be killed.' I feel very sorry for her, sitting in her tiny, pretty room feeling her bad heart.

This morning news of the bomb at Munich which nearly finished Hitler.* 'So Mr Nasty has had a fright,' observed the village postmaster in a laconic British voice, as he took Harry's air mail letter from me.

To tea with the Shrapnell-Smiths. Mrs Shrappie and I cried together over Tommy's death, only twenty-three, in a mimic battle in the air. She has had nearly 400 letters. Tommy was very popular – lucky she has a first class photograph of him. It was sad to drive away from the fine old house with its clipped

* On 8 November Hitler survived an assassination attempt by Georg Elser, a committed opponent of Nazism. Elser had planted a bomb in the hall where Hitler was scheduled to speak, but owing to a last-minute change in his travel arrangements, Hitler left the building before the bomb went off.

hedges and red-berried creeper high round the old windows, where we have had such hospitality, such happy tennis parties. No use to write like this. The house is up for sale.

Winston made a splendid speech yesterday. He said in a memorable sentence, 'We shall have suffering, but *we shall break their hearts*.'

Friday, 10 November

It is a fine, still, thoughtful November evening, with veils of mist round the green fields of Newlands and winding about the golden woods. Everything now is governed by black-out time. The post to my sorrow is deteriorating here, as in the last war (and we only restored it about ten years after). The postman comes while it is still daylight and there is already only one delivery round Dorking. People are writing much more than they did I think, and the troops in France manage more than one letter per head per day.

Saturday, 11 November

Holland has flooded her fields, afraid of the German advance. I keep thinking of the Low Countries where I was only a year ago in June. I admired the sober, sturdy and independent-minded people and their neat, clean houses, shining windows and crimson shutters. Ada, my Dutch friend, said then that they were very much afraid of the Germans.

Sunday, 12 November

May B. to tea. She said they had spent all Friday rehearsing an air raid; so when the actual 'I pass you the yellow warning'

ATS anti-aircraft artillery spotters learn to use an identification telescope at No.7 ATS Training Centre at Stoughton near Guildford.
Photograph © IWM H14189

came on next day on the phone at her Aldershot office, she found that her troops simply took it to be a joke, and received it as a signal for another practice about which they could go slowly. It was hard to convince them. They had the All Clear signal in about half an hour.

Monday, 13 November

I had the piano tuned. The little tuner explained how he had lost his job in London, all his clients having gone into the country. One lady wishes him to go on tuning her grand, now in a furniture store, 'probably lying on its side. How can I? It wouldn't pay me.' This war hits people like this severely.

He smiles and says he doesn't notice any more the noise going on in his back garden. Over the wall are the barracks, and recruits firing all day, volleys and rattles and in the adjoining wood the raw buglers practising horrible blasts.

Robin is reading the White Paper on German concentration camps, ably written and painful.*

Wednesday, 15 November

Diana and I went to visit the communal kitchen and saw a pleasant scene, three happy ladies peeling potatoes (with the new patent knife), and another carrying buckets. Smart black and white lino, good stove, and so on. Pretty Mrs Coppinger in a striped overall says that her husband is very cold at Harwich now on a mine-sweeper, and also sometimes in a chilly office at Parkstone Quay. He will be glad to receive the 100 Balaclava helmets for his men which the ladies of Shere are knitting.

We went to lunch with Mrs Rayne at the Farm; a lovely room, big white chrysanthemums, huge chimneypiece, and log fire. In the farmyard was a man with a brilliant blue shirt, piling logs. 'That is the national shirt of the Sudeten Germans,' said

* The first officially published account of German concentration camps, released on 30 October 1939.

our host.* The foreigner, happy-eyed, was piling the logs with great art. Dr Benes,† they think, is not keen that his men should join our army, and many have no jobs: lawyers and doctors. Mrs Rayne had just got permission for a young doctor to 'observe' in Guildford hospital, and was fighting to get a Czech boy into the technical school at Guildford, already overrun with evacuees.

Back through the leaf-strewn lanes. Diana and the Tuckwell girls at tea, all of them wondering when they will be called up.

Basil phones at five to say he will be stationed with the Royal Engineers at Codford, Salisbury Plain, and will get seven days' leave for uniform.

Robin looks at the calm sky and the young moon and says that the Hun may easily be with us tonight.

I think more and more of compromise. That is very likely to be the end of all this war – an unsatisfactory peace!

Thursday, 16 November

My husband is a perfect war-time companion – all house repairs quietly and efficiently done. Today a ventilator carved out of some wood for a certain wall; the black-out speedy and complete.

I think generations after this will be amazed (if they ever have the inclination to read of the past) to note the extent of our precautions against air-raids. People living week after week away from home in the most annoying conditions, desperately

* Many of the Sudeten refugees were ethnic Germans fleeing forcible repatriation because they were Social Democrats or other political opponents of the Nazi regime.

† Edvard Benes, President of Czechoslovakia from 1935 until 1938, and again from 1945 until 1948. During the war Benes was head of the Czech government-in-exile based in London.

unhappy, yet not venturing back, when everything points to their going back as the only solution to their misery.

Friday, 17 November

Basil went to town to buy uniform, and there was a great discussion re how many shirts, how many boots and so on. His overcoat tried on makes him look like a thoughtful Guardsman, so very bunchy and waisted.

Rumours in the papers and on the wireless that Germany is torn by dissension in its higher commands and councils. 'Of course the best Germans have lost faith in Hitler and his government,' says Robin.

Rotterdam has lost 72 per cent of its trade through the war; no wonder the Dutch long for peace.

Everybody has been sulking about the black-out trains and the long terrifying crowded journeys back from London to the suburbs. 'Hell with the lid on,' cries the *Evening Standard* tonight.

Saturday, 18 November

The papers are full of guesses why the Germans do not attack.

Woke early, and thought of Clive Modin, the timber merchant, now at Sandhurst, training to be an officer in the Royal Fusiliers, of Mickey Robinson now in the ranks of the Coldstream Guards, of Basil, off next week to Salisbury Plain.*

* Connie added after the war in a handwritten footnote: 'Only Basil got through. Mickey was killed by a Japanese bomb thrown at his brow and hitting it, in Burma, when due for leave. Clive died on D-Day on the Normandy Beaches, gallantly leading his men.'

Sunday, 19 November

Tonight there is no more Summer Time, so we shall be in the black-out well before five.

Went to call on Mrs Barlow, in bed, knitting a Balaclava helmet. She showed me a charming letter of thanks from a mine-sweeper on the *Florio*, saying that four helmets (of the first Shere contingent) had been dealt out to each ship, and they were furiously competed for. 'I was one of the lucky ones,' said the writer, 'and I can assure you it is very welcome. When we come off our watch we are like blocks of ice, and have few comforts.'

I read the *Life of Adler* by Phyllis Bottome last night. Adler's gardener knew Hitler as a boy, and used to say Adolf would never play with the others, but would watch them from afar. Once the schoolboys made a snowman, and Adolf suddenly darted forward and placed his own hat on top, as if he had had a share in the trouble of making it. This story highly intrigued Adler.*

Monday, 20 November

Robin says he feels that there must be a big air raid on London tonight or tomorrow in the moonlight, or 'they may never come'. As we came out of the cinema after seeing *Goodbye Mr Chips*, the placards said, 'Enemy airplane over the Thames'.

* Alfred Adler, influential psychologist and co-founder with Freud of the psychoanalytic movement, best known for his theory of Individual Psychology and the concept of the Inferiority Complex.

Tuesday, 21 November

The days seem to slip past pretty quickly: everybody is wondering why Hitler does not start the offensive, and is not entering Holland after all. The neutral countries are in a most terrible state, their sea-borne trade is vanishing; the Danes have laid a lot of mines.

Basil will soon be gone; I dread it. It seems so far away, Codford St Peter, and the chalky Plain so wide and dreary.

Wednesday, 22 November

At dinner Basil declared: 'I am fighting against three things in this war. One, against the War Office with its ridiculous archaic system of red tape. Two, against discomfort. Three, against Hitler!' I told him that I had a very shrewd suspicion in the last war that Alice in Wonderland and the Dodo had got into the War Office, turned everybody else out, and were running it, with the Red Queen as their messenger; and I believed the same thing had happened again.

Thursday, 23 November

Forever to be remembered as the day Basil went into khaki; and it is Eudo's wedding day in Shanghai.* I did not see Basil in uniform, save for the pullover and tie, as he went up to town to try on the tunic again. The packing was at long last completed. His military cap came complete with the noble badge of the RAMC as worn by his uncle before him; the cap was too

* Eudo Andrews, one of Muriel Andrews' three sons. Peter and John were the other two.

small for me, too big for Robin, tight for Basil, but immensely becoming.

After his departure, everything fell very flat, and I was grateful to my kind friends who carried me off after lunch to see the Gracie Fields film, *Shipyard Sally*, which swung along in very amusing fashion. Felt much more cheerful after it, driving home most cautiously through the dark roads to Shere. It is not much fun when you see a big mass looming right over you – a bus!

I was horrified to read of the Gestapo methods with the Czech student suspects in Prague. Rousing them at three a.m. and making them come off to prison (many must have been perfectly innocent) in their night clothes; pouring cold water all over them when they arrived. It is admitted, it seems, in Germany, that there were 1,700 executions of these students. What a time we live in, yet all seems so safe in this little Surrey community tonight, where supper slowly warms in the oven, and there is perfect stillness outside. Not one glimmer of light can I see in the village.

Saturday, 25 November

An extremely interesting article today in the *Telegraph* by one Villard, an American journalist. Some points are that the Germans are saving up for a terrible smashing of England in May, when our seaside towns will be attacked.

Well-informed Germans consider that the submarine which got into Scapa Flow and torpedoed the *Royal Oak* sailed boldly on the surface with its searchlight going, and deluded the British sailors into believing that is was one of their boats that was approaching and it never submerged.

Mr Villard found many German people ashamed of the Polish campaign.

This morning in the village I met Mr Dodds, who was beaming: his sailor son has come on leave from the Far East; their boat sailed in a great loop from Gibraltar right out into the Atlantic to avoid mines and U-boats. Tony has been away nearly two years, and looks 'much taller and very brown, and he's full of beans'.

Sunday, 26 November

Joy Annett to lunch. I hoped we could avoid a long and fruitless discussion on politics. I know she is very unhappy about the war. However, nothing would keep the charming, beautiful being off it and we talked gloomily till dusk began to gather and were no forrarder. Joy thinks we should not be patriotic, we should have no country, but belong to all nations.

Monday, 27 November

The papers are full of the sinking of ships. The Davidsons came back from Cyprus on the *Rawalpindi*, and are much distressed by her loss. So many went down with her.* The pictures in the press are constantly of a great boat just being submerged, looking very pitiful.

Tuesday, 28 November

Basil writes that he has been continuously busy since he has been on the Plain, six or seven hundred men of the Royal Engineers in his charge, vaccinations and innoculations to

* HMS *Rawalpindi* was a former passenger ship converted to an armed cruiser. On patrol off the Faroe Islands she encountered two German battleships, and her captain, 60-year-old Edward Kennedy, elected to give battle rather than surrender. He and 237 of his crew were killed: there were 48 survivors.

tackle; also the questions of poor, overcrowded billets, scabies, etc. First sick parade is at 8.30. It sounds overwhelming.

Every night we hear of some ship mined, and we are losing count of even their names.

Wednesday, 29 November

The war seems pressing on us here, especially this week. Robin walks about pouring out floods of talk and I listen with my mind half on the widows and children of the *Rawalpindi*. Feel very cross and touchy, and a great longing to get away.

I try to send two guineas to Canada for my sister-in-law's Christmas gift but it is too difficult, the thing would have to be put before judge and jury (says the post office man), who would decide whether a money order could go. 'Besides,' he adds gloomily, 'you know, ma'm, with them U-boats about, it might never get over.'

Thursday, 30 November

The one o'clock news told us that Russia has invaded Finland.

What of the poor little country? What of Norway, what of Sweden? What shall we do? Will Germany ally itself with Russia, and shall we automatically be at war with Russia too? What of India? What will the neutrals do? How insolent are the Russians, never pausing to reply to America's offer to intervene before taking action.

Friday, 1 December

Soon we will have had three months' war, and I will have my journal bound up for this period. I hope it has been worth keeping. I hear 12 per cent of the printing trade is out of work, alas, and not likely to get it.

Madge says she is bored to death with the war. But there is a huge amount of local bridge going on. Everybody is knitting, and wool is difficult to get.

Barbara says Miss J., ruler of the *Children's Hour* on the BBC, returns her engaging story of a mouse air warden who dealt with bats (and spoke in rhyme all the time), saying that she hopes that children don't know anything about air raids. 'I suppose their gas masks are to keep fairies in!' cries the irritated author.

Monday, 4 December

Down to Hampshire by bus. Most exciting; my first journey to stay with anybody since the war started.

It gave me a queer feeling, coming down the hill into Winchester, to see an aeroplane immediately above the grey ancestral tower of the cathedral. Shall I live to see our cathedrals bombed from the air?

Arrived to find my sisters-in-law's main preoccupation the six or seven red setter dogs. The stables are almost empty, and the business of letting horses out to people who want to ride in the New Forest has vanished. Molly was up in London being interviewed by the Admiralty. They offered her small pay to be a dispatch rider in the WRNS. Molly, aged forty, declined.*

* Robin's elder sister May and younger sister Sibyl lived in the New Forest not far from Muriel Andrews at Picket Post. Molly (elsewhere referred to as Molly W.) was clearly part of their household, but whether she was a friend or a relation is not clear.

Tuesday, 5 December

Muriel Andrews called for me.

The school at Picket Post has gained pupils through this war, and the house is full of jolly, well-mannered little boys. This year, owing to the black-out there can be no performance of the usual Gilbert and Sullivan as parents could not do the journey. So all will be taken to *The Lion Has Wings*, the propaganda film, instead.

I heard of Peter in France (whose scarlet mess kit hung in the wardrobe of the spare room); he has been digging trenches with his men. Every morning the cordial French landlady at his billet puts a dash of rum into his coffee.

Friday, 8 December

Left with great regret as always. At Southampton it was pouring with rain, but men were digging away manfully at underground shelters in the park.

Robin, surveying the shelters from the bus with critical eye, considered their structure was faulty and that they would 'fall in' by and by.

Sunday, 10 December

May B. came in the afternoon in khaki straight from Aldershot. She described the work she is doing with the FANYs and told us many stories of girl recruits, and of many well-to-do married women, who after a time come to her weeping that they are being 'wasted'; jibbing at the menial work they have to do to begin with.

May told one rebellious maiden that she must regard herself

as merely 'a cog in a machine'. Later on wrathful letters arrived from Pa, saying his girl possessed 'originality and personality' and that she was certainly no cog. The CO laughed heartily with May over this.

It's interesting to hear May's idea of the war. She thinks this is Armageddon. Before we have finished she believes that the whole world will be ablaze. She thinks the Arabs will rise and the Russians pour into Asia.

Tuesday, 12 December

I am writing at eight o'clock and the German wireless is giving over marching songs sung with great élan. They don't seem in the least depressed! Fine young men are obviously shouting them.

Yet all is not well. I read in the *Readers Digest* that the health bulletin of Germany, taken from Germany's own statistics, shows that rickets is prevalent, and diptheria more common. In 1935 and '36 only 75 per cent of the men called up were found fit for active service. By last year only 55 per cent were acceptable. Dysentery has increased 300 per cent under Hitler. Heart trouble and tuberculosis are increasing, and so on . . .

Every now and then one feels the greatest pity and love for Germany, so strained, so chivvied, so much afraid, and so mechanical.*

Heard from Mickey, a private in the Coldstream Guards. He says that two very nice chaps deserted from his squad on Friday night. They just couldn't stand the roughness of the life.

* Connie was widely travelled in Europe and knew Germany well. Her hatred for Hitler and for the conduct of the war did not prevent her from sympathising with the German people, at least in the early part of the conflict, before its later horrors became apparent.

Wednesday, 13 December

From the news of the Assembly at Geneva today*, it is clear that the neutrals are by no means sure that we shall be the victors. They fear to offend Russia and, behind her, Germany. Would not Sweden, Norway, Denmark and Holland help poor Finland if they could do as they longed to do? Obviously they are not certain that Germany and the Soviet would not crumple them up and never get out, while we possibly made a compromise to suit ourselves, and left them in the lurch.

Thursday, 14 December

I am sitting by the fire; the tenants below are dressing for a dinner party at High House with bridge to follow. This is very delightful: the Davidsons are refusing to be depressed by the war.

Shere has achieved its 100 Balaclava helmets for the minesweepers. Glorious!

Friday, 15 December

So the year creeps to its close – the days still shortening, the north wind bitter, Christmas a burden. I got a magazine with a first instalment of a serial [written] by me, and I wondered if the war would permit the serial to be finished.

Tonight the German broadcast is one long boast as usual.

* The twentieth Assembly of the League of Nations, forerunner of the UN. The following day, the League formally expelled the Soviet Union for its acts of aggression against Finland.

They shot – they say – ten out of twenty of our aeroplanes over Borkum. Our Admiralty says we lost three. Will the *Graf Spee* sail out of Montevideo harbour or stay in it, interned? The Germans are very silent about that tonight.*

Went to *The Lion Has Wings*, a perfectly amazing film about our air force. A triumph indeed. It mut be a new creation, this modern airman. Clouds and guns, brains and nerve – utterly astonishing to one of my age.

Sunday, 17 December

I note various prophecies. The American *Saturday Evening Post* says Germany will eventually be (a) starved for fuel and (b) starved for materials. German artillery and aeroplanes top the Allied strength, but these are not of much use after ammunitions and petrol give out – and these will give out, says the US Department of Commerce, in two years. Denmark already lies helpless before Germany, and it is likely that Hitler will seize it; also Holland for its air bases, agriculture and shipping; Sweden for its indispensable iron fields, and Rumania for its oil.

And what of Finland, where in the Baltic north the few hours of light flit like a phantom? Some of the Russians, they say, have perished in the snow.

Ten p.m. Now the *Graf Spee* has moved from her moorings, and all the world waits and wonders.

* Following the Battle of the River Plate in the South Atlantic, the badly damaged *Admiral Graf Spee* was penned in Montevideo harbour, Uruguay, by two British cruisers, who managed to bluff her captain that theirs was a superior force, to the extent that he ordered the *Graf Spee* to be scuttled.

Monday, 18 December

Everybody pleased, and most of us surprised that the *Graf Spee* is scuttled. 'I cannot get down the chimney this year,' says the German Father Christmas. 'Why not?' cry out the little Hitler Youth. 'Because there is a scuttle in the way!' Idiotic, but the joke of the moment.

A Shere man has been killed in the black-out in the lane outside, and I knew the girl driving the car, cool and capable Joyce Stevens. He got right in front, apparently.

Tuesday, 19 December

The Eusti came to lunch.* Shoulder of lamb, lots of delicious onion sauce, browned potatoes, suet pudding with hot black treacle poured over it, and a few mince-pies from Guildford. A good deal of story-telling and laughter – I think we were all very happy to meet again.

Bert turned out an ARP warden, and at any moment may be called on the telephone to be told to distribute to various centres the words: '*Red Warning*'.†

It was noble of them to come, with their last petrol ration, and to bring me a plum pudding and a Christmas cake.

It is well worth taking the *News Chronicle* as well as the *Daily Mail* and *The Times*. Today Vernon Bartlett is back from Geneva, and tells in an article what the neutrals were talking about. It amounts to this:

* The Eustaces, old friends of Connie's. *Eusti* is a humorous 'Latin' plural: one Eustace, two Eusti.

† Meaning that enemy aircraft were five to ten minutes away.

1. The overwhelming mass of Germans are sick and tired of this Hitler regime.

2. But, there will be no revolt – there's not enough vitality left, except possibly in the higher ranks of the army.

Harry has been down a tin mine at Kuala Lumpur. The air mail this time has taken only eleven days.

Wednesday, 20 December

So grim and dreadful a day, foggy, icy, that I got Robin to stay in bed with his cold. Felt very bad myself, writing in a fireless room.

A woman choosing bacon from the very slender stock at the Forrest Stores cried that she wanted *collar*. The man serving, amazed at her obstinacy, and her lack of realisation as to the conditions of the bacon trade, just threw up his hands and said: 'Oh *gosh*!'

Sunday, 24 December

This will be rather a brief week's journal, as one's mind is completely weary with the effort of organising Christmas without any help from any other brain. The menfolk are entirely uninterested, but drop brown paper on the floor and sit down joyously to nice hot meals.

Joy and Otto came in: he is an Austrian refugee from Vienna, a very learned art critic. It is not known if he will be allowed to work here permanently, but since the Aliens Tribunal* it is

* The tribunals were set up 'to deal with all enemy aliens of registrable age who have not already been interned, of whom there are about 50,000' (*Daily Telegraph*, 9 September 1939). Most were refugees from Germany or, like Otto, Austria, and 'aliens with anti-Nazi sympathies may be found work in the service of this country.'

easier, and one hopes that such a specialist will be used over here.

Wretchedly cold, so cold that in every room practically of our little flat fires burn all the time.

Christmas Day

Church, and cheerful carols.

Madge's turkeys failed to appear from Aberdeenshire. Our little local station, Gomshall, had heard nothing of the band of three noble twenty-five-pounders, travelling south.

The King's speech was painfully delivered, but he got through it better at the end than the beginning. I wonder if his speech specialist, Mr Logue, was by his side.*

Boxing Day

The speech tonight by Georg Gripenberg, the Finnish Minister in London, was the most moving of any I have listened to on the wireless since Hitler's War began. He drew a swift graphic picture of his little country with its brave modern towns, enlightened ideas, care of the poor, absence of unemployment. Now they are hoplessly outnumbered, and alas they have not enough ammunition or guns. It was a brave, tragic speech, spoken with great dignity and self-control. Cannot the neutrals brave all and come to help? This fear of Russia is terrible.

* As depicted in the 2011 film *The King's Speech*, which portrays the relationship between King George VI and Lionel Logue, the therapist who taught him how to overcome his stammer.

Wednesday, 27 December

Woke early to wake Basil, who had to leave early for Salisbury. Very cheerful idea, this journeying in the morning, instead of the gloomy night. Tony Dodds called for him at 8.30 and the dark blue naval overcoat walked with the khaki overcoat down the village street in the morning air. I missed him all day dreadfully.

Madge is down at the canteen, getting ready roast beef (her turkeys from Aberdeen still linger mysteriously) for the evacuees' parents who are being entertained by the village. She makes Yorkshire pudding for the very first time and is thrilled. The parents come: there are forty-five. They eat, they smile, they make speeches of thanks. They leap in the fields with their children (for it is fair) and return to eat again. Madge returns, exhausted, and has a hot bath while the parents travel back Fulhamwards and many of their sons and daughters go to bed in the cottages weeping.

Thursday, 28 December

Snow and muffled roads and white boughs, and the village nurse in her car slithering about the hill.

I hear from Margaret Dell in America. It is a vivid, agitated letter. They seem to listen in to Europe a great deal. 'Our young,' she says, 'do not understand, but my husband and I agree that we are letting others fight our battles and that the fight is for the retention of all the things we hold most dear in life. One's whole heart aches over the war and you.'

My article on our village in wartime is in the *British Weekly*. The number is a very, very thin one. I wonder how long it will live.*

* The shortage of paper caused difficulties for many magazines and periodicals. The *British Weekly* survived the war, however.

Bey came to sherry, and tells me that a baker, an elderly Czech refugee, is allowed to work at last in Guildford, and is radiantly happy. His wife is to have a little home again of her own; they are leaving their sad haven here at last and taking lodgings in the town.

Friday, 29 December

I feel much overwhelmed by the state of things. Shall we win – can we *ever* restore Poland and Czechoslovakia?

Saturday, 30 December

Pipes frozen everywhere. A terrible earthquake in Turkey. So ends the year in angry frost and wintry rain.

Sunday, 31 December

I hear from May that twenty-two FANYs are volunteering for Finland and are taking out a complete ambulance there quite shortly. Some of them will not come back, she says.

1940

Monday, 1 January

I think people are getting much more grave about the war, feeling we are up against a wonderful, highly trained war machine. Nothing will ever induce England to get ready in good time. Slovenly, happy-go-lucky place.

Tuesday, 2 January

Robin has just read out that 'the most horrible warfare is the kindest', a great Hitler saying, quoted by Rauschning in *Hitler Speaks*, a most illuminating volume which I must read.* Hitler would be much annoyed if he could hear the calm tone of voice in which Robin is reading out some of his more trenchant ventures.

* Hermann Rauschning, a former National Socialist who had repudiated Nazism, claimed to have had many hours of conversation with Hitler. His book *Hitler Speaks* was later denounced as a fraud, or at very least an exaggeration both of the time he had spent in Hitler's company, and of the Führer's behaviour. Nevertheless it made a vivid impression on readers at the time and was influential in creating the image of Hitler as a madman.

Wednesday, 3 January

Here is an extract from Barbara's letter about going round to see Donoghue, who has had flu:*

'He is really a very nice little man. Jack suggested that if he provided a pair of old riding boots for the auction on behalf of the Red Cross and lettered them, "I rode Brown Jack" then he might make a lot, and he agreed.

'His bedroom was all clean apple-green walls – tiny shoes by the bed, a tiny dark silk dressing-gown on the bed and a gas-mask slung on the radiator.'

Thursday, 4 January

Our gardener is still out of work, but for his three days here. I fear the war is against gardeners. Everybody coughs, looks hideous in the ghastly cold, and suffers, and the very idea of all these frozen people in Finland makes the reality of war cut us more sharply to the heart.

Friday, 5 January

A better day. Mrs Murray called, to bring some Balaclava helmets for the Surrey Regiment, and her face lit up when I gave her some more wool. We started off for Guildford, the back of the car full of books, etc. for the soldiers. Drank at Lyons a glorious glass of hot blackcurrent juice, reminiscent of cosy nurseries at night, with a fire glowing in the hearth, and a rosy

* Steve Donoghue, ten times champion jockey between 1914 and 1923. Brown Jack was a hugely popular racehorse in the early 1930s, who had a locomotive named after him in 1935.

face on the pillow. I ignored placards announcing that a great spring offensive was imminent.

Saw a film with Charles Boyer in it. There was a picture of the *Graf Spee* scuttling herself, and blazing down the sea, absolutely awe-inspiring and full of doom; a magnificent, dreadful sight, smoke mantling the huge turret . . . What history these films are writing for generations yet unborn!

Saturday, 6 January

Robin has finished *Hitler Speaks*; it gives an amazing impression of a mad, bad neurotic gangster, surrounded by opportunists. Sometimes Hitler sees some demon he dreads in the room, and points at him, screaming with fear. It is a terrible and serious indictment.

Sunday, 7 January

My poor Ebi von Brunn, of Tübingen, I think of you, gallant young Nazi, who, your mother told me in Germany, so hated the Labour Camp, when you put in your service there, that you would roam the woods and pick wild flowers to send back to your loved home, and write often and long to her. No Hitler can turn *you* against a peaceful, settled life, with love and beauty in it. We in England make you suffer longer, since we have been so slow to move, so late to prepare.*

Monday, 8 January

Dora said that her husband, a miller, is only having one third of

* The von Brunn family were friends of the Mileses prior to the outbreak of war. Basil had stayed with them when he was a student.

his stock allowed to him by the government. How are they going to live, when their full business only just paid them? Everywhere people are having to put down pigs and hens owing to lack of food. The manager of the grocery stores today bitterly criticised the method employed, and showed me three tins filled with tiny tickets like postage stamps in size, which are the ration coupons that must be checked by the young ladies in the Guildford office. What a life! If they sneeze, they will blow away.

Robin and I both think the war may be ended by mutual difficulties and boredoms and wilting enthusiasm of the troops . . . it is a kind of nasty deadlock . . . and the expense horrifying.

Sunday, 14 January

Last night Captain Dodds* informed us that there was a grave shortage of coal in this country. The great power-houses have only a week's supply.

I see, by the way, that cold has made the mutton-headed ones of Germany (as Hitler so engagingly describes his flock) rebel for the first time in ages and ages. They were so perishing cold – owing to the great coal shortage in Northern Germany – that crowds of them appeared in stations and entered the still-warmed waiting rooms, and insisted on camping out there. Not even the tough Nazi boys could get them out. So that was that. Well done Karl, well done Anna!

On the other hand I suppose nobody did anything in Berlin about the fact that so many thousands of poor old Jewish

* Connie refers to Tony Dodds' father sometimes as Captain Dodds and sometimes as Mr.

women and Jewish children in thin clothes were ordered onto the streets to shovel away the snow. It makes one's blood boil to read some things in the paper.

Monday, 15 January

Drove with Robin and some army comforts, books and mittens, over to Stoughton barracks. It was an unusually frosty morning. As I waited outside the 'Old Comrades Hut' I saw about twenty young recruits in the very act of arriving. Nice lads, I should say twenty-one or twenty-two, in grey flannel bags, dark blue and brown overcoats, each hanging on to either a paper parcel or a small suitcase.

I wondered what the mothers and sweethearts of the newcomers were thinking.

Tuesday, 16 January

Robin reads out as I write that nearly 800 Czech officers have been arrested lately in Prague and may be shot. Three of our submarines have been lost, and there are many who go to rest tonight in England heart-broken.

The wind is rushing round this ugly old house, but we are very comfortable inside it, and have so much to be grateful for. Mrs Dodds is very nervous about Tony and told me on the phone that each time she says farewell at the weekend is like dying a little death. I advised her to get sleeping tablets from her doctor.

From a textbook of English phrases for the guidance of German troops, prepared by a German officer to use when they finally arrive as conquerors in England:

Tell me, please, Mrs N.!

Tell the truth or you will be killed. But quickly clergyman, write down on this paper the number of the English Army corps.

I want thirty workmen tomorrow.

Every driver that drives the wrong way will be shot.

You will be paid now, later, after the war.

Friday, 19 January

Basil wired that he is coming for twenty-four hours tomorrow.

Miss Beck and I walked in the black and white landscape shivering, and trying to avoid talking about the war.

Saturday, 20 January

Expecting Basil. The cold is paralysing.

Dutch Ada writes at last from Doorn. She has many soldiers billeted in her great hostel, and is running musical evenings for them, and is very busy. She implores me to send her news. I can imagine the Dutchmen hurrying up the fine oak staircase of the great house with the long glossy black shutters by the well-proportioned windows, and the comfort dear Ada will dispense to them.

Barbara has lost her gas mask, and thinks the ghost in her house may have taken it. You see hardly any in the streets of Guildford now.

Monday, 22 January

The iron frost continues. Everybody is feeling thoroughly put out. The newspapers seem to be full of bad news – the Germans obtaining a corridor through Russian Poland to

Romania to get at the oil wells there, the *Grenville* sunk, and so on.*

We can't hear about Italy, from which I hoped much, without the wretched words, 'increase of armament'.† The world is raving mad, and bent on destroying itself.

Tuesday, 23 January

Entered London about eleven, sped to Piccadilly and dived into Swan and Edgar's basement, only to find it was empty and made into an air raid shelter. The statue of Eros is now wholly concealed by a wooden cone and sandbags. Very small stock in the shop, I thought; a display of warm stockings which would normally be two shillings and elevenpence were four shillings and elevenpence. The girl in the coat and skirt department said that prices of materials go up every day, not every week.

Lunch with Mildred in Fortnum and Masons, as in a fairy palace. Green gold walls, mauve curtains, sweetly pretty or finely discreet waitresses moving quietly about the thick carpet. I saw the piles of glittering sweets, and as I went out, the sprays of real white lilac and pink roses, and I could not for the life of me find any trace of war. But I heard later that the firm has closed down several departments, and is fighting for life like the rest.

* HMS *Grenville*, a G-class destroyer, struck a mine off the north Kent coast and sank with the loss of 75 men.

† Italy, while it had allied itself with Germany, did not enter the war as an active combatant until June 1940; partly because it had insufficient armament at the outset to take part.

Piccadilly Circus, showing Eros boarded up and covered in war savings posters.
Photograph © IWM D9785

Wednesday 24 January

Terrible news: The *Exmouth* has been sunk and all lost.*

As a war-time companion Barbara has a small black kitten. It likes cheese straws and cabbage and it spends most of its time purring as mine does. It fitted itself into a blue glass vase

* HMS *Exmouth*, an E-class destroyer, was torpedoed in the Moray Firth on 21 January by German submarine U-22 while she was escorting a merchant ship.

the other morning and went whirling round and round. It was in an ecstasy. I should like to meet it even more than Goebbels.

Thursday, 25 January

Wireless news says that Lloyd George* declared today in Parliament that we must dig up all the parks to plant food.

Friday, 26 January

Sir Neville Henderson, formerly British Ambassador in Berlin, last night said that the war might last a long time. There was not going to be any early collapse in Germany. This is beginning to soak into many minds in Britain.

Sunday, 28 January

A very strange day, so much ice after the thaw. The sprays of creeper leaves up the house are curiously encased in sparkling frost.†

Monday, 29 January

Snowstorm, and as I write at two p.m. more snow direct from the east. There are sixteen little icicles hanging from the dining-room window which do not vary. Spent the morning

* David Lloyd George had been Minister of Munitions, Secretary of State for War and then Prime Minister during the Great War of 1914–18. Aged seventy-seven in 1940, he was still a major political figure.

† Connie adds in a handwritten footnote (presumably tongue-in-cheek): 'So I hear later, a live peacock was encased in ice. *And* a whole haystack!'

writing to Harry, and to Basil. Robin is very miserable, slowly knitting a khaki scarf with chilly fingers.

'The shops here,' writes Sara from Weymouth, 'are bursting with bacon but none can afford to buy it.'

Tuesday, 30 January

Snow muffles the village. Some of it has washed through Nancy's ceiling and made puddles of ice water all over her nice green carpeted floor. The men are brushing it off the roof with huge hand-brooms and heavy lumps of white are thrown onto the frozen yard.

Rather too cold to think well. I'm listening in as I write to a furious hissing, screaming shout from Hitler on the German wireless. I can translate a bit, and know that the speech is full of hatred and lies against England.

Every day brings dreadful stories of torpedoed and mined ships, of ships bombed from the air. And many perish in the waves, making for a shore they are never to see again. A strange destiny indeed for the neutral sailors who are at war with nobody; to be caught by the hand of grim Fate and to find it a death-grip, without time for a word of explanation, expostulation, or message of farewell.

Food is scare in Russia, scarcer in Moscow and Leningrad* than for many years. Bread queues everywhere. 'The bread queues are due,' says the irrepressible Soviet, 'to irresponsible elements in the transport and bakery services.'

* The name by which St Petersburg was known under the Soviet regime between 1924 and 1991.

Wednesday, 31 January

Water is now rushing into the coal cellar and scullery. Miss McF., unable to get back to London as the trains are irregular still, shows me the white helmet she has completed for a Finn, with a tiny window for the face; it is very delicate and warm. Fog covers Catherine's Field, and the broken oak tree.

The paper seems to be full of pathetic single sentences such as 'The London ship *Eston* (1,487 tons) is missing, with her crew of eighteen.'

Thursday, 1 February

This is the day we should have been leaving Hôtel des Thermes in Aix-en-Provence after coffee and rolls; lunching out of doors in the sunshine at our own special restaurant at Fréjus, on the village square perched high above the neighbouring villas and the slope to the turquoise-coloured Mediterranean. Then on to our hotel at Mentone. But for Germany![*]

Ajax has arrived at Plymouth. A great welcome from thousands.[†]

Basil writes that his men in unwarmed billets shave with snow and melted water. He asks for bedroom slippers for the patients, and roller towels.

* Connie and Robin spent several weeks each winter in Mentone in the South of France, a tradition they inherited from the Miles side of the family. Robin's grandfather had retired to Mentone, and had had a house there.

† HMS *Ajax* was famous for her role in the Battle of the River Plate and the eventual scuttling of the *Graf Spee*. Although heavily outgunned, she managed to survive a number of hits from the German warship.

Friday, 2 February

Telegraphed to Pam and Prue for their fourteenth birthday* and did up a mixed parcel of books for them, including *The Fifth Form at St Dominic's* by Talbot Baines Reed, as it is good for even fourteen-year-olds to forget the war atmosphere in a wonderful story.

Sickness is everywhere. The many FANYs at Aldershot having the fashionable German measles are only allowed two days' sick leave now, instead of the customary four days.

To Guildford, where I saw that the usual shilling layer cake bought at Lyons had much shrunk.

As I write, I hear:

Twenty places in Southern Finland were bombed today.

The Russians are using armoured sledges.

All the world seems to be sending money to Finland.

Phyllis Hazeldine asks me to start saving all my halfpennies for War Saving Certificates.† Yes, I will.

Saturday, 3 February

Too cold to venture forth.

Winston's motto, written in his own hand for Harry just entering Sandhurst, stands forward on the mantleshelf:

'In War, Resolution, in Defeat, Defiance, in Victory,

* Two of Connie's nieces, the twin daughters of her sister Mildred.

† Government bonds issued to raise money to support the war effort. National Savings schemes were promoted with posters exhorting people to 'Lend to Defend the Right to be Free' or 'Save your way to Victory' and so on.

Magnanimity, in Peace, Goodwill.' (Chartwell House, Westerham, Kent, April 1931).

In this village of mine nobody talks of enlistment – nobody expects to volunteer. The place is stiff with men between twenty-five and forty-five, all without any idea of adventure, one supposes. 'When I have time, I may have to go and give 'em an 'iding, certainly,' remarked our news-agent.

Here is a sad little notice from the front page of *The Times*. What a world of suffering lies behind it:

> NEUMANN – At Warsaw, driven to death by German cruelties. Aleksander Neumann, barrister. Funeral service at Polish Catholic Church, Devonia Road, London N1 (Angel). Feb. 3, at 11 a.m.

Sunday, 4 February

'And where is Victor now?' I asked a cottage friend. Her son joined the Army some time ago.

She stood in her garden in the fierce north wind gathering her scanty jacket around her. She is nearly seventy. She spoke with a great sense of the dramatic:

'He's on the water!'

It was as if, coming from her innocent country lips, Victor had gone to his execution. The water holds every sort of terror for her. The dull grey sky, the general atmosphere of fog, gloom and ice were all in keeping with the mournful news; the poor grey hair of the mother brushed back over a brow with yet one more wrinkle of care, for Victor is her darling, her favourite, 'what always brought me a cup of tea when I felt bad'.

Many different posters were produced
to promote the War Savings scheme.
Photograph © IWM PST 15586

The Hydes to tea. Bey, who teaches the local Czechoslovakians English, tells me four peasant boy weavers are going at last to be allowed to weave, and depart for Manchester immediately. Also one toolmaker has got his permit and travels off to Kent to a factory with his wife and children. It is to be hoped that all will one day be dispersed, of the sad little companies forbidden to work.*

Monday, 5 February

What a book of War Stories could be made! Here is one in a nutshell:

> Fraulein Christel Zimmerman, 26-year-old 'learner' in a Mayfair fashion house, fears that her own brothers may drop bombs on her.
>
> She is a Catholic refugee from Germany. The Aliens Tribunal here gave her full freedom.
>
> Three of her five brothers are in the Nazi Air Force, only because, she told me last night, 'the penalty of refusing to fight for Hitler's Reich is death'.

Tuesday, 6 February

The German propaganda speaker known everywhere as Lord Haw-Haw was acting in a dialogue last night aping an English lord with terrific and old-fashioned gusto, showing that he seriously fancied himself in this part! It is really very

* It could take some time for permits to be issued, since there were approximately 170,000 non-enemy aliens, as well as the 50,000 enemy aliens, all of whose cases had to be considered.

funny and interesting, this. He evidently regards our scornful British nickname as a compliment. What next?*

I wrote all morning, and judged a big competition for an original short story to be called 'The Emerald Ring' this evening. I gave the prize to the writer of a sad little story about a man who went to the Front without proposing and without having a chance of giving the ring he had bought to his girl. He was shot, and she never knew about his plan, and the emerald ring was returned with his effects to his mother, who had never heard of the girl. Possibly I am influenced by my slight fever to select this melancholy effort as best. It's so utterly possible.

Thursday, 8 February

I did not write yesterday as I spent the day in bed, but I took one or two things from the papers. Lloyd George, pleading for the draining of millions of British acres, said we must vote more money to it lest 'through prejudice, stubbornness and lack of vision' we neglected one indispensible contribution to winning the war, and found ourselves suddenly faced through hunger with inevitable doom or humiliating surrender.

I glance through the window at the great neglected bit of land opposite us in this lane, Catherine's Field, and wonder.

How terrible it is to think that the Germans are doctoring

* William Joyce, who was hanged for treason in 1946, is most commonly associated with Lord Haw-Haw, but the name was coined before he became the main announcer on the Nazi propaganda programme *Germany Calling* in February 1940, and it is not certain which of his predecessors was the original. The most likely candidate would seem to be radio producer Wolf Mittler, who later fled the Nazi regime, although there were others in the early months of the war.

their men up with injections of a certain vitamin to make them brave before they begin to fight. Are we doing it too?*

Mickey says forty men have volunteered from the Guards Depot to go to Finland. 'Thank you for your help,' said a Finn, quoted in *The Times*, 'but you cannot send us the gift of sleep.'

My charwoman tells me of the return to London today of her evacuated children. Pat, aged fourteen, had trouble at school and came back saying that the teacher had slapped her face and that she was going home. The billeting officer, after consultation, said, 'Don't stop her.' Her little brother Bernard, aged ten and beginning to enjoy feeding the chickens, etc., was to go home too. The other lodger in the cottage, a big nice lad aged seventeen, who works on the land, had got so upset and jealous with the presence at close quarters of the two evacuated children, that he had turned quarrelsome and has gone back to Wales. What an effect human beings have on one another!

The fishman was very scornful when I asked if he had any fish below one and sixpence a pound today. Cod was two shillings a pound. Imagine being in his power! It was take it or leave it, and you're damned lucky if you secure a piece of anything. Finally I got enough for one person for one-and-fourpence, fresh haddock, and also a little bit of cat's fish as a tremendous favour.

Rachel says her husband can get hold of no coal to sell, but only has raw green logs to offer.

* Fanciful stories such as this spread widely. Connie was no fool, and the fact that she took this one at face value indicates how easy they were to believe, at least in the early months of the war.

Friday, 9 February

Robin's birthday. I gave him a box of dates. We drove over in the dim winter day to Haslemere, where they had a lovely birthday lunch for Robin, pheasant with mince pies and delicious coffee in light gold lacquer cups from China. We drank his health before the meal in gin and lime.

Our hosts' three children are widely scattered – the elder boy in Tanganyika*, the second a Marine prowling round Australian seas, the daughter in Malta with her little girl. The Eustaces, old Hong-Kongians, are full of steadfast faith in Chiang Kai Shek.† I am afraid their dividend from China slips lower and lower. Seventy pounds less the other day. We discuss economies. They have already arrived at the 'little supper by the fire'. Kitty eats bread and butter then, so was very pleased with my gift of a half-pound of butter from Scotland.

May writes that in Romsey, troops are lying on the floor in the local Town Hall having pneumonia, each with one blanket only.

Recently the Germans stopped a train in Poland and shot one passenger out of every five, and at about the same time seventy-two Poles were hanged near the beloved city of Cracow.

Monday, 12 February

Shopped. No pork sausages in Sainsbury 'because,' eagerly exclaimed a shop girl, 'pork is impossible to get.' No rabbits.

* In 1964 the union of Tanganyika and Zanzibar formed the United Republic of Tanzania.

† The Eustaces had money invested in China, which Japan had invaded in 1937. Presumably their hope was that Chiang Kai Shek, the Chinese leader, would repel the Japanese and restore stability.

They have suddenly assumed greater dignity. I bought 1lb beef sausages for tenpence.

From my letters:

Diana, WAAF, to her mother, from Pembroke Dock:

'It is marvellous here. I love it. I am on duty five till midnight, was also on last night, and two other evenings in the week, also we get one day off a week, so our hours are very pleasant. Occasionally we get a rush, taking down messages or sending them by telephone or teleprinter, entering them up or popping about the place with messages.' Of a sixpenny hop, Diana says: 'It was a tiny little hall and only an old piano, only airmen of course – having the Australians here adds variety. I struck some wonderful dancers: best I ever have ... We have decided to go dancing mad.'

From Margaret Dell, Princeton University, USA:

'We are heartily ashamed of our Congress for its lack of action in helping Finland (or anyone). It seems degrading, just as though one's good friend and neighbour were being robbed and one wrote a polite note of sympathy.'

Florence Dell, the daughter (twenty-two) writes from New York that she finds 'all ideas about the war over here are muddled. No one knows how we can keep out, but all think we should ... We now hear no one *wants* us, anyway, which no one had thought of.'

There is no hot water in Denmark owing to the fuel shortage, and you can walk on the ice over to Sweden! Here we have our little coal store freshly replenished, and sit by a fine red fire.

Tuesday, 13 February

The cold has come again with a vengeance. Snow and frost and shivers. We have just been laughing over a broadcast ridiculing German propaganda – nobody in this country can pay attention to Hitler, Goebbels and Himmler. This may be our great misfortune.

How wonderful to think that one day the loathed Stalin and Hitler will be creatures of the past and other historians will arise and write of them intimately, and they will stay harmlessly enough within the pages of the diary, and even beguile the hours of some invalid, robbed forever of their thunder, which is uncommonly violent at present.

Wednesday, St Valentine's Day

In the *News Chronicle* it describes our recruiting office in Smith Square as being besieged with volunteers, which is refreshing. A middle-aged man who had driven to London in an expensive car to volunteer was sitting beside a young man wearing down-at-heel shoes and a ragged suit. They were helping each other to answer the long list of questions on the form.

A still day. Robin is actually up on a ladder sawing off the branch of a tree, thank goodness. All this weather has been disastrous for his activity.

I wonder how Basil is getting on. His difficulty is in assembling the men for their innoculation. He gets hold of, say, seventy who are due for the second after an interval of ten days. Back they come, but thirty have not turned up because they have been spirited away, say, for a course at Chatham. He can do 300 innoculations an hour, which seems marvellous, assisted of course by orderlies with filled syringes.

Thursday, 15 February

A very evil, piercing day of cold. It reminded me of the peevishness of poor Mr Attlee, our Labour leader. The wind was querulous.

How I long today for some fresh flowers. It is a flowerless winter.

Friday, 16 February

Received a rather miserable letter from Cis up in a grim little Scottish town waiting for the coal merchant. 'I've only two lumps left.' Ian hears that they are not employing officers of over fifty-five.

Madge says their egg man has just told them there will soon be no eggs. Barbara says knuckle of veal makes soup for three times for her and Jack.

The wind is howling round the house and my hands are red with cold even by the ample fire. The *Spectator* says that Germany is full of tinned stores which will keep them going for ages.

Saturday, 17 February

Deep snowfall.

We hear Hitler is thinner, working harder than ever, and more nervous than of yore.

At at least one East Coast port, says the *News Chronicle*, the crew of minesweepers about to set out to sea go through this little ritual. All hands group themselves round the master at the helm. 'Are we all here?' he asks, and the reply comes to him, 'Yes, in God's care, Amen.'

'Of what, then, are we afraid?'

'We are afraid of nothing,' comes a second reply. And the ship beats her way out of harbour to do as unpleasant a job as any on the Seven Seas.

Sunday, 25 February

I write in great excitement at 6.30, because, as Summer Time came in today, it is still light, and how extraordinarily blessed that is. Yesterday came spring. Sunshine actually streamed in, the first happy-looking day we have had for months. Hikers sprang out of towns and aconites came out in their pretty green ruffles, and the pale cold azure of the perfect grape hyacinths in a vase by my bed whispered that possibly they might soon be seeing some of their sisters in the garden borders.

The lift to the spirits of *more light* is amazing.

The journal has been discontinued for a whole week owing to an attack of influenza and laryngitis, prevalent all over Britain. The doctor says it has taken the form for the most part of a very sharp pain in the chest – I felt as if I had a whole heap of knives in mine cutting me.

Prince George Chavchavadze played Chopin the other day to some troops. They listened politely and then a voice was heard enjoining him to 'Swing it, George!'*

Monday, 26 February

Tried to get spaghetti, baked beans, beetroot and celery today and failed in getting any of them.

* Prince George Chavchavadze was a Russian exile and occasional concert pianist. As a general rule, the troops tended to prefer jazz and swing to classical music for their entertainment.

Singing (yes, I'm afraid so) 'Roll Out the Barrel', the first squadron of the Canadian Air Force arrived in England yesterday.

Tuesday, 27 February

Mrs Dell wrote to me from Princeton, New Jersey, today about the war. She says: 'I feel in perfect agony over the war, and sunk in shame at the indifference and spinelessness of my government and many of my acquaintances. We are all doing most footling Red Cross work and at long last a private committee has been formed in New York called Fighting Funds for Finland, and I am engaged in organising the local branch ... We Americans are giving millions of dollars for Finnish relief, but until last Friday everyone was hoping that the Government would give the Finns credit with which to buy guns, ammunition and planes for their defence. Now it is quite evident that the Government will do no such thing. They may eventually lend them money for more food, etc., but not for arms.'

Barbara writes from her Berkshire village: 'The housekeeper of a friend of ours here still thinks we are fighting the French. She said, when Sibyl told her of the discomforts her nephew had had in a French ambulance after being wounded: "Well, what can you expect of the French. It's a wonder they didn't murder him, poor boy!"'

Such are our voters.

Wednesday, 28 February

Robin and I talk a great deal in the firelight, sipping glasses of sherry, about the mysterious element in this war. It is as if the Germans are playing a very deep hand indeed, keeping us all on the alert and not attacking. Is this going on indefinitely?

True, spring is not yet very far advanced, but it is surely light enough for the Great Air Raids to begin. Are all the people in England now on guard going to get quite sick of the inaction and the deadlock? Will there not be a huge cry going up for compromise?

One thing seems certain. The Germans can get on very well with their food supplies, limited though they may be. It must pay them to play this waiting game.

I had a postcard from Winnipeg from my old Nanny to say she was at the head of sixty-five women sewing garments for the poor evacuated children in England. Sad and shameful that it should be necessary.

Thursday, 29 February

We should normally be finishing up our Mentone month and saying goodbye to the yellow walls and the bougainvillea. Robin says we must pretend we have been.

Anthony Eden made a speech which was given on the wireless. Did not bother to listen much. I feel he is only a façade – nothing of importance behind that graceful manner.*

Friday, 1 March

March comes in with a bitter wind.

Phyl writes that when the searchlight unit near her cottage got flu they had no hot water bottles, so she put half-filled

* Connie was fiercely partisan in her likes and dislikes and had little time for Eden, who had resigned as Foreign Secretary in 1938 and was at this time Secretary of State for Dominion Affairs. Her opinion may have been coloured by his policy disagreements with Neville Chamberlain, whom she greatly admired.

sandbags which they had into her oven and warmed them and they retained the heat for a long time.

There is a great deal of talk as to whether the Germans will bomb us or not. Everybody seems to think not, till we remember they may 'get nasty' and let us have it hot and hard. Yesterday in Guildford a great aeroplane passed, it seemed, roaring northwards almost over my hat.

'No dripping,' says the butcher firmly on the phone. 'No, we can't be sure of letting you have a pound and a half of sausages. You shall have what we can spare.'

Sunday, 3 March

Basil and I walked over to Mrs Theobald's and heard her tell some stories of her evacuees. The two little boys are imps. One day during the bad winter weather they turned off the water at the main without saying a word. Mrs T., their kind hostess, found herself having a very tiny bath at midnight. Her husband warned her that the boiler might burst. He went up into the chilly loft to inspect the cistern, poor man, while Helen in night clothes toiled away at dispersing the boiler coke in buckets and carrying it across the freezing yard. In vain did they ask a plumber to come next day when no water. He was so busy he couldn't get to them. The secret was not discovered for many hours.

Tuesday, 5 March

One of May's great friends has committed suicide, a deaf, rich, lonely batchelor of forty-eight. He cut his throat, fearing none of his friends would have time for him during the war and knowing he could not go on travelling. Poor C. H.!

Eileen's father has had to kill off many of his chickens owing to lack of foodstuffs. It's very lamentable and makes a great difference to them, as they are hard up.

Sunday, 10 March

Tomorrow starts the quite alarming meat ration. How to manage, is the question. Take what you can get and when you can get it, is the reply.

What is going to happen about Finland? Everybody Robin met today in the village spoke with anxiety about its fate.

Monday, 11 March

Ursula says this morning in a letter: 'We are supposed to be guarding the Chelsea Power Station from the IRA.* We patrol all night in turns. When Molly and I were on patrol the night before last, there was a terrific explosion. We rushed round expecting to be stunned by falling masonry at any moment and were awfully relieved when the police rang through to say it was in Park Lane.'

The whole of the men's and women's armies seem to be screaming for cooks. Many good men and true of forty-five and upwards are unemployed. Why set Ursula and Molly, frail girls, to guard the great power station?

Ray says in her letter: 'I got a shock when glancing into the Yeovil Town Hall today to see where hundreds of the soldiers

* The IRA were actively involved in a bombing campaign in England in 1939–40 known as the S-Plan or Sabotage Campaign, at the height of which five people were killed and fifty injured in Coventry on 25 August. Two of the bombers were hanged on 7 February 1940, which in turn triggered further bombings in London and Birmingham in February and March.

People were encouraged to save their kitchen scraps for much-needed animal feed. This municipal pig bin was at Kingston upon Thames.

Photograph © IWM HU36203

sleep, just within a yard or two of each other, and on ground sheets on the hard floor.'

Robin says, however, he thinks the men would have 'biscuits' to lie on – some sort of mattress.

Wednesday, 13 March

Woke feeling so much oppressed by the Russian victory over Finland. Everybody feels dreadfully depressed about it. Four hundred thousand people will have to be evacuated from the part of the world now ceded to the Russians. God help them all, and forgive us.

Thursday, 14 March

Prices all up in the village shop. Stockings a shilling up, chocolate getting rare. Indeed a day of discomfort as well as mourning. As I write, Robin is lamenting bitterly that we did not force our way through Sweden. The *Evening Standard* says that even if our Franco-British force had gone to Finland, Germans would have poured in and the little country would have become a Flanders. I wonder.

Friday, 15 March

Motored to Brighton, still full of depression over Finland, feeling it so much more than one felt the misery of Czechoslovakia or Poland.

Glorious March sunshine. Truly you would never know at Brighton that there was a war. Certain terraces want repainting, but crowds move about and there is traffic on the front and lots of buses.

Monday, 18 March

Who was James Isbister? The unfortunate first civilian to be killed by an air-raid bomb in the United Kingdom. Aged twenty-seven, an employee of the Orkney County Council, poor James perished, leaving a wife and baby, up in the remotest of islands, standing at his cottage door.

'*Hitler and Mussolini meet in a blizzard at the Brenner Pass*' – so runs the evening paper placard (yes, there are still placards, though we are so short of paper). I wish generations to come, if they ever read this, would realise that to us in England these are not Napoleonic names. We despise Hitler as a little and nasty man. Mussolini we hesitate over a little, but he does not cut any real ice, and his prolonged flirtation with the German powers alienates us. The ladies of England in this March of 1940, believe me, are sick of these two men, and weary of hearing of their sinister plots and hateful designs.

Says a newspaper correspondent:

'A night-flying RAF machine, its petrol running low, landed in Germany. Its crew were given their position by a German peasant, got back in the plane, and flew off! The story was told to me today by the pilot of the plane. He said:

"The second pilot, who spoke French very well, said to one of the peasants, 'Is this France?' and received the alarming reply, 'No, this is Germany: France is over there, about twenty miles away.'

"We did not stop to say 'Thank you'. We bolted for the machine, and started up."'

Wednesday, 20 March

Had Harry's room cleaned out, and am longing to see him, but think it must be another month to wait.*

Am reluctant to read the paper full of Stalin bestriding Finland, and shouting that they must have no pact with Norway and Sweden. (I wonder if I shall be able to force myself to read it?)

The description of the air raid up on the Orkneys sounds dreadful. A ring of red flame from the guns spread round Scapa Flow and the earth shaking 'as if all creation were rocking', said one old woman.

I think with pleasure of Brighton and the many gay girls staying in the hotel, and outside the wind tearing down the esplanade and blowing colour into many middle-aged cheeks.

Thursday, 21 March

I got herrings – three for ninepence. Delicate Mrs G. said when I met her at Guildford that it was very dull being poor, and her pension arrived this morning docked considerably for income tax. And, furthermore, she thought we should begin bombing German cities – yes, civilians.

The Sylt raid must have been tremendously exciting, but what a strain on the flyers.†

* Harry was invalided out of the 2nd Battalion, The Loyal Regiment, who were in Singapore, as a result of spondylitis, a degenerative bone condition, and was awaiting passage to England.

† On Tuesday 19 March the RAF attacked the German naval base at Hoernum on the island of Sylt for six hours in order to disrupt German mine-laying and attacks on British shipping.

Good Friday, 22 March

Here is something from *The Author*'s current number, in which many writers express what they think about wartime conditions.

'When war is declared,' writes the ancient Bernard Shaw, 'we all go mad. We assume that all who are doing anything must stop doing it, and do something else, and that wherever we are, we must go elsewhere. We forget, if we ever knew, that a war is only a ripple of slaughter and destruction upon the surface of the world's necessary work, which must carry on without a moment's intermission, war or no war.'

Osbert Sitwell says: 'When the bombs begin to fall, there will be a slump in reading even of *Gone With the Wind*.' Everybody, he goes on, is in for a hard time – authors included. But authors were in for a hard time in any case. The old reading public is dead, and the new one which will be made by the Penguins and kindred enterprises is hardly awakened.

Easter Saturday, 23 March

Mickey arrives to spend Easter, bringing a ration card. I and my Coldstream Guard proceed to the grocer's, where we are given half a pound of butter and half a pound of sugar for the one night he spends here.

The manager of the village stores looks much older since the war. He had 8,000 coupons to count last week and is foaming at the mouth at the whole system. 'There's a woman up the street who has nine children. She can't afford four-and-a-half pounds of butter. The lady next door with two chidren longs for more butter and can't get it.'*

Easter Monday, 24 March

Saw a lot of hikers. Scores of young men in unbecoming brown suede golf jackets, all looking as if they ought to be called up. I suppose the war has thrown its shadow over every one of them.

Wednesday, 27 March

A letter from the Finnish Troops Comfort Fund, very grateful for my grandfather's ancient gold seal and an old watch-chain. They say they have packed already 2,800 bales of comforts and are in daily cablegraphic contact with Finland.

Sibyl writes that capable Molly W. can't get a job in this war, yet she is a first-rate cook. She can't be prepared to enter the Army, I think.

All the beans in the garden are destroyed. We have no vegetables now save potatoes, and tomatoes are tenpence a pound.

Thursday, 28 March

A delightful surprise by this morning's post. My godchild Ursula (who has been guarding the Chelsea Power Station) is

* The Ministry of Food introduced ration books for every individual, including children, which contained coupons for set amounts of various rationed goods. Shoppers could only buy from shops with which they had registered, as shopkeepers had strictly limited supplies, and had to take their ration books with them so coupons could be checked off.

betrothed to one Kenneth Steele, a policeman. She will have a war wedding, but I am sure it will be pretty.

The bank assistant is exceedingly caustic as he cashes my little cheque, about the strange goings-on at the Ministry of Supply. He has some remarkable ideas about Mr Neville Chamberlain, past and future. I tell him he is 'very cynical', and I go on my way.

My thoughts very much on Harry today; possibly he is starting [for England].

Went to see Mrs Hopgood, back from St Briac. She is very interesting. She loves life in France. She says the French are full of a spirit of revenge, and fear we may go all soft and forgiving after the war. Marna* is stationed at Folkestone, the billet a boarding house full of aspidistras and beds. She lies on a lilo mattress on a frail camp bed. The rations are rather scanty. But her eyes shine, it's an adventure; and there are no doubt affairs of the heart.

Last night the young airmen on the wireless explaining about their fight with German Messerschmidts were amazingly calm and bold. But can flesh and blood stand this aerial warfare for long? The casualty list is very lengthy.

Friday, 29 March

To the dentist. He said his old father was getting depressed with the war, and that old people should turn their faces in another direction when it was possible, and not think war thoughts all the time.

The Times says:

'In Mariendorf, a small village near Aix-la-Chapelle, the cor-

* Connie adds a handwritten note: 'Mrs H's daughter, in the ATS'.

respondent visited the cinema. There he saw the official film of the Polish campaign, which contains harrowing shots of executions and other brutal happenings of the war. During the interval the correspondent was struck by the effect on the audience; women were in tears and men looked pale and stunned. This type of propaganda, intended to impress people with the ruthless power of the Nazis, is being used more and more.'

Dr Ley* has informed the German workers that the 'Strength Through Joy' holiday tours will at the end of this summer include trips to the South Coast of England – I suppose Bexhill, Bournemouth, Torquay!

Hardly any parents in danger areas have replied to the Government paper about evacuation of their children in the event of air-raids. *Nineteen thousand* people have not answered in West Ham!

Saturday, 30 March

Olive's young man told her that our soldiers in France are drinking far too hard. He brought back a bottle of champagne for Olive's unemployed father.

Sunshine, cold wind. I think of Basil, settling in to his new billet by Father Thames. I wrote a short story this morning at top speed – no war; love, and brown eyes.

Monday, 1 April

To London. Men busy in Kensington High Street digging shelters. Ursula and Kenneth think they will have no difficulty in

* Robert Ley, head of the German Labour Front (the *Deutsche Arbeitsfront* or DAF) from 1933 to 1945. Ley committed suicide while awaiting trial for war crimes.

getting a flat in these days of a deserted London. They hear existing flats are to be made smaller (so poor are we all to become) by halving them.

I bought an American dress – 'positively the last shipment, madam' – and dashed to Waterloo.

Tuesday, 2 April

A letter from Harry. No departure in sight. I long to see him.

Mrs Beck and Mrs Wilkinson to tea. Mrs Wilkinson talked of the Lyttons' kindness to the girls now at Knebworth. The Froebel School is there. The room belonging to 'Antony', the son and heir, killed flying, is kept locked.*

Wednesday, 3 April

We hear the Canadians near us are very restive and complaining of the inhospitability of Guildford. They don't understand there is now a layer of gloom over our natures, spread by winter.

I wonder if I should have bought those two garments in London. I could have done without with difficulty. One hardly knows in what world one is walking, and there is no commoner sentence in this village than 'We must live from day to day.' Women always say it, as men do it, anyway.

Eva's letter just in says: 'I hear it is really very nerve-shattering living in Dover now that the gunfire is almost ceaseless night and day. How much of this is practice one doesn't know; nor do the people of Dover.'

* Edward Antony Bulwer-Lytton, Viscount Knebworth, pilot, MP and eldest son of the 2nd Earl of Lytton, died in a plane crash at Hendon in 1933.

Thursday 4 April

Olive demands a rise in wages. Housekeeping very difficult. Winds howling about. Neville Chamberlain still lets old stagers like Hoare* look after the modern and fiery Air Ministry and so makes our loyal hearts sick. Why not appoint somebody young and ardent and up-to-date?

Words we have now taken from Germany are: *Lebensraum*,† *Ersatz*, *Gestapo*, *Blitzkrieg*.

We seem to be forging ahead in the air. Every day come accounts of fleeing Germans. Nobody seems to think that we will attack by land, and in my opinion it is likely to be a long, slow war.

Saturday, 6 April

Basil came last night straight from Reading to Gomshall. He looks extremely well, save for the ever-weary aspect of the eyes, got from late nights. He is more resigned to the army forms, fills them in in a more obedient way and says it can't be helped – 'This is a paper war.'

Spoke with old Fellowes, a village workman, for long without regular employment, now at seventy-four pitched into the

* Sir Samuel Hoare, a staunch Chamberlain supporter, had been Secretary of State for Air in the 1920s before serving as Foreign Secretary and then Home Secretary in the 1930s. He was Lord Privy Seal in Chamberlain's War Cabinet until his resignation in May 1940.

† Literally meaning 'living space', the concept of *Lebensraum* underpinned the Nazi expansionist ideology, which required that the German nation should possess as much land as it needed to grow and prosper. *Ersatz* passed into English usage as a result of the Great War, when prisoners in German camps were given *Erzatskaffee*, inferior substitute coffee made with grain or acorns, or *Erzatsbrot* – bread cut with cheaper substitutes for flour.

job of Church Clerk, since the youth who held it has volunteered as an army baker, and has been snatched into the gunners as an artillery-man.

I heard some of our naval prisoners of war speaking from Germany on the German wireless. Their voices were broken and lifeless, as if somebody was standing over them, poor chaps.

We are all waiting, waiting for a spring offensive, but none of us seems to expect the British to do anything but sit tight, and many expect a quiet summer.

Sunday, 7 April

Have just come in from seeing Basil off – Gomshall to Reading. We walked up to Netley Woods all among the bright green yews and glossy hollies this afternoon, and he told me a great deal about the re-grading of the men from a medical point of view. He considers this a great improvement – so many more categories than there were – and the power to grade entirely his at first. He described the case of a young man who was afraid to kill anything. He got him boarded out, after a bit of an argument with the Adjutant. He says the fifty-year-olds are not really much use, and he is pretty well convinced that those who fought through the last war are not very happy in this, among the young recruits.

'Today over eighty million Germans,' interrupts a voice from Bremen, 'are willing to carry out the wishes of the Führer.'

The voice from Germany now says that we in England are in despair. I don't think we are! There were so many cheerful hikers strolling through the Park today, under an azure sky, and cars galore going cheerfully along the road.

Monday, 8 April

'Those Germans are downright cruel on the sea, not saving the drowning. Did you read about the U-boat in the paper today?' asked an old fellow serving me out with my weekly sugar ration for Robin and me this afternoon. 'I couldn't hurt a cat myself.'

'Specially not a cat,' I said, remembering how devoted he was to his huge puss out in the warehouse.

Two bulky parcels arrived for me today from New York. Some caster sugar was trickling out of one. Great merriment on the part of the postmaster. 'They think we're starving there, madam.'

Surely our propaganda service should put through to the Americans the news that we are not short of food? I am sure the German propaganda must have seen to it that America thinks we are suffering more than we do suffer.

Just had a friend to tea who has had two children, boys, aged nine and nearly thirteen, as evacuees from Fulham for the seven months of the war. The youngest had never seen a lamb before – there are so many in the fields now – and he came home in great excitement to tell Mrs Turner: 'It was a little animal, no larger than the *Daily Sketch*!' She says they say they go either to the swimming baths or the cinema every night at home. When they are cross here, they sit together on the staircase calling out, 'Shan't we be glad to get out of this blinking house!'

Tuesday, 9 April

One o'clock. Astounded by the wireless news that the Germans have occupied Denmark and landed in Norway.

This indeed sets the chariot wheels of war, long inactive, rolling round.* What will it mean to Basil? Will he have to go to Norway? Will troops selected for Finland be landed there?

Six o'clock. The wireless tells us that there is a naval battle raging. It is hard to listen to *Vanity Fair*; and a sonata by Lizst merely makes one feel terrible.

Wednesday, 10 April

The dentist told me he had heard from a friend that Norway has capitulated to Germany this morning. A horrible moment! This war is so paralysing in its complexity, that one had never thought of this very likely surrender. If it takes place, what will happen?

Is our army already on the way? As I write, the cold April weather dismays us with its sharp, unfriendly wind. The garden looks dumb and stricken. Probably there is a naval battle waging now, and in any case the hearts of the mothers and wives of the men in the *Hunter* and *Hardy* are beating wildly, hoping and fearing and waiting for the truth.†

* The invasion of Denmark and Norway marked the first stage of the ending of what was known as the Phoney War, in which there had been no significant land offensive against Germany by either Britain or France for the seven months since war was declared in September 1939. Hitler's move against countries over which Germany had no valid territorial claim resulted in Allied troops being landed in Norway from 14 April. Less than one month later Germany had invaded Belgium and Holland and the full scale land war had begun.

† HMS *Hardy*, an H-class destroyer and flagship of the 2nd Destroyer Flotilla, was badly damaged and run aground in the attack on Narvik on 9 April, capsizing next morning after her crew had managed to get ashore. HMS *Hunter*, also an H-class destroyer, was torpedoed and sunk during the battle with the loss of 112 men.

Thursday, 11 April

'Lots of young Nazis are busy learning Welsh,' says Robin, 'preparatory to coming to rule over Wales,' and he doubles up with laughter, he who, half-Welsh and very proud of the fact, knows no Welsh.

Friday, 12 April

Very cold today. Relinquished very sadly the idea of going to be near Muriel in her caravan. The news is too serious to be parted from Robin just now.

Madge and Edie left for Eastbourne with carefully saved petrol. Could just get a small piece of liver for Robin's dinner tonight in the butcher's – 'no pork'.

Saturday, 13 April

The war is now on our doorsteps. Nothing stands between us and the Germans save the British Navy. Nora W. says people are going about again with gas-masks in London. To me, the spirit appears very firm and cheerful.

'My sons,' says the local builder, 'are over thirty. They don't care whether they do 'ave to go.' This queer, lackadaisical English speech of ours is just a disguise for something quite different. He would rather have died than have said, 'They are mad keen to save their country', and how embarrassed we should have been if he *had* put it thus.

King Haakon says he has not had his boots off for days, is worn out, but will never leave Norwegian soil. In Denmark some of the Danes are hitting their own soldiers with missiles, so disappointed that they have not resisted the Huns.

Sunday, 14 April

Alice's birthday, Sibyl's birthday.* Alice has a son in this war, Sibyl nobody much to care about. What a sharp difference that makes!

Monday, 15 April

Had an early lunch of cold roast beef and then off to Reading and Pangbourne. Much enjoyed the drive, though it was cold and thundery. Basil was waiting, very well, very young, beside the pretty George Inn.

I sat in the George talking to a young officer's wife who was unsuccessfully looking for lodgings. How well I remembered the familiar quest! She was thankful to leave Edinburgh as it had been so full of air-raid warnings, and 'the German planes flew so low over the house-tops'.

Thursday, 18 April

The *British Weekly*, already very thin indeed, announces that it will get thinner yet. Will they cut away my competitions? If so, I shall lose three guineas a month.

To Guildford. Spent about ten shillings – long envelopes (up fifty per cent) ninepence a packet, mackerel one-and-seven for four fillets, threepenceworth of cat's fish, very rare indeed.

Friday, 19 April

The papers give an alarming account of the German

* Alice was Connie's cousin; Sibyl was Robin's younger sister.

thoroughness in Norway. Their blowing up of bridges is complete. Villas on the cliffs are full of gunners ready to bombard any of our troops that try to land. They have instructions as to how to deal with the Norwegians.

Joy comes in and tells me that I have not grasped that the head of the Norwegian Church is pro-German, and many high officials also.

Sunday, 21 April

Basil's birthday. He is twenty-six. *What* will have happened by his twenty-seventh birthday? I feel he may be ordered overseas at any time, and it may well be Norway.

Shadows darken over the war horizon. The great chain stores are being affected by the difficulty in getting goods in great quantities. You would have said six months ago, watching the high price of the shares, that it would be everything to have an investment in Woolworths. It will struggle, though.

The idea that the Germans might try out an invasion by parachutes on Britain is more likely to be grasped when the Hun sets foot in Holland. At present we do not seem to realise that troops could be moved into Britain by air.

Glorious sunny day. In church this morning during the communion service, the parson's voice was drowned constantly by the odious drone of aeroplanes.

Monday, 22 April

This evening I went into the Forrest Stores, and feeling sure that there would be a new tax on spirits in tomorrow's Budget, I asked for a bottle of whisky. There was a long, reluctant pause. The manager was then called, who immediately gave me one of the very few he has left. I said I wouldn't have it if he would rather not, or if it weren't right for me to get it, but he was very hearty about it. I will put it away for the winter days. Today has been joyously warm, and I have had a little posy of the very first pansies given to me, dark deep purple, pale yellow and velvety mauve, and it is as if Summer herself had come into the room.

Tuesday, 23 April

Overjoyed to have a cable from Harry, announcing in suitably veiled language his departure. We ought to get him in five weeks' time, anyway.

The shadow of the Budget lies heavy and ominous on us all today. 'I do think they should keep the postage low on the letters to the troops,' says the shopkeeper, 'to make the parcels worth sending.' It was interesting yesterday to hear Mrs Norton, aged about eighty, telling of the lack of men in Shere in the last war. 'They even took the village idiot, and *he* came back.'

Wednesday, 24 April

Am rather staggered at all the new burdens, including the Property Tax.

Sweden is very much alarmed, and Germany is using most abusive language to her. Malmo is being evacuated. Poor mothers, poor wives and daughters!

Just heard the Admiralty's account of how our old friend, Geoffrey Stanning, dragged himself with one wounded foot to take charge of the *Hardy* when everybody was wounded or killed. He did magnificently. What a quiet, earnest schoolboy he was, so kind, beaming behind his spectacles. There must be great joy in the Rectory at Meonstoke.*

Thursday, 25 April

Went to London. At Waterloo young airmen with bundles labelled Capetown bade farewell to wives and sisters.

In St James, Piccadilly, a young curate conducted a short serice at noon, the church empty save for two women and the sacristan. Behind the altar Wren's church is hidden high up the wall by massed sandbags, over which somebody has hung a large piece of red damask.

Friday, 26 April

'Why doesn't Sweden call in our aid at once?' complained Mr Pethick-Lawrence today, 'and let us get her airports. I can't quite understand it.' Mrs Pethick-Lawrence is the kindest-hearted woman; she looked tired, I thought, but her lovely blue striped velvet coat was becoming. She took a great part in the matter of women's votes.† This is not much use as yet. *We can't yet stop war.*

'The war gets one down,' he observed. 'Intangible things ... the feeling of such an accumulation of hatred. Yes, it presses in even on one's quiet moments.'

* Paymaster Lieutenant Stanning took command of the *Hardy* when her captain was mortally wounded at Narvik and ordered the badly damaged ship to be run aground, thus preventing her from sinking until after the surviving crew had abandoned ship.
† Both Emmeline Pethick and her husband Frederick Lawrence were active in the cause of women's suffrage. They each served nine months in prison in 1912, during which they went on hunger strike and were forcibly fed, and when they married in 1901 each took the other's name, rather than Emmeline taking his as per the usual practice.

Sunday, 28 April

The Shrappies* to tea. He has at last got a London job. 'I found it myself,' he said, with his bright, alert look. He is in control of the National Savings Association poster distribution. But he does not get a salary, and has to pay his own secretary. Also, the Paper Controller himself† has recently said that there would be very little paper left soon, so the job may vanish. Meanwhile, he is pleased and satisfied at having occupation. I so wish Robin could get something that really suited him.

The Shrappies are camping out, as it were, in a corner of their large historic house, and Mrs S. is doing a lot of their cooking. How common this is just now all over England. Such a lot of weary women!

Monday, 29 April

My wedding day. Thirty-one years ago I was married at St Andrew's, Frognal, Hampstead.

On the radio tonight a comedian reported that the cuckoo had been heard in Berlin and had been arrested for insubordination.

Robin in a tone of malicious triumph reads out of the *Evening Standard* that various celebrated young men crooners have been called up.

Tuesday, 30 April

Tomorrow letters are to cost twopence halfpenny each. Everybody, I think, will use the twopenny postcard at first.

* The Shrapnell-Smiths

† Ralph Reed, later Sir (Albert) Ralph Reed, a paper industry magnate, served (unpaid) as Paper Controller for the Board of Trade during the war, monitoring paper stocks.

Very little news comes out of Denmark, It is reported to be fairly full of Nazis, but thousands must hate their guests.

Wednesday, 1 May

Today bought five shillings' worth of the expensive new letter stamp – the bright blue twopence-halfpenny. It seems an enormous sum for a letter. This morning's news about Norway not good. Hitler issues a manifesto crowing with joy at the Germans' advances.

As I write (9.30 p.m.) the Lord Chancellor is explaining to us that Germany is uneasy, because opinion in other countries is hardening against her.

Thursday, 2 May

Nine o'clock. Mr Chamberlain warns us that the Germans may make a lightning attack on our country.

To Guildford this morning – dazed by the high prices in the cheapest food shops. Tomatoes, mushrooms, cauliflowers etc. out of my reach. Got three herrings for Robin's supper – I shall have a bowl of bread-and-milk.

Robin visited the Air Raid Precautions office in Guildford, talking about the importance of arming men in villages. Two colonels there appeared rather surprised; they may be less so after Chamberlain's admission tonight.

Stavanger has been bombed again. The Norwegian woods where German aeroplances were hiding were set on fire too. How can these young airmen stand all this? It beats me entirely.

Mr Eden has been saying our resources and those of our Allies and the Dominions are infinitely greater than those of our

People got used to long queues every day to buy basic foodstuffs.
This queue is at a greengrocers in Wood Green, North London.
Photograph © IWM D25035

enemy. But nothing less than the greatest effort of which our people are capable can ensure victory.

I see Hess* says the German dockyards are filled with U-boats.

Every now and then one has a shrewd suspicion that the Germans are really revelling in the war, that it is their natural element. I say this to Robin, who contradicts me at once.

Saturday, 4 May

I am afraid this has been rather a dismal week for the journal, and our spirits have been none too good over Norway. Robin

* Rudolf Hess, Hitler's Deputy from 1933 until his attempt to broker peace with Britain in 1941.

fears that the German airplanes will give our troops at Narvik no rest.

Monday, 6 May

'Women,' says a book on psychology I have just opened at random, 'specialise in feeling; men rather in thought.'

How gloomy the papers are. Thus yesterday's *Observer* on Norway: 'We know of no parallel for this collapse of a military expedition, like a castle of cards.'* This sort of talk is perfectly useless.

The German wireless last night, by the way, was curious. The speaker – new to me – announced with joy that a bomb had fallen straight on a British battleship, destroying it completely, carefully mentioning no name – liar!

Thursday, 9 May

The debate in the House last night must have been electric. It is evident that many people were so anxious over Norway that they lost their self-control and shouted. It must have been horrifying for Neville Chamberlain, our Prime Minister, who is a sensitive man, tired and seventy.

Winston Churchill, I think, touched the heart of the whole matter in his speech. *Why* did we not get hold of Norway. *Why* are the Germans in triumph there today?†

* The Allied response had been unable to prevent Norway from falling into German hands, although fighting continued in the north of the country until June. The resulting recriminations saw the end of the Chamberlain government.

† Churchill was still First Lord of the Admiralty, becoming Prime Minister the following day on Chamberlain's resignation.

The reason for this serious disadvantage of our not having the initiative was one which could not speedily be removed, and it was our failure in the last five years to maintain or regain air parity in numbers with Germany.

He ended with a great plea for unity. Let all energies be harnessed; let the whole ability of the nation be hurled into the struggle. At no time in the last war were we in greater peril than we were now.

The pity of it is that this debate, with its wretched recriminations, had to take place.

Mr Pethick-Lawrence, I hear, has come back to Peaslake for the weekend, thoroughly sick and ashamed. What is going to happen is not clear.

To tea with Miss M., who sometimes lectures on relaxation. She looked as if she could not relax any more; wrinkled and anxious and grey. The young Lieutenant at tea was happy and carefree, just off to an unknown destination. This is a queer war.

Friday, 10 May

Comes the awful news that Germany has invaded Holland and Belgium.

We had no idea of it until pretty Nancy came in to my kitchen and told us. We listened in at eleven and were told of invasion in the early hours of this morning, parachute descents in Dutch uniform, and so on. Brussels, it seems, had an air raid. Antwerp also, so prosperous and so fine. Will they bring down my belfry at Bruges?

Basil wrote saying how he was looking forward to a tiny walking tour in the New Forest. He has been working fourteen hours a day. Shall I see him before he goes into the unkown?

Afternoon: If we must drop Chamberlain as Prime Minister, I hope we may get Churchill.

Later: Mr Chamberlain has just broadcast a message to tell us that the Labour party will co-operate in a Coalition Government 'provided I am not Prime Minister'.

Saturday, 11 May

Churchill has slipped into the Prime Ministership in a very quiet atmosphere. Public attention is completely arrested by the progress of events in Belgium and Holland, and there is only the most meagre amount of space in the papers devoted to the new regime.

I cannot help thinking that the children and mothers will soon pour again out of London.

Vernon Bartlett says that Hitler boasts he will have his men in Great Britain by the end of June. One fact keeps emerging – that in Holland we have a doughty ally, one we can respect and trust with all our hearts.

Robin hears from a man just back from Norway that the Germans shot Norwegian prisoners and fired on women and children. The Norwegians begged that we should shoot the German prisoners we took.

Later: very delighted to hear that Tony Dodd has gone to Iceland. A great relief to his parents.

Saw Mrs P., who is very anxious about her husband in France. She has been polishing furniture hard to take her mind off her worried thoughts.

Sunday, 12 May

I wish Sinclair and Eden were not in charge of Air and War. Gentle, foolish fellows I call them.* What a weight is on Winston!

Just passed an army lorry, one of a great convoy stuck on the hill outside, on which is written the name 'Connie'. 'My name,' I said to the youthful driver. 'There now, we've been waiting to find somebody called Connie!' and he beamed.

The news is good. The Dutch are full of what their sturdy, fine Queen calls 'a flaming protest'.

Whit Monday, 13 May

Professor Trevelyan† (who years ago told me his private opinion of Mussolini when we sat side by side at a Literary Fund dinner – not favourable) writes in *The Times* today:

'This war is full of bitterness. The thought of Norwegian mountains and fjords in the power of the dog is scarcely more bitter than the thought of the lovely, quiet, old brick streets of Holland, full of art, civilisation, and history at its best, crumbling under bombs. But if freedom were to perish in Europe, what would even they any longer be worth?'

Holland and Belgium are turning into infernos. That Queen Wilhelmina should come over to England seems to me a very wretched piece of news. I am sure she hated the idea of coming.

* Sir Archibald Sinclair was appointed Secretary of State for Air by Churchill, which position he held until the end of the war. Anthony Eden was Secretary of State for War from 11 May to 22 December 1940, after which he resumed his former role of Foreign Secretary until July 1945.

† G. M. Trevelyan, noted historian and prolific author whose *History of England* (1926) and *English Social History* (1944) were among the most widely read textbooks of the age.

Tuesday, 14 May

Woke to the most appalling news on the eight o'clock wireless; the Germans advancing, air raids everywhere. It is a very bad plan hearing it all at the break of day, I think, when one's brain is still clouded from sleep.

Mr Struben telephoned very anxiously about the volunteer police force proposed to combat parachutists. Millions of imaginative people in Britain are picturing the air above the countryside full of parachutists disguised as nuns and clergymen, armed with machine-guns, rifles, cycles and heaven knows what.

On the contrary, the air has remained clear all day in these parts anyway.

I wrote to Ada Maartens at Doorn, asking her to take refuge here should she wish to do so. The vision of the peaceful Dutch lads and lasses coming in and out of the Youth Hostel that Ada has installed in the stable gateway of her stately mansion haunts me.

Wednesday, 15 May

Learned with *utter* dismay this morning that the Dutch had laid down their arms and that only Zeeland is still fighting. The odds against them were too tremendous and the heart of the country was laid open to the enemy.

What is Ada doing? Utrecht and Doorn lie in enemy hands. I have looked up the letters of Maarten Maartens, her novelist father, to verify the fact that he was Jewish. I hope she does not suffer personally through the insolence of the invader, though that proud heart will be severely wounded.

Robin heard last night on the wireless that the Local

Defence Volunteers were to be formed which would actually – poor, eager Robin! – include men of his age. He went this morning to put his name down at the Police Station, and the form asked if he were prepared to go anywhere. He answered yes, if the details were satisfactory.

Two members of 32 Surrey Battalion show how the Home Guard developed from their early beginnings as Local Defence Volunteers. Photograph © IWM HU18501

Everybody is talking about parachutist troops. We are told not to let our cars be available for German soldiers, but to take out the ignition keys, etc.

Saturday, 18 May

I have never felt so acutely a sense of impending disaster. The Germans reported in their official communiqué that they had broken through sixty miles of the Maginot Line.* This is none too clear in our news, we are only told that the Germans have made a big bulge in the line.

It is a war of detonations. Apparently the bombers go first, the new battleship tanks go after and their shells are so huge that they stun the wretched soldiers.

Our gallant Air Force, for which prayers should be put up every five minutes, are performing miracles of skill and bravery. Gamelin's† orders to his troops are so grave that one feels the end may be near at hand: 'Every unit which is unable to advance must accept being killed rather than abandon the nation's territory entrusted to it.'

This comes from a man obviously almost beside himself. Yet today in our village I saw, on this critical day, a young man carrying in his hand a book which was the script of a play he is going to take part in on Monday, going to rehearse it under a large may-tree in a pleasant garden.

A lady searching for some nice corner to sketch in.

In the afternoon the usual sight of a cricket match on the village green, everybody in white flannels.

'Oh,' says Robin, all on edge, 'why don't they invite some

* Mirroring the German Siegfried Line, France's Maginot Line was a system of concrete defences, machine gun emplacements and tank traps along the French borders with Germany and Italy. A hasty extension along the Belgian frontier in 1939–40 was insufficient to halt the German invasion of France.

† General Maurice Gamelin, commander-in-chief of the French land forces in 1940, whose inability to mount an effective defence against the German advance contributed to the withdrawal of the British Expeditionary Force and its evacuation from Dunkirk.

parachuters to come and play them next Saturday? They could lay down their hand grenades and give us a game before killing us . . .'

I sometimes think we really deserve to lose this war. Boys of twenty-six are not yet called up. A look of infinite boredom breaks over many faces when Robin urges that trenches should be dug.

In our peaceful street this evening twelve men advanced upon us. They were rather elderly and carrying strange foreign luggage. Was this then a band of Germans who had desecended neatly in the woods and abandoned their 'chutes'? I was worried enough and tired enough and anxious enough almost to think so. All vanished, as I turned to look at them, into the White Horse Inn.

Everything at tea-time, watching the slowly waving branches of our great green beech-tree, seemed worthless and life no longer worth living. Thousands to be blown up and to die in the most horrifying moments of terror. Everybody is paralysed with anxiety, and I hear letter-boxes are often empty when the postman comes to call.

The Maginot Line!

Editor's note. Six weeks of the journal are unaccountably missing here, from 19 May to 31 June, 1940. During those six weeks, the situation worsened:

By 20 May the Germans had reached Amiens, trapping the British Expeditionary Force, which retreated to Dunkirk. Between 26 May and 4 June 200,000 British and 140,000 French troops were evacuated by a combination of Royal Navy warships and 700-odd fishing boats, merchant ships and pleasure craft which had answered the call to rescue the waiting men from the encroaching German forces. Nine destroyers and 200 civilian vessels were lost during the evacuation, and the RAF suffered heavy losses covering the operation from the air.

On 10 June Italy entered the war.

On 14 June Paris fell; the French government fled to Bordeaux and a new administration was set up under Marshal Petain.

On 22 June Petain signed an Armistice at Compiegne, north of Paris (the same place where Germany had signed the Armistice ending the Great War twenty-two years before) which surrendered two-thirds of France to Germany and disbanded the French Army.

Between 30 June and 2 July Germany occupied the Channel Islands, the British government having decided, albeit reluctantly, that they were not strategically important enough to be defended. Some 30,000 islanders, roughly one-third of the population, had been evacuated earlier in June as the German forces pushed through France, but the remainder had elected to stay.

At the end of June, Harry arrived in England from Singapore. The journal resumes on 1 July.

Monday, 1 July

Six o'clock. Hot sunshine, the vases full of red sweet peas. Robin is in town fetching Harry. More than a million French people are unemployed in Paris, and stop others in the street asking for food.

Tuesday, 2 July

More about occupied Paris. Fruit stalls and flower barrows are again in the streets. The opera may begin. Life is more normal. In Holland they say food is scarce and rations are small. In Belgium, much unrest.

A heavy day, very hot. Felt dreadfully low over the

Channel Islands' occupation by Germany. I am so afraid the Islands will think us powerless, as we do not send anything to protect them. Grover the fishmonger was very heated on the subject this morning: 'We have the men to send.'

Cis reports that she waited half-an-hour in the queue outside the Passport Office to see about Christine, sixteen, going to America, where she is offered her education free at a Boston college. The man who interviewed her said rather brutally, 'Oh, Bevin will soon see that she is hoeing beetroots.'*

Wednesday, 3 July

General Fuller says tonight in the *Evening Standard* that invasion will come on a grand scale, beginning all over the place on little beaches, and then at our big ports. It is bound to come, he says, probably about Friday. On the other hand, it was expected yesterday and today!

Thinking a great deal about Sark, and the sunny hours spent there. Will they ever forgive us for abandoning them without a blow, logical though the reasons may be?

The village is full of Canadian soldiers. They speak a queer French patois, hailing, some of them, from Quebec and Montreal.

Thursday, 4 July

Delighted to see in the *Daily Mail* that the Dame of Sark announces that she is staying on the island, with her 471

* Ernest Bevin, previously first general secretary of the Transport and General Workers' Union, was Minister of Labour in the wartime coalition government. As the war went on, unmarried women were conscripted to work either in industry or on the land, taking the place of the men who had been called up for military service.

subjects. They have coal enough for a year, and they are full of confidence that Britain will win through.

I feel much happier. Sarkians would die if moved.

Bombs have fallen in Haslemere, Witley, etc.*

Saturday, 6 July

To town to a war wedding: my goddaughter Ursula. The bride had met her groom through ARP work in Chelsea. Everybody there seemed infinitely relieved to forget the war for a while, and to return to normal life, eating a happy wedding lunch in a Kensington hotel. We waved goodbye to the bride and her husband in his car, she very pretty, hatless in her grey coat and skirt. The best man had tied on a tin can at the back which trailed after them.

Travelled up with a woman in the act of leaving her home in Portsmouth, unable to endure the nightly alarms.

Sunday, 7 July

Many soldiers in church, quite unable to join in the Psalms, owing to the high pitch of the organ. They rolled out 'Oh God, Our Help in Ages Past', however, with great gusto.

Monday, 8 July

The sun sinking in pale watery gold. A notice has just been brought in, imploring men to go and dig defence trenches at Guildford, bringing picks and shovels.

* Thirteen miles and nine miles from Shere respectively.

Tuesday, 9 July

Tea is rationed now, and the charwoman is very vexed, as she usually drinks many cups a day. Feebly listened to the German news in English, although I don't believe that I ought. They were gloating over the tea ration and announced that we haven't the faintest chance of winning the war.

Shere is full of passing tanks. Even the oldest inhabitant raised an ancient hand to wave to the merry Canadian faces peeping out of the waggons this evening – yes, quite a sour old fellow, carried away by the movement and the excitement.

Wednesday, 10 July

Heard from Arthur that his nephew Lionel, the airman,* flew a bomber back from Dunkirk, a bomber that had lost its crew. He had no experience of bomber-flying, but gallantly volunteered. It saved the Government £40,000. He had no compass, but got it to the Isle of Wight.

Found a soldier writing a letter by the roadside, and got him into the garden. He pulled a photograph out of his pocket of himself and his bride. He has been married two months. 'I've been moved here, and I've lost all my mates,' he said. 'I shan't make any more friends in case I lose them.' He looked very fair and young. He told me his health was much better since he had been in the Army. I hope he will come again.

Friday, 12 July

Christine, aged sixteen, writes an ecstatic letter about life on

* Connie says in a handwritten note that he was lost in 1941.

Peewit Farm. She milks Damsel, Blackie, Cherry, and loves it. Bless her. What an innocent, useful day it is for her in the fresh air of Berkshire, the wind blowing roses into her pretty cheeks.

Robin has gone down to deposit on the aluminium dump my passionately loved preserving pan, and a case for motor papers. The local bone dump has had to be put on a high pole, as the village dogs conceived the idea that we were doing war work for *them*.*

Harry has taught me how to identify a Lysander aeroplane and a Defiant (a very fast variety).

Woke exceedingly sleepy, and hear in a haze the wireless announce that Pétain at *eighty-four* was to be supreme Arbitrator in France.† I felt I was in a mad sort of world. 'Think of the old men round hereabouts of eighty-four!' cries Nancy to me as we discussed it later, going down the street.

Fifty more children arrive to be billeted here next Sunday! Fifty more for dinner at H's communal kitchen. Poor Helen's car was full of *her* five little boy visitors yesterday evening, and a free fight, arms and legs flying, was going on, and a great bawling came from the junior (usually an angel) when we went to see.

Mickey writes from Sandhurst that he is worked almost to death, digging, in his spare time, the outer defences of London.

* The aluminium from cans and pans was used in the manufacture of Spitfires and other aircraft. Bones made glue for aircraft and glycerine for explosives. In addition, kitchen waste helped to feed pigs and chickens, paper was used in munitions as well as to make new paper and rubber went to make tyres.

† Marshal Pétain was revered in France for his defence of Verdun and reform of the French Army in the Great War, and to some he remained a hero even after he signed the Armistice with Germany in 1940. After the war, however, he was convicted of treason and sentenced to death, a sentence which was commuted to life imprisonment. He died at the age of ninety-five in 1951.

Sunday, 14 July

Went with Robin and Harry to look at our Shere defences. Robin was fascinated as usual by the sight of the concrete mixers, incongruously placed at the very entrance to one of my dear favourite walks, where they are hewing down ancient beech trees.

Monday, 15 July

Very wet. Uncomfortable thoughts of the winter come into my head. Churchill said that we should have to go through the years 1941 and 1942 in this war. Is it really possible? Can we endure, all the world, the strain? We shall, I suppose, look back, if we are spared, on this time with amazement.

We are trying to take in that we are in a village where a line of defence (is it for London?) nearly cuts into us.* 'We might have to stay in our shelters for days,' says a Colonel's wife. 'It would be very cold.'

Maurice Ainslie, an acquaintance of ours living at Monte Carlo, is missing. His poor old mother is advertising for news of him.

Tuesday, 16 July

From *The Times* front page advertisement: 'A lady (young) wanted to cook for six convalescent officers in private house,

* The Surrey section of the GHQ line, the longest of Britain's Second World War land defences, followed the Wey, Tillingbourne and Mole valleys. Traces still remain across the county. Impressive dragons' teeth (concrete tank traps) run alongside the River Wey in Stoke Park, Guildford, and there are six pillbox machine gun emplacements in Netley Park alone.

Wiltshire, good cooking essential, no other duties: useful drive car, play tennis.'

One can imagine many pretty and efficient damsels hastening to answer.

Wrote a glowing character for my goddaughter Christine to present at Radclyffe College, Cambridge, Mass., if she goes to America. At present she is perfectly happy milking Cherry and Damsel.

Wednesday, 17 July

Phyllis Twigg says she can live on sixpence a day: she has just practised this for six days.

Thursday, 18 July

To London with Basil. We got seats for the ballet, and it seemed rather too good to be true to be lifted suddenly from the everlasting round of food problems and to have a holiday. Who knows what ugly war thoughts were banished by the exquisite dancing and the lovely colourings?

The trip to Sadler's Wells was made via St Pancras. The arched station roof, entirely blacked out, made the place look like a great dark cave.

Going back to Piccadilly in the darkened bus was most interesting. The buses at night are shrouded and mysterious, and our conductor did not announce the names of the stops. A huge moon rose solemnly over Hyde Park.

Saturday, 20 July

All day catching up with tasks left undone. Hitler's speech is a hollow mockery, full of lies and insults. After alleging that Mr

The blackout made streets extremely hazardous both for pedestrians and for drivers. This was one of a series of posters produced by London Transport.
Photograph © IWM PST15477

Churchill had ordered the bombing of civilians, he said that the German reply, when it came, would bring upon the British people unending suffering and misery. 'Of course, not upon Mr Churchill,' he added, 'for he no doubt will already be in Canada.'

Monday, 22 July

Great despair on the part of the local grocer over the new fat ration, so difficult. All day long yesterday, Sunday, he spent cutting up rashers for the troops and is exhausted.

Saturday, 27 July

Do we really need 20,000 tanks to win? General de Gaulle says so.*

Letter from Basil. One of his dispatch riders has died of a fractured skull.

Sunday, 28 July

Colonel P. came in to have some sherry. He said he felt that to avoid all the miseries of stagnation in the disagreeable cold months, our regiments should be sent to make raids on the enemy coasts, 'even if we did not come back,' he said sturdily.

Major Thomas came, and also mentioned the problem of the

* The future first President of the French Fifth Republic, General Charles de Gaulle rejected the Nazi armistice with France in June 1940 and escaped to Britain, where he became the leader of the Free French.

coming winter. He dreads it for our army and for the colonial troops.

Mrs Thomas said she was at Guildford station when the Dunkirk men came through. They all wanted postcards and pencils. 'And they all wrote to Mother – none was addressed to Mister,' she said gleefully.

Monday, 29 July

Lunch with Edna. She is working at the American Embassy, interviewing people about getting their children to the States. She says there are about 2,000 names down. Some of the people are exceedingly difficult and fidgetty.

May Browne came about three and we motored to her new flat in Lancaster Gate. She said one thing I shall remember especially: 'Hitler has got the right way with the Germans; they respond to his touch. But wait and see, it will not answer with any other nations.'

Thursday, 1 August

Last night I went to a concert in the village hall, given by some RASC men. Mrs Isherwood allowed one to have her violin, as he had left his at Dunkirk. It was an excellent show; all the music, however, of the jazz variety. Audience of troops and villagers. A little later Canadian soldiers visited the hut where our canteen for the children is, and stole the clock and also a lot of jam, and left the place anyhow. A pity. The Canadian boys are longing to let off steam. 'Where's this — battle?' they roar, lurching along the road.

Interesting in today's paper to hear the numbers of those who chose to vacate the Channel Islands:

Jersey: 6,000 out of 50,000.

Guernsey: 17,000 out of 42,000.*

Not a word comes. Not a plane escapes, to tell us what is going on.

Saturday, 3 August

If only I were an artist, I would keep a war scrapbook. Today my pictures would be:

(1) General de Gaulle smiling over the news that informs him that the Pétain Government has condemned him to death.
(2) The eighty-six children on board a ship bound for Canada making friends with everybody in two hours, including the Captain.
(3) A sad one. In French country places the refugees poke listlessly into heaps of rubble that were their homes.

Monday, 5 August

People who up to now have disdained all mention of dug-outs are ordering them to be made in their gardens. Mrs M., who is not well off, ruefully confesses that she had ordered one 'five-foot deep hole'. Robin is dying to go round and do it for her.

I notice also that great hatred for Hitler is abroad. It flies like a fiery cloud over England; hate and loathing.

* Of the other two islands, on Alderney, where the authorities advised evacuation, most of the population left, whereas on Sark, following the example of the Dame of Sark, they chose to stay (see the entry for Thursday, 4 July).

Tuesday, 6 August

Listening to Haw-Haw tonight from Bremen, we hear that we are desperate, and that our shipping is being slowly destroyed. He seemed particularly angry tonight.

'When they told me,' said my charwoman today, 'that Hitler plans to be crowned at Winchester Cathedral on 25 August, I saw red. You couldn't *believe* what I said!'

Wednesday, 7 August

Ruth F. here tonight in black satin and flowered blouse. She has been back to Folkestone where her house is. A raid warning sounded and all the aeroplanes in our aerodrome mounted immediately into the blue. No sign of the enemy.

Robin prepares for his first Home Guard patrol. I have supplied chocolate and a thermos of tea for the joyous return, when dawn is breaking over the downs, and Muff, our cat, begins to stalk the starlings.

Thursday, 8 August

Mr Forbes called about organising a rota of workers for the canteen about to arrive here. A horrible job. Impulsively I consented.

Friday, 9 August

Heard from Betsey F. at Haslemere about the beautifully run evacuation of officers' wives from Malta. It was something like this: 'You are requested not to think,' ran the notice that was sent to them. 'We will do the thinking. All we ask you is to be at a certain place at a certain time with a certain amount of luggage.'

Saturday, 10 August

Much interested in Sir Ronald Storrs' *The Second Quarter*, a history of this war from December 1939 to February 1940. I had not grasped before that we habitually import 90 per cent of our fats and flour and 50 per cent of our meat and 40 per cent of our eggs. Before the war about a million tons of foodstuffs were thrown into dustbins every year, Sir Ronald reminds us!

Tuesday, 13 August

I suppose an air battle begins with a great hum of engines all round. I have just been out – 8.30 on a rather sullen summer night – and found the air full of noises. You felt as if planes were approaching from every direction and converging. Harry is out with glasses identifying them, and Robin also. I can hear them now buzzing past. They are huge Whitley bombers, with crews of five.

The air war certainly intensifies.* I was in London today and oberved placard after placard written in big letters in ink or chalk on white slips of paper: 'Air battle raging – more raiders down.' Twenty-eight Germans are down and we have lost four.

Saw Muriel at the Strand Palace Hotel – lovely. I am much afraid regulations as to closed areas will prevent my visiting Picket Post for the duration – a great blow.† There was standing room only at the National Gallery Beethoven concert. I consoled myself with another good look at the war pictures exhibition.

* This was the Battle of Britain, which went on until October.

† Areas of open countryside such as parts of the New Forest were liable to be closed to the public for military purposes.

How tiresome it is to listen to the wireless bulletins about the air fighting. One gets perfectly dazed with the 'south-west towns', the 'south-east towns', the 'north-east towns', the 'north-west coast' and so on. Nor can one identify the separate battles or their separate days. Haw-Haw tonight was lying vigorously over the results – remarkable numbers. 'It cheers me up, it is all so piffling,' said Harry afterwards.

Wednesday, 14 August

To see Mrs Palmer's dug-out for herself and family. In it is a box. Lift the lid and you see every preparation for a long stay. Syphons of lemonade, chocolate, children's books to read, vaseline, cotton-wool. She reminded us that the tide is just right for Hitler's invasion tomorrow.

Thursday, 15 August

And sure enough, some parachutes have been found. In a Midland village they discovered them, and felt that the Hun soldiers had descended and were about. The church bell was rung as an alarm. Nothing more has been heard.

Eva says in her letter this morning: 'Sometimes, in spite of all the magnificent bravery of the Forces, the tireless planning of Churchill, and all the determination of the people, it seems almost impossible to think of the end. Germany – yes, we shall beat her well and truly, but at the end of that – to force Russia to give up her half of Poland! Well, one can only hope for the best.'

Saw Mrs Rayne at Ponds Farm. She told me she had had a pessimistic letter from a friend in the Near East. His Air Force boy has crashed twice lately in a bomber, the last time in the cold North Sea. The rubber boat they carry holds four, but there are six on board. John swam for help for an hour, not at his best because he had had a land crash just three days before. He was rescued, unconscious, and has been in hospital for weeks.

I hear that one of the survivors of the torpedoed *Transylvania** came on shore with a cat in his arms, purring contentedly. Good!

Friday, 16 August

An air raid warning sounded about an hour ago, and the dim grey sky was filled with an enormous dull roaring. Nothing to be seen. Machine-gun fire. I was glad to have my cotton-wool ready in the little green bag around my neck. I went into the dug-out and thought how beautifully Robin had done the bricklaying. I laughed when I saw him standing outside gazing up, just as he had expected the foolish public to do. 'Oh, I should throw myself down directly,' he always says.

Another plane is zooming above now and there are thuds. The charwoman arrives saying, 'I don't want to die yet.' I had no idea that we should not *see* the fighters in a raid, that they would be so far up.

Saturday, 17 August

In the bank this morning a stranger, a young man, was showing the people present a scrap off a German parachute which he

* HMS Transylvania was a liner converted to an armed merchant cruiser which was torpedoed by submarine U-56 off Malin Head, Ireland, on 10 August. She sank while being towed to land, with 36 lives lost.

had obtained at Northchapel, not far from Petworth. A Heinkel had come down in flames and the airmen were blown to bits. 'Did you fetch a doctor?' 'Oh, no. They were dead – smashed to pieces, bits of their bodies blown up in the trees . . .' 'Did it make you feel sick to see it?' The young man replied readily: 'I'm joining the Air Force myself on Saturday. I'm very glad I did see it. It showed me what I was up against.' 'All the best to you,' murmured the small crowd of us, awed and impressed by his resolute manner.

Monday, 19 August

In the evening Bey came in, and described her ride home from Oxfordshire to Guildford on Friday last. In Slough she found German planes overhead and took shelter in a baker's. The man exclaimed defiantly: 'I'm not going to let the Huns spoil this batch of Madeleine cakes,' and continued to bake amid the roar of guns. She left after a time, and saw people's heads popping out of air raid trenches like rabbits coming up out of burrows. At Brooklands there was a big raid, and she was allowed to shelter in the Vickers works shelters, long tunnels elaborately planned with a trained Red Cross man every few yards. There were huge jokes going on and many, seeing the haversack on her back, enquired gaily if by any chance she had a frying pan and some sausages in it. The din of our guns was tremendous and she was delighted to find she did not mind it. So far as I could make out, there were no casualties or damage.*

* The Vickers Armstong aircraft works which occupied the disused motor-racing circuit at Brooklands, Weybridge, Surrey possessed one of the largest deep shelters in the country, consisting of multiple passages each 180 feet long and protected by a 50-foot entrance tunnel with blast doors. According to Subterranea Britannica the tunnels are still in good condition, although there is no public access.

A lady called, to offer her services at the canteen. She escaped from Paris to St Nazaire only a few hours before the Germans arrived. She said it was awful on the blocked roads in her car, just creeping along in the chaos. She said the reason France collapsed was *fear*. I must find out more.

'Four hundred killed at Croydon,' said a little grey-haired wife at the butcher's this morning. I don't believe this for a moment.*

Thursday, 22 August

Yesterday at a meeting of women MPs Lady Astor expressed the complaint which I personally have felt for so long – that women have not got a word to say in the policy of this country. 'Women of ability,' she cried, 'were held down because of an unconscious Hitlerism in the hearts of men.'

Friday, 23 August

We had a very restless night, a plane zooming and throbbing over us with great persistency. It seems exactly as if the Germans wanted to alarm us, insolently flying up and down, up and down. We go back to bed about 1.30. In the morning I find Harry has again been up about 3.00, when bombs dropped and red flashes were seen as they fell.

* Before Heathrow was built, Croydon Airport was Britain's largest commercial passenger airport. At the start of the war it became an RAF fighter station. Six airmen and 62 civilians were killed when it was bombed on 15 August, and among the outlying buildings hit was the Redwing Aircraft factory, which repaired fighter planes and bombers on behalf of the Air Ministry.

Saturday, 24 August

To sherry with the F—s. Their son is a bomber observer and flies constantly to Italy and Germany. The bomber crew carry each two Thermoses of coffee, chocolate and raisins and barley sugar. He likes the job very much and said that the moonlight over the Alps was wonderful.

Mr F. shows us his very expensive dug-out, a work of art with £7 of sandbags, electric light and an electric fire. He tells me the Canadians are going to have a baseball match next Saturday here to show the village boys what's what.

Sunday, 25 August

Captain Dodds came in and said he had been to see a lot of French soldiers now resident in the White City, some longing to get back to captured France, to stand, we will suppose, at their families' sides. There is great boredom – it is a difficult crowd.

One's feelings now are these. The atmosphere of the world is poisoned, there is something wrong with the happiest moments. Day follows day almost indistinguishably. The wireless news – often completely concerned with air raids – is nauseating. I feel one must be careful now not to write and talk of air raids all the time.

Monday, 26 August

As I write, a talk is going on from Germany telling us we are starving. Also that we are using girl pilots in the air, as we are so short!

Tuesday, 27 August

It is nearly nine o'clock, a sultry night. Robin has spent hours today over a device to be given to the Home Guard for observation.

In Guildford today the fishmonger bitterly said that since the Channel had become a 'No Man's Land', as he expressed it, he would have to shut up shop. No kippers, no herrings, no nothing! He pointed to some dried haddock and said, 'If I sell that at one-and-eight a pound I shall have made a penny profit.' The shop was certainly very empty and the fine, stalwart man was extremely worried.

Sibyl writes that there has been a big raid on New Milton. Crouching by the road for shelter, she saw lorries coming past full of dead.

Wednesday, 28 August

Rosemary's and Ellen's birthday today. I wish I could be in Scotland to see them. When will one go north again? Great rumpus in the night, aeroplanes hovering and the house shaking and distant bumps. I woke Robin, but we didn't go downstairs.

I saw the billeting officer, Mrs L., looking very determined, driving rapidly along to *enforce* some householder possibly to take children in from Portsmouth.

Thursday, 29 August

Last night about ten we suddenly heard an enormous explosion, apparently just out on the lawn. I took it to be gunfire, but it was bombs. Harry appeared in pyjamas and we all went into the hall.

I couldn't sleep. The noise was so constant and so extreme. Robin got up at 2.30 and dressed for the Home Guard duty. Still there were thundering noises.

When I went out after breakfast, I heard that the bombs had fallen two miles away, near a searchlight.

Went to serve the evacuated children in the canteen. They all seemed very little and shabby and held their spoons in a

This canteen for evacuee children is at Hindhead, Surrey, but the canteen at Shere would have looked very similar.
Photograph © IWM D21631

firm grip. 'No cabbage!' cried so many of these tiny mites. I said severely to some little girls, 'You will never grow up pretty and get big unless you eat cabbage.' One looked up and said: 'Shall I grow pretty if I eat cabbage?' 'Yes indeed,' said I. 'Then I don't want to be pretty,' she replied firmly.

Olive goes into a factory on the Kingston by-pass next week (Oh, Olive, what a good cook lost!). She will get two pounds, better money than service. She tells me that her name has been down at the Labour Exchange since June and it is exceedingly difficult to get work. 'If you're over twenty-one nobody needs you.' She described how many women were fruitlessly seeking work and faking their ages.

Here is a true story I like. During a raid yesterday ninety-two-year-old Mrs Turner was assisted from a train to a shelter in a London distict. On reaching the entrance she turned to the warden and said: 'An Ancient Briton returns to her cave.'

Saturday, 31 August

We are getting to understand the necessary technique for air raids slightly better, and no doubt we shall get infinitely more skilled at it than we are now. At all costs we must not keep awake all the time we are being haunted by German machines. If one person in a large household is naturally more alert and wakeful than the rest – and there is generally one – let him or her undertake to call the others.

Sunday, 1 September

We are bombing Chartres aerodrome and Stuttgart, two towns well known to me. Is the damage repaired at Orleans? Is the cathedral at Auxerre hit? I hear the place is badly damaged.

Tuesday, 3 September

This evening I went to teach French Canadian soldiers English. They were hungry to learn, much to my astonishment. I had expected boredom and fidgettings. Instead I received earnest stares of attention. One showed me a letter from his people received that day postmarked Lewiston, Canada. Inside were two little medallions of glazed paper, on which were written the names of the man and his brother – 'I am a Roman Catholic. If I am hurt, please send for a priest.' I thought of the anxious sister over the Atlantic, sending them, and wished she could have seen her brother's satisfaction.

In a letter from Nantucket, Jackie says she finds it hard to write as her heart is so full. 'It's like a log-jam where the key log can't be found to loose all the rest which are tangled and caught. Over here,' she continues, 'there seems to be utter confusion. I don't think that there are two people in the USA who can agree as to what ought to be done.'

Wednesday, 4 September

There was an air raid today just as we were sitting at lunch. The charwoman and I went down to the cellar and invited the postwoman (who was calling at that moment) to come down also. Robin stood by the open door and was amazed at the speed of the dog-fight. One plane came down on Netley Heath. We saw the smoke coming out over the hill. Later Robin went up there, and a Canadian soldier told him how they went to secure the airmen, as it was quite near their camp. Apparently some of the crew were blown to smithereens and a hand of one of the Hun fliers was proudly carried round the tents by a French Canadian soldier. How terribly sad – how often had that boy's mother held his hand tenderly!

Thursday, 5 September

A most lovely letter from Rhodesia, bidding Harry go there.*

Saturday, 7 September

In Edna's letter this morning she says that the London shop-girls are getting very weary, in and out of shelters all the time, and nobody is venturing out to shop, so trade is miserably bad. She lies on her Sussex balcony looking up at the stars at night and feeling their benediction.

What is going to be the end of all this air-raid warfare? It seems totally inconclusive. One cannot get it out of one's thoughts and comversation and letters.

Sunday, 8 September

The papers do not arrive. London has had a terrible time – a reprisal for our raids on Berlin, the Germans gleefully announce. The names Shoreditch and Fulham are heard as having greatly suffered, as well as Dockland.

It is said that some of the searchlight personnel are longing to learn astronomy, gazing up at the starry sky un-understandingly every night.

* Robin's brother Bevis and his wife Evelyn had a tobacco farm in Rhodesia (now Zimbabwe). It was felt that the climate of East Africa would be beneficial to Harry's health, which was worsened by conditions of cold or damp.

It's six o'clock and there is a great noise of planes. It gives one a headache.

I like this: London householder, looking at searchlights and parachute flares: 'Very good in its way, but I still hold that the old Crystal Palace was better.'

Berliners go to bed wishing one another a splinterless night.

Bey came in. She had danced with a Canadian sergeant, who had been first on the scene when the German plane crashed at Netley Down. Only the pilot was recognisable, and he had been shot between the eyes. The Sergeant took his papers, his bottle of vitamin tablets, his wad of money (quite a lot), the picture of his girl, etc. He was twenty-one. All these things will be sent back to Germany, to his mother.

Monday, 9 September

Harry reads out from the *Aeroplane* that Germany has about 7,000 bombers and 4,000 fighters, two-thirds of which might be used against us. It is imagined one side must crack, probably in October.

It is difficult to write about the great air raids over London. Various men and women with suitcases appeared in the village today, trying for rooms. They have been bombed out of their homes.

Tuesday, 10 September

A very disturbed night – zooming of planes without even five minutes intermission. Many thuds. At the canteen this morning I had a chat with a woman whose husband has come down to see her from Fulham. The hospital in Fulham was hit once or twice and the scene was indescribable, he said. He himself was in the demolition squad who rescued some of the patients. The young nurses, he said, ought to have had VCs, so cheerful and efficient.

Everybody is tired but determined.

Later: Harry comes in from a tremendous journey back from London. He saw great damage, just escaping Baker Street Station and Madame Tussaud's. Firemen were being very brave, clambering about ruined tenements. He said people's faces showed distinct signs of strain. It of course must get worse, and we must brace ourselves.

Thursday, 12 September

Robin went out on Home Guard duty about 3 a.m. He said the firing over London was terrific, more tremendous than ever before.

It is reported that a Hun airman down at Dorking apologised, saying: 'We had no intention of bombing Dorking. We did not know where we were.'

Friday, 13 September

Ruth F. says she is sure Folkestone will be compulsorily evacuated, and what shall she do about her furniture. They are poor, but I am sure have lovely, carefully collected things. Their house stands near the Links, which has had 100 bombs.

I got hold of May B. on the phone, waiting in the new ATS canteen at Aldershot to give an Inspector lunch. She had time to tell me she had been in London during last Wednesday's raid and the barrage was terrific. She rejoiced in it, as noise always stimulates her. She was dining out with two men in a fashionable restaurant and nobody was allowed to emerge, such was the danger and the racket. One of her hosts was a General high up in the War Office, so possibly he had to go out among the bursting shells and red gun-flashes.

Sunday, 15 September

Miss B., the shopgirl, yesterday spoke with suppressed and dangerous excitement of her mother's shattered house in Kensington. 'Oh, I went up to fetch her, and you wouldn't believe the damage. Mother was down in the basement with the others. There was a crash. She said, "Now all keep quite calm. We will go next door." But there was no next door!

'We saved a little of the silver and came away,' she said, with a queer, hysterical laugh, as if it were great fun.

Monday, 16 September

A bad night. An enormous explosion. First a plane rushing past low down and near my window, it seemed, and then the bombs. Poor Mrs Burton, who lives about three-quarters of a mile away, and who had felt so unhappy about everything, as if danger threatened, was right in it. It has made her deaf. She still feels 'as if among horrors'.

Nevertheless, looking very pretty with her forget-me-not blue eyes, she drove off in a Canadian waggon with other ladies tonight at six o'clock, to give the last lesson in English to the men from Montreal. They are moving, to an unknown but heavily bombed neighbourhood.

Four letters this morning. E. writes from Ross-on-Wye, where they have had several raids. When the noise came close, she says, 'My first thought was, "I must take this seriously."' The only damage, however, after a lot of shells had fallen, was to one small pig and two partridges.

Tuesday, 17 September

Harry left the house at 8.15 and reached London at midday. The line still terminates at Wimbledon and there are many, many changes.

Mrs F. came in with some tomato sausages for me. She said that she had heard from her niece in a famous club. The young secretary related that two waiters had phoned through one recent morning, to say they were sorry they would be delayed, as their houses had been demolished! When they eventually arrived, they were smiling.

Thursday, 19 September

The stream of German aeroplanes over us towards London began about nine o'clock last night and there was not so much as five minutes' silence till, I should say, two a.m., and one woke constantly to noises. Two lots of bombs – one lot disagreeably near us. It seems quite wrong – nay, appalling – that the Germans are masters of the air at night.

Friday, 20 September

May B. on the phone from Aldershot: 'Walking along Cromwell Road yesterday, I saw a large house on a corner completely wrecked and a big piece of parquet flooring suspended in the air and some beds in the road. I shall never forget Wednesday night in London. The bombs just *rained* down.'

Last night we had bombs within a quarter of a mile. Pulling

aside the heavy curtain of the library window, Robin showed me a fire in the rainy dark.

Said the butcher boy, leaving half a pound of liver this morning, 'A great many incendiary bombs were dropped right on our farm in the Silverwood. One was on our porch, and burned the creeper. Dad and I went out and beat out the flames.'

Saturday, 21 September

Summer still lingers, the garden gay with tall golden sunflowers and purple Michaelmas daisies. Basil writes, wishing to volunteer for Africa. Many men are going East.

The announcer on the BBC has just told us that a new interceptor Lockheed machine can fly 500 miles an hour and take off the ground at 100 miles an hour.

Sunday, 22 September

Harry is very pleased because a huge plane – an Avro Anson – came rather low over the fields.

Women, it is said in London, choose red frocks, hats, coats and flowers after air raids, a device to keep up the spirits.

Monday, 23 September

Shere is filling up with Londoners. Two invalidish, very old ladies in a large red brick house have been presented with two platinum blondes and their babies. Old Miss B. offered to take a party of them – she is an exquisitely neat spinster of nearly seventy – and suffered agonies of apprehension as to where the man should smoke and shave.

Tuesday, 24 September

Harry has been to the War Office, trying to arrange to get out to Rhodesia. He is put on half-pay from 9 October.

Six men of the HAC* arrived begging for baths. Two went next door, two to the doctor's and we had two. 'I feel quite human,' declared one lad, emerging.

Wednesday, 25 September

To Guildford to see Harry's doctor, who told me St Thomas's Hospital had been very badly hit, again. They will rebuild.

A dreadful night. Instead of the usual couple of bombs, there were constant thumps and they were all in the neighbourhood – thirty in all. I pity the middle-aged Air Raid Wardens who are darting about here and there in the dark, visiting the cottages, and on the look-out for fires.

Thursday, 26 September

Moving things about in the flat below. It nearly got taken by the military. The rent – all important – would have been much reduced.†

Muriel writes that she had bombs dropped 400 yards away. In a friend's house a grand piano was blown over a field.

* The Honourable Artillery Company. An HAC unit was billeted at the time at Netley Park.

† The long-term tenants, Madge and Edie Davidson, had gone to Scotland. For the remainder of the time covered by the journal, the downstairs flat was sub-let first to Mr Stevens and his niece Miss Scott, then to Captain and Mrs Pakenham, then Mr Brook and his invalid wife.

Friday, 27 September

Preparing for the tenant in the flat. Poor old fellow, if he thinks he's coming into peaceful nights. I hear he brings a nervous niece.

The news seems rather bad. Japan has thrown herself into the arms of Germany and Itály.

Today Mrs Murray said to me: 'Yesterday we decided to go into our dug-out as an air-battle was on. We looked everywhere for Byng, our Pekinese. No sign. After calling, a pale little face appeared at the dug-out entrance, saying: "Why on earth are you not coming down?" Byng is palest golden colour, but oh, yes, he got paler, and I heard him mutter, as he ran down again, "Let the women look to themselves, it is I that matter!"'

The sharp tang in the air, whispering of winter, usually rouses me to such joy, such plans for work between October and Christmas; but now this poor disjointed diary is almost all I have to write.

Later: I was half asleep when an army waggon drove up with considerable noise. Went to the window, and saw a policeman carrying a small leather case, and a soldier. They rang the bell and asked for Major Miles. I asked what they wanted. *Billets*. 'I think I should be able to get four at least into this big house,' said the NCO. I did not care for his manner. I felt as if they were rather Gestapo-ish.

It might be very pleasant to have one lively officer for the winter to talk to in the long dark evenings.

I have come to a conclusion. We cannot win this war unless America is fully and actually with us.

Sunday, 29 September

Last night there came an appalling crash – I thought a bomb was in our roof and threw myself down.

The murky lane outside was soon full of hurrying footsteps, and our good Head Warden was soon at the side of the household of women only, next door.

Robin dragged down my mattress into the cellar and the bombs continued to fall – it was impossible to count them. I thought the ticking-over of the electric meter was a rat, but felt anything was better than to go back to the life upstairs.

Robin lay in the hall without taking off his clothes. Harry slept unperturbed. The bombs so near us fell on the Men's Club five minutes away; a great beech tree uprooted.

Monday, 30 September

Spent a very happy, peaceful time in my cellar bedroom, though it was a rough night.

What is going to happen to all these old ladies and old men who are steadily being deprived of sleep? As I write, heavy German planes are going past, and probably the beastly humming will not cease until dawn.

A bomb has just fallen, preventing me from writing much about the approaching partition of poor gallant Switzerland, which is foreshadowed.*

Tuesday, 1 October

Mrs M. Crawford of Hampton has subscribed £5,000 for a

* In fact the proposed Nazi invasion of Switzerland never took place.

Spitfire to be called *Mabel.* The Dorothy Fund is slowly progressing, and now a George Fund has opened.*

To help at kitchen. Pandemonium. Teacher who simply couldn't keep order. Suet pudding most popular.

It is expected that within the next few weeks, when we are all drawing closer and closer to the fire, the war will quicken all along the Mediterranean.

At Cannes and Nice, those once spoiled cities of pleasure, there is now a great scarcity of milk, butter and cheese, fats and coffee. Sometimes hotel-keepers refuse guests because they have no soap to wash their sheets.

Worst of all is the apathy which spreads everywhere under the German yoke.

Thus the Norwegians tear up every paper connected with their Trade Unions. They have destroyed their lists of members and burned their documents, and wrecked their whole machinery, a characteristic Norwegian act planned and carried through thoroughly by disciplined and organised labour in a spirit of profound despondency.

Then along the Geneva border of France, shops are almost empty, and the peasants do not want to make the autumn sowings. This means much indeed. Oh God, grant us one good victory at least soon, to turn the tide.

Wednesday, 2 October

Guildford in the morning, dentist, talk entirely of bombs, where and how. When the history of this war is accurately written, there

* Spitfire Funds raised money to help finance the production of the fighter planes that were needed. Communities, businesses and individuals contributed and had planes named after them. Donations came not only from people in Britain but all over the Empire and Commonwealth.

must be stress laid on the fact that the conversation of the English, high and low, rich and poor, was about where and when the bombs fell. We hear so little, and conjecture a lot. Not a word has appeared in the press about, for instance, the great aerial torpedo which fell right into the YMCA hostel in Tottenham Court Road. Jacky Browne,* aged seventeen, was standing with a cup of coffee in his hand at the entrance to the lounge and escaped, but there were nine young men killed just inside.

Sara J. came to sherry and said she could not possibly sleep in my cellar: she would have an attack of claustrophobia. I love it, and feel perfectly secure.

Thursday, 3 October

Edna tells of a sojourn in a tunnel in Villiers Street during a bad raid. 'All very murky and like *Les Miserables*. Tired people unrolling mattresses, newsboys selling newspapers, cockneys going out to the local pub, wardens shouting "Put out that cigarette!" On the whole, a quiet atmosphere of good temper, I thought, but I'm not the stuff that heroes are made of.'

En route homewards Edna bribed a taxi-driver to take her to Croydon. When she paid him largely he thanked her, and smilingly said he was glad of the money, as he had just been bombed out of his house.

Friday, 4 October

From Nantucket Island, Massachusetts, came an anxious letter from my friend Margaret. She says: 'The days are utterly indescribable to us. What must they be to you! We hang over the

* May Browne's son

radio with our hearts in shreds and tatters, and we can do nothing. The reports make our blood run cold, and the hours are endless, and our hearts are with you.'

Saturday, 5 October

In the *Author* there are various laments about the plight of writers today. The publishing world is passing through the most critical period in its history, says St John Ervine: 'Authors are assailed from every direction. The shortage of paper affects us vitally. Our opportunities of earning a livelihood are everywhere curtailed or stopped.' Don't I know it – not a single review book comes nowadays.

Tuesday, 8 October

Waited on a hundred at the village hall. I think it would be a good thing if the children were trained to march out quietly table by table instead of running (today knocking over and breaking a tray of tumblers).

Wednesday, 9 October

We hear that Denmark, the placid, the apparently most submissive of all countries, is now in a ferment. Says *The Times*: 'The Danes look across the Sound nightly to the lights of Sweden, showing them that Sweden is still intact, and inspiring them with envious gladness.'

Friday, 11 October

It was a ghastly night of aeroplanes up and down. This evening

The shortage of paper was one of the reasons why Connie gave up her journal for almost eight months in 1941.
Photograph © IWM PST14656

went up in the car to look at some of the craters. It was quite a scene for a war painter. The westering sun shone in a sky all rich gold over a lonely and lovely heath. Down a sandy lane, two humble farm cottages, semi-detached. A shed by the lane had all its tiles knocked about. A lorry in front of the gate, and a young couple with a little child, busy assisting a man who was heaving on the furniture, poor, flimsy stuff. The family had only just returned, as they had had a time-bomb in their field three weeks before.

One shell was actually only three yards from the other in the field. I dare not ask where they were going.

I hear the Poles are winning great opinions in Scotland. And Scotland has risen to the occasion. Large groups have formed, sometimes a hundred strong, to study the size and work of the countryside around them. Visits were paid to farms of all kinds, to market gardens and large garages. The charm of the Poles broke down the reserve of the Scot. 'These very men had the hospitality of an old, whitewashed house in which Prince Charles Edward had lived, and no doubt talked of his Polish mother.'*

Ruth F. tells me of her visit to Folkestone. She found the windows blown out of her house, and the curtains wet in the rain. Fetching a tarpaulin, she tried to fix it up in the drawing-room. There were seven warnings while Ruth was there. Everybody in Julian Road has evacuated. Poor Folkestone! It's almost impossible to find a safe storage room.

* The mother of Charles Edward Stuart, otherwise known as Bonnie Prince Charlie, was Maria Clementina Sobieska, granddaughter of John III Sobieska, King of Poland 1674–1696.

Saturday, 12 October

Barbara sends a despairing letter about her boys from London, and heads her letter, 'Little Hell, Blewbury'. The elder boy wrote home to say that bombs were dropping all round him, and couldn't he go home? He packed his suitcase and has been bellowing loudly. Barbara thinks the LCC education they have received is very bad. She writes: 'I wish one could see any end to this war – it seemed to be spreading so violently. And what is going to happen afterwards? How are people going to be housed again? And what of education? The public schools are bound to die, but I hope the public school-masters will be able to leaven the lump of the LCC. It is a deplorable education. One discovers the terrible laziness of it when dealing with these children – no attempt made to show the reason of anything, all parrot, parrot, parrot.'

I should have been at Paddington Registry Office today at 10.30 to see my dear May Browne married, but the danger of air raids being so intense I did not venture.

Sunday, 13 October

The year slips away and the woods are becoming red-gold. Basil arrived this evening for a spot of leave.

Monday, 14 October

Borrowed the book I had sent Basil, *The Neuroses in War*, edited by Emanuel Miller. 'All cases of neurosis in wars are not curable,' says Dr Maurice Wright. 'Many thousands of broken, frightened men are still drawing pensions as a result. This fact must be faced squarely and honestly.'

Tuesday, 15 October

Walked with Basil to look at the beautiful and death-struck year. It was lovely, walking under the brown beech and green yews. Unfortunately, we were obliged to remember the war, as we came upon a large barricade made of huge logs and a dull green pillbox in the background. I brought back a bough of golden maple. It is such a pity he has to go back tomorrow.

Basil talked of the London air raids and the feeling of anger they provoked, and of the physical processes that go on when the human being is agitated. He said it was a thousand pities that no form of revenge could be taken by the citizens to avenge themselves. He even thought that to hit savagely at medicine ball would be better than nothing, and wished there could be some put up in the tubes. He thinks, contrary to his father, that it will be a long war.

On polishing buttons. I was saying what a pity it was that brass was not abolished, but Basil said: 'Oh no; what relief women get from knitting, so men get relief and interest and change of thought in cleaning and polishing their kit.'

Robin is feeling very low with the approach of winter. A large bomb was dropped this afternoon, much to the indignation of the tenant below, who was resting to make up for lack of sleep during the wretched loud night.

Olive's husband, a noted chef, is out of work. I suppose people are not using these rich hotels like the Connaught or the Dorchester so much.

A dark rainy night. Harry has gone to bed with a pain in his shoulder-blade. Miss Scott and I are uneasy, she in her flat below, I upstairs, at the unending loud hum of Hun planes. Old Mr Stevens tells me from his armchair by the fire that he has heard from Hythe, where he lives, that several people he knew in the little town have been killed – a gardener, a tailor's wife who used to do repairs, and so on.

I must say I feel pleased that the Berlin authorities are evacuating 75,000 children. It must bring it home to them.

Thursday, 17 October

Very much depressed at the news of Jack Bower's sudden death.* He had not been ill long. He was a true poet and a true sailor, with an adventurous spirit that never lost its daring. One of the best-informed men I ever knew, deeply versed in history and a vivid good talker. I hate to think of the deep loneliness of his wife.

Friday, 18 October

A horribly bad day for Harry as so foggy and damp. London begins to look rather damaged. The cook has arrived late as 'a young lady came to the door and begged me to put her up. I said no. She nearly collapsed. I felt sorry and let her in and said I wouldn't cook for her or anything, but that she could sleep here. She said she came from New Cross.'

Saturday, 19 October

A mild morning. If there were no war, I should be trying to get to Paris to sit outside a café and drink coffee in the sunshine on the quay.

* Commander John Graham Bower, RN, who had married Barbara Euphan Todd in 1932.

Felt rather desperate on hearing that Japan had already begun to bomb the Burma Road. Can't we frighten them?

Sunday, 20 October

A glorious morning. I found a maid, lurking in a field cottage. As I brought her back in the car, she said: 'My young man is a prisoner of war. He has written to me and on the postcard he put, "Please send me a cake".'

Monday, 21 October

'I always thought,' says a writer in today's *Chronicle*, 'that the mother-lynx defending her young was the fiercest animal in the world. Worse, much worse, is the Englishwoman fighting for the last silk stockings of the war.'

Dinner punctuated by gunfire. I move from the window.

Thursday, 24 October

Sibyl writes from the New Forest: 'We had a bad scare at lunch time yesterday. Molly rushed in. "They are machine-gunning the house – lie down!" Reg had thrown himself on the floor after shouting "Down!" to us, which we did not hear. The noise was simply awful. I thought a plane was coming down on the house. Really it skimmed over the porch end, chased by two Spitfires (which were doing the machine-gunning), and eventually was brought down a flaming wreck in a field at Hordle.'

Saturday, 26 October

Wrote my Xmas story, 'Mrs Halliburton's Trouble', and a

column for the *Home Messenger*. There were bombs within a mile of two of us.

A letter from Ray full of bomb news of Yeovil, where they are closing the schools.

Harry sent a cable to Rhodesia today and so did I. He extracted the necessary letter from the War Office yesterday.

Monday, 28 October

The great news is that Italy has declared war on Greece. How quick this is! What of Yugoslavia?

Imagine Hitler choosing Florence for the scene of his meeting with Mussolini. Poor desecrated Florence!

Hear of the bombing of Athens with sharp alarm. What barbarity!

Tuesday, 29 October

Muriel writes that the great double and treble searchlights keep her awake, as they flash across her face and light up the room. When she comes back from Bournemouth there is 'usually an air raid and the searchlights light up all the inside of the car in an extraordinary way. One can see everything, which is rather convenient in the black-out.'

Went to call on a Paddington evacuee cat in the village, a sweet whitish kitten. The two dressmakers accompanying it are humbly grateful for their one room, where they can just squeeze in.

Friday, 1 November

Another month has started and we have a strong hope that

there will be good news for Britain before it ends. Greece seems to be holding out well at the moment.

Sunday, 3 November

I write actually on All Souls Day. I think of the masses of French people wending their way to pay homage to their dead, and I am pretty sure that in many minds there must be a strange and quite new thought. They must be glad, many of them, that their near and dear ones are out of this disgusting war of conquest; that their brave mothers and bright, dark-eyed fathers had not silently to watch the Gestapo preening by.

We have landed troops in Greece.

Monday, 4 November

Went to see Miss B., whose niece is training to be a 'roof-spotter' in Buckinghamshire. She can now identify thirty-six aeroplanes and has 'a nodding acquaintance' with others. This enterprising young Englishwoman has three small children and intends to take America's offer of hospitality if she can for her elder girl, aged seven, for California. The offer is of course not open just at the moment. In fact, the news about our shipping is very grave.

Robin went to Guildford hospital this morning to give blood. He enjoyed the whole show, resting and having a cup of tea. He said to one nurse: 'Do you ever take a conscientous objector's blood?' 'If I did,' replied the warlike woman, 'I would take five or six pints and do him in.'

I don't have the slightest feeling against the conchies, but Robin has a lively emotion of rancour.

Joan Hoffman has just rung up to say they have had no gas at their Harley Street house for ten weeks.

Thursday, 7 November

We had the most alarming evening. Again and again I descended to the hall to talk to Miss Scott below. We spoke lightly and foolishly, planning that I should give a party in 'Montmartre', my cellar, which is decidedly Montmartrish with its card table, gas meters, meat safe and empty jam-jars and chintz chair.

Robin went out on Home Guard duty early in the dawn, heavily dressed. Hundreds of machines seemed to drone past all the time.

Have just rung up the grocer's. No biscuits, no marmalade, no currants, no figs.

Ray writes that she and her husband go from Yeovil nightly now to seek a good night's rest in a village called Yetminster, where in a rich and obliging private house they have a big spare room. Poor Ray hates 'the turn out into the cold eve and morn – back for an 8.45 breakfast.' Her husband takes a bath at home as the other water is lukewarm. She says: 'We drove the other night steadily through gunfire and flares, a bright light, white, almost like being on a battlefield, it seemed to me.'

Friday, 8 November

I see Cummings of the *News Chronicle* says that through the election of Roosevelt again all is signified.* In fact *we cannot now*

* Franklin D. Roosevelt was elected to serve a third term in November 1940, the first President of the United States to serve more than two terms.

lose the war, being firmly assured of the support of the USA. They say Hitler listened to the figures of the election feverishly, and was constantly informed.

Friday, 15 November

Last night several people I know didn't go to bed. The planes over us were incessant: and there was a devilish raid on Coventry, about which we have not yet got the facts. I went to sleep about two.

Saturday, 16 November

Did not properly undress last night. It was weird standing on the terrace at midnight, unusually light, with just a sinister vast throbbing of plane engines all round; and you couldn't see a single machine. London must have had hundreds of visitors. The noise never died.

Harry was delighted to get his entry permit to Rhodesia. Now we wrestle with the Passport Office.

Sunday, 17 November

As I write, there is a BBC lament going on for the lost folk of Coventry.* Coventry and Hamburg – these are the cities on our minds. The Germans will get even more violent.

I long for flowers. They are so dear now, and many for sale

* Over 500 German bombers targeted Coventry on the night of 14/15 November 1940. More than 550 people were killed and 1200 injured, and the cathedral was destroyed, as were around one third of the city's factories. The following two nights saw major raids by British planes on Hamburg, foreshadowing the almost total destruction of that city in July 1943.

look broken by the wind. The British officers in Crete were carried shoulder-high the other day, and their cars filled with fresh glowing chrysanthemums, pink, bronze, white and gold.

Harry thinks he may not get a ship to South Africa for many weeks. As phones and telegrams are so bad, he will have to get a friend in town to bring him a message down if news comes that there is a vacancy.

Friday, 22 November

This is a very poor journal this week, as every effort is being put forth to help Harry pack his things for what may be life settlement in Rhodesia. I am so very bad at packing, and hover round Harry, who appears to me to be equally bad. But I have the sense to get help always in sorting and folding and he, being twenty-seven, will not have it.

Sunday, 24 November

Basil arrived. He says Dover is not so badly knocked about as one might think. He is sad that he can't go East at the moment as there is a shortage of doctors in his Division.

The brothers cooked sausages together for Sunday supper. Harry kept exclaiming 'It's gone!' when one burst, as if it were a death.

Basil returned to Kent in a friend's aged car. Having no signposts is ghastly. England is full of people gaily motoring up the wrong turning.*

* All signposts had been removed from road junctions in June 1940 so that parachutists or other invaders should not know where they were.

Men from the Ministry taking down signposts
at a Surrey junction.
Photograph © IWM HU4925

If we find the secret of defeating the night-raids, so will Germany. That is a thought that haunts me today.

Monday, 25 November

No ticket for Harry. Passage cancelled till early December.

From *News from the Outpost*, a paper issued from the Americans in London, this story:

Dear old lady of seventy-five: 'I don't think we are doing so well in this air war now. The Germans are dropping their bombs nearer every day.'

'Nearer to what?'

'Nearer to *me*.'

Wednesday, 27 November

Much distracted by the Christmas gift question, deciding, in view of our heavy expenses, to give nothing, but not able to screw up the courage. Women live by getting gifts, and count on them, and there it is; women also enjoy giving them to the full.

There was apparently a heated discussion of the Trade Unions this week, as to whether they should insist on extra wages. This thoughtful comment was made by one Jenkins: '. . . in Portsmouth, when the men stood at the guns during air raids, dockyard workers went to their shelters, and some of the gunners said after the raid: "Look at the £6-a-week men coming out of their shelters while we stand by the guns!"'

Feel rather dismayed tonight. Have been out on the terrace, as there was such a roaring of planes. If only one could see them, but tonight we only shuddered in the bitter winter air, and looked at the stars and the roofs and the spire of our little village against a murky sky. The murderers were hidden; tonight's victims as yet comfortable by their fires.

Took two notes round tonight, one to a newly-made widow of a flying officer, one to a mother whose only child has just rejoined his ship after a very glorious leave.

Friday, 29 November

Went into an old cottager's house this afternoon to find she had made me a good Christmas cake, for which I shall pay her five shillings, although it was offered me as a gift. She had saved up her rations very carefully to get the material for the cake, which it is a triumph to possess these scanty days.

I observe with dismay that all the professors of the Faculty of Law in the University of Utrecht have been sent to concentration camps in Germany 'because of their loyalty to the House of Orange and their preference for a democratic form of government'.

The Germans have no idea of how to govern! You never hear of any wise, just measure calculated to win the hearts of the new subjects.

As to news, Greece seems to be doing well, but the shadow of our shipping losses is still heavy on us, and my one idea is *when will Harry go*, and will he be safe when he is on the deep?

Sunday, 1 December

Everybody seems to think Italy is dished by the Grecian triumphs. It is amazing.

Monday, 2 December

It is terrifically cold, alarmingly cold.

Robin reads me a long and deeply interesting account of the French in occupied France from the paper while I rush about over morning jobs. Harry's fiancée in Singapore has leave to resign and marry him. This is a great matter. Now we must just wait for his small Dutch vessel to receive him on board.

Later: the Greeks seem to be wonderfully successful and their triumphs are cheering us tremendously. For rations they have sardines, hard bread, thin soup and cheese.

Southampton, that pleasant town, has had two dreadful air raids. When you know all the main streets, it makes your heart turn over.

All news from all sources reports a rising feeling of annoyance with Germany in France and speaks of the low spirits of the homesick German soldiers.

Catering gets pretty difficult. Barbara writes: 'I managed after much labour to get four eggs, rang up the farm and was half-promised three.' There have been egg queues in Woolwich.

Wednesday, 4 December

This afternoon the telephone rang, and it was a telegram from South Africa House to tell Harry to be on the quay at Liverpool by nine o'clock on Monday morning.

Heard that when the Hun was busy over Southampton our poor friend and ex-cook, Mrs Smith, hid under a kitchen table and put a large saucepan on her head as a tin hat.

The news of the shipping losses is exceedingly serious. I must keep calm and controlled during the next difficult week.

Thursday, 5 December

A strenuous day of jobs for Harry in Guildford. It is all a lucky dip now in the shops. 'Have you any sausages?' 'No.' 'Any tin-tacks?' 'No.' 'Any slab chocolate?' 'No.'

The insurance agent called from Croydon and was eloquent about the sufferings of that unhappy place through bombing. He himself lives in Streatham. Much has been destroyed. 'You get used to it, of course, but if a bomb whistles by you quite near, it is a sound that you could never forget all your life.'

Friday, 6 December

So afraid that the phone will bring news of a fresh cancellation of shipping, now we are all set and screwed up to bear the parting. The usual brisk and cross drama over keys and straps, in spite of idle days.

Saturday, 7 December

The great day of Harry's departure for Rhodesia. May the Dutch vessel start and sail safely into port! There will be little peace of mind for the next fortnight; so many U-boats, so many enemy bombers.

Sunday, 8 December

We have just been out on the terrace to look at a couple of incendiary bombs burning themselves out in the lane below, so near I could have shied a ball at them. Crowds of little fires all over the village. Now a man has reported that he has picked somebody up on the road with a bad burn, and the doctor has been rung up.

Harry struck the one bombless night in London, and must have been disappointed. He wished to hear the barrage! He must be sitting in Liverpool now.

A cold bitter wind. Asked Miss B. about billeting soldiers. She finds hers pretty good; they never make their beds, apparently, but that's their pigeon.

Monday, 9 December

Last night slept in my clothes. The stream of German planes going to London was loud and incessant. It was very chilly tripping up and down stairs to take refuge in the safe corner, and 'Montmartre' felt very damp.

8 p.m.: Mrs Rapson, my charwoman, arrived in a state of almost perfect incoherence about the incendiary bomb that fell on her daughter-in-law's house last night. 'I knew something was going to happen. I was that uneasy, I told Robbie, our London child, to put his clothes all ready in a case, just supposing he had to quit in a hurry. Then it all happened, and the village was lit up something beautiful. Went through the roof, quite a small 'ole, slanted across to James's bedroom, then made a bigger 'ole and exploded and went through the scullery below. My son was ever so handy at putting out the fire, but everything's scorched and a chair's burned out, and you'd never believe the black smoke on everything. There's a bucket of sand I have standing in my hall, and in normal times it's so heavy I can't lift it, but you know I just seized it, and I dashed over the road to my son with it!

'Mrs Mensil had one come right down her chimney and

lodge in the copper, and it didn't explode. Jerry don't seem to be here tonight.'

It is blowing hard. Is Harry feeling it on board, or will he walk in tomorrow? I hear Beryl's ship from New York was cancelled six times before she got away.

Tuesday, 10 December

Tonight's *Evening Standard* tells us of a Greek Lance-Corporal named Tassos, only thirteen; an amazing boy and a dashing leader.

May wrote that Southampton is a sad sight. Many forsaken cats sitting on the rubble, and piles of stones and bricks.

I stop writing to listen to Churchill's speech about our success in Libya.* It is glorious news. The Italians seem to have been surprised.

Thursday, 12 December

Just rang up Kitty Eustace. She has heard neither from her daughter-in-law in Nairobi nor her son at sea, nor her son-in-law at sea nor her daughter in Singapore for ages.

Friday, 13 December

Felt a great sense of relaxation that dear Harry was finally on his way.

From Mother's letter today from Aberdeenshire: 'Last Wednesday at our Women's Institute Red Cross meeting I

* This is actually the victory, in Egypt, not Libya, that Connie refers to in more detail in the entry for Friday, 13 December.

found a table covered with little piles of presents for each of our village men in the Forces, not yet abroad. Each pile had a helmet or scarf, chocolate, cigarettes, soap, pencil, handkerchief. The relations came and carried off parcels to post themselves.'

Mrs Burnett Smith writes that farming conditions are so arduous in Scotland that she is afraid her farmer host, who has worked so hard all his life, will have to come out of it next year. Too sad.

We have a glorious and clever victory in Egypt.* The troops were silently moved up across the desert during the darkness of Saturday and Sunday nights and spent the whole of Sunday lying motionless in the open – a very trying test of endurance. They had their reward in being able to spring a complete surprise on the enemy. It is difficult to know how we are going to supply 20,000 prisoners with water.

Saturday, 14 December

The news this week is excellent. We are all waiting to see what Hitler will do next – he is bound to make a leap. We take more and more prisoners in the desert.

Harry has now been at sea five days.

Monday, 16 December

Everybody is wondering if Hitler will march into Italy, or try an invasion here. Last night I dreamt that I saw German troop-carriers landing their men on a solitary English marsh.

* The Battle of the Camps. At Nibeiwa on 9 December, where the Italian General Maletti was killed, Sidi Barrani on 10 December and Buq Buq on 11 December a total of 38,000 Italian prisoners were captured, along with 73 tanks and 237 guns.

Then, later, another dream. The Germans were in possession here, and we all had to go to Selfridges and give in our gas-masks. I had lost mine. When I arrived in London, the whole of the great shop had been stripped by the Germans, and we had to queue past empty counters behind which stood triumphant Nazis in uniform. I felt I would be shot, then woke.

The outline of the future does not yet emerge, and all talk about our war aims seems to be lifeless and unreal.

Went to see D. She says her son, a policeman in the Air Force, was mad keen to get abroad, but now he has fallen in love with a girl six foot high with fair hair, so he would rather stay at home! Both, I think, are twenty-one.

Tuesday, 17 December

Letters in at last from Rhodesia. Our letters took two months to get out to them, and theirs one month back to me. They welcome Harry and are so kind. Lucky Harry! I hope his ship is out of the danger zone.

Wednesday, 18 December

Frost and fog this morning. The R—s were coming to tea, but wrote to say that their elder boy, RAF, whom Robin met last week, had been killed in the air. The husband has been waiting for a boat to India for months, but must be glad to be in England now, to comfort the poor, broken-hearted mother.

Harrods' man came with some orders. He told Doris that he had been bombed out of his home, and his missus had been killed.

Columns of docile Italian prisoners are marching about in the desert. They do not try to escape. But obviously the Italians never dreamt they would have to retreat. The slightly malicious story is going round military circles in London, that when GHQ Egypt asked for 50,000 sandbags from England, they were sent filled.

Thursday, 19 December

The Greeks are fighting in appalling weather. 'Conditions at the front,' says a *Times* special correspondent in Albania, 'are almost tougher than can be endured by men who had been softened by the life of modern cities before they turned soldiers. If it were just plain snow or plain cold or plain wind ... but the three combined, and the high peaks with their rarified air, make it a white hell. It is worst for the Italians, with their heavy equipment.'

Mrs P. told me more of her sister-in-law's flight from Paris just before the Germans entered. They took eleven days to get to a port. Crowds of refugees were lost and separated, and in certain shop windows agonised notices were placed asking for news.

Shere is humming with traffic as I write in the softly falling grey evening. What would I not give to have a talk with my cousin Alice by the fire? But she is in bleak Edinburgh this afternoon, giving a wedding reception for her daughter Dulcie, who is marrying a brilliant young soldier with examinations before him when he emerges from the army.

The streets of Rome, I read, are thronged today with German officers and men. High German officers are crowding into big Rome hotels, where they very curtly demand special service.

Olive* has just rushed in to say that Miss Scott in the flat below reports that our light is showing in the kitchen window.

Friday, 20 December

Mrs Heath came in. She had had a terrible time, she told us, in her Sydenham flat. Apparently their blocks stood on a hill. The other block was smashed by a direct hit one October evening at seven-fifteen. Their own flat had doors blown in, windows blown out, and they could not stay in it. One girl only (in the top flat) was saved in the other block, and she miraculously slid down the falling wall. Many people were sheltering in the basement, but they were all killed. 'Such a pile of rubble,' said Mrs Heath. 'They only dug out the last body five weeks later.'

Italy is at last, we hope and pray, cracking up. Posters printed on cheap paper have appeared on the walls in Turin, Milan, Genoa, Florence, etc., saying one word, '*Basta*' (enough). People going to work wrote on them '*Bene*' (good).

Saturday, 21 December

Basil sent a beautiful Xmas gift to me, an RAMC badge, circular, glittering with bright stones. He refused a chance to take administrative work in India last week, and still hopes for Egypt. He says great preparations are being made for a jolly Xmas with the troops. 'The officers are giving the beer.'

* This is Olive Sutton who was the daily maid, not Olive the cook who had left to work in a factory in September.

Sunday, 22 December

Phyl writes amusingly of a War Fare Cookery Week at Bampton, Devon. Robin was very pleased with the idea of children's cookery dances. One between two teams, the leader of one side, General Slackness, with accompanying demons clearly labelled Stomach-ache, Nightmare, Hiccoughs, Collywobbles; and General Efficiency, whose team would be made up of Delight and Health, Taking Trouble, and Comfortableness. There should be a dancing battle, and the good side produces arrows to slay the rotters. Robin suggests executions for all the demons with a cardboard axe.

I thought of the Nourishing Soup Dance, to be performed by Mesdames Potato, Mutton-Broth and Lentil.

The papers are full of interesting debate about the immediate fate of Italy.

Later: So Christmas dinner is going to be quite different for different Allied soldiers. It is said the Czechs will eat the traditional carp (no doubt elaborately cooked), the Dutch a goose, the Belgians chicken and sweet tarts.

The German troops occupying countries where they are detested must have hard hearts. How can they listen to the strong yet piteous community singing of the Danes, singing national songs, thousands of them, regularly, together, without feelings of distress?

Monday, 23 December

Perishingly cold. We have two huge logs on the fire. Muff, all soft grey, is settling down on a piece of golden-coloured brocade for the evening. The only food I could get for him today was 'chicken's 'eads fourpence a pound.' No fish, no lights.

The butcher says on the phone as regards a joint for Christmas already ordered: 'We will see if we can find you something of some sort.'

There has been a fearful air raid on Manchester, and one or two dreadfully bad ones on Liverpool. In one a market slab of turkeys was set on fire and some of the birds were cooked to a turn. These, I read, 'were given to the needy'.

Ellen McR. writes: 'Donald is home for seven days' draft leave before going to the Middle East. I am terribly sorry for his parents. None of us is thrilled and neither is Donald. You see, we are all home-loving and not at all military, and this whole time is revolting to us, but what can one do? We are only one family in thousands and very, very grateful to the many brave souls who are defending us, and of course, must carry on and do what we can.'

Christmas Day

I had a marvellous surprise from Harry. It appears he gave Miss Scott, below, some money to buy me 'white wine and biscuits'. The gift was so magnificent that a chocolate cake from Fullers was included and a tin of shortbread from Harrods. The wine is Barsac and Graves. This delighted me so much, and took away the loneliness a bit.

Went to church, and observed that all the priceless old glass has at last been removed and replaced by plain glass.

Boxing Day

An artist's palette would only need the most sombre colourings, if he tried to paint a country lane as I have just beheld it. Dark greys and browns and dull greens, even the ivy leaves a subdued hue. The ancient church looked extremely aged and parchment-coloured. I remember how pale and aged the cathedral at Chartres seemed when I looked at it last under a March sky of freedom.

Sherry party. Mr F. asks me if I will sell my piano. He says he can't find one for the troops. He lent the village hall instrument to the soldiers for Xmas and it was duly returned with five or six notes silent, and a piece of its woodwork inside. Visiting the piano shop in Guildford, he found many, but they were all booked.

So a war-time Christmas ends. The Rector says that, owing to the exodus from London, the parish has doubled in population.

Saturday, 28 December

Harry has now been at sea nineteen days! How I wish I knew just where he was, and how far off that mysterious African coast. He must be under deep blue skies now, I think.

Sunday, 29 December

The planes have been pouring over us all evening. There are fearsome vermillion flashes glancing in the dark skies over London.

Suddenly we see a light, naked and unashamed, at Netley. Somebody has honestly forgotten to turn it off. Robin rushes to the phone to warn the ARP, who reply alertly that they will inform the police.

Monday, 30 December

Ursula and her husband came about one o'clock. He is in the

Metropolitan Police and was most interesting. Every other occupant of their block of flats near Battersea Park has gone save the caretaker. Ursula used to sleep at the Lavender Hill Police Station in the bad raids, but now she goes round to a basement at a friend's flat five minutes away. She hates turning out and leaving her warm hearth. Kenneth has assisted in many of the fires in his district, helping to dig people out, and says it has been very awful. He thinks one of his hardest tasks has been to evacuate compulsorily the people round about any time-bomb that is due to explode. He says none of them want to get out, and the police have to be very firm: Kenneth, with perhaps half-a-dozen men, putting in his head at the doors. 'Is everybody out – are you sure nobody is left?' These people are taken to Rest Centres in the London schools.

Kenneth tells me that although bits of parapets have been bombed, all the bridges are intact. This is pretty wonderful, considering the enemy uses the river as a guide. He said when he hears bombs dropping, he at once becomes anxious about certain factories and power-stations, and when it's over he satisfies himself that they (and Ursula) are safe, and feels thankful. One of their great friends has been killed in Dolphin Square.

Later: It appears that the raid over London was perfectly devastating. They sent thousands of incendiary bombs hurtling over the City and dozens of fires were blazing for hours. More Wren churches and the Guildhall are gutted.

I am very sad about St Bride's, Fleet Street, which is damaged fatally. Went to bed very unhappy. Will Winston get angry? The tame little talk on this vast, hateful fire given by the BBC made us feel sick. No details; everything about the bravery of the firemen and the capital way ARP behaved. We should rub in our great irreparable losses. Dr Johnson's beautiful house in Gough Square has gone. Feel very miserable.

Tuesday, 31 December

The ghosts of Wren and Dr Johnson are tonight pacing the streets of London. Wren has been sorely bereaved. Eight churches were either destroyed or severely damaged in Sunday's raid. They had many historical and beloved associations, and with one exception were built on the site of ancient churches that perished in the Great Fire. By fire they have perished again.

1941

Thursday, 2 January

It is eight-fifteen and Robin is down in the Village Hall trying to tell some of the Home Guard about map-reading. I am longing for it to be popular, as he badly wants to help and is rather too old to be guarding bridges, etc. (Later: he came back – they were too busy to have the lecture at all.)

What is happening in Switzerland? There is little news.

We now have Hitler's New Year message to the German people. It is wonderfully blasphemous. He shouts: 'Because we are fighting for the happiness of the nation, we are convinced that we shall be the first to earn the blessing of Providence. Up to now the Lord God has given his approval to the fight. If we carry out our duty loyally and bravely, he will not desert us in the future.'

Friday, 3 January

May Sinclair* came to see me at last. We had both been under duress so had not met since her wedding. Her Farnham shop is still struggling on. But she is worried about the future. 'If I did what the Government wished,' she said, 'I would shut up my

* Née Browne.

shop tomorrow. We are throttled by restrictions. We have a quota of goods only ... I generally sell some specially choice little linen handkerchiefs at Christmas. I went to the warhouse in the City in November to see if I could have my usual supply. They said, "Oh no, merely a quota, a proportion of what you generally have." I saw a whole stack of them on the shelf. "You haven't enough?" I questioned. "Oh, we have masses of them, but it is the law."' (That warehouse is now burned to the ground.)

She explained how it was that the City warehouses were, many of them, burned out in the Second Fire of London owing to the lack of roof-spotters. Take the case of the great carpet manufacturers she knows near St Paul's who lost eight thousand pounds worth of carpets in this very great fire. The manager, a friend of hers, is not young, and was almost distracted by the loss of so many of his assistants to the army. He had ten men's work to do, and also had to contend with all the dislocations war had made in his trade. He is delicate, with a nervy wife down at their home at Westcliff, who wanted him back early to be with her, so he had to leave London by a train that would reach home ere the blackout. How could this tired, worried, overworked man roofspot himself? And he could not obtain reliable fellows that would do it. Possibly he was too dejected to exert himself. Anyway, May thought it was a clear case for the army to take over the roof-work.

Her husband, who executes orders in the printing trade, has had very bad luck lately. Again and again deliveries have been held back through enemy action. You get your order printed and thankfully put it on the train for York at King's Cross, and then lo, there is an air raid and it's destroyed, or the train is delayed by air raids and so delivers the goods too late to be any use. Or you can't get zinc plates for the printing, the supplies have clean run out, etc., etc.

Joy Annett came to tea. Her brother's factory at Coventry is burnt out and they are taking it some miles out of the town. Looms will be hard to replace.

Unless one talks to business people, one has no idea what is happening all over England. It is very serious.

Sunday, 5 January

Robin very melancholy, what with having seen the Home Guards playing darts, when he would like to have taken them to map-reading, but chiefly with the cutting icy weather. There was a gathering fog as we went off to tea. I was so concerned at his cries about his cold state that I forgot to post my Sunday mail.

Monday, 6 January

Paper full of Bardia.* Italian officers and armed troops wished to surrender to a car driven through by Richard Dimbleby (a name suggesting a nursery rhyme) of the BBC. Not an Italian who, when interviewed, didn't say they were sick of war and Mussolini.

Wednesday, 8 January

Two mothers of airmen called on me, both having come down from houses more than a mile away. Both refused tea, cocoa, or ginger wine.

One mother had already lost her son. The other had two flying sons. One has suffered with nerves ever since he crashed badly in the sea. The other was a pacifist, but is now delighted with flying. Brave mothers both, and ready for any blow, but

* An estimated 36,000 Italian prisoners were taken after the Battle of Bardia, in Libya, which took place over 3–5 January 1941.

life for one is changed for always, and you can see it in many little ways, though she is so cheerful.

Mrs R. is entertaining two boy evacuees from the East End. They arrived with only one of every garment. They had never used a toothbrush. Their mother, being requested to do something about it, posted one 'to use between them'.

Mrs S. talked much of food in war-time. She insisted on me writing down a recipe for a war-time pudding made with flour, a little margarine, a pinch of salt, a pinch of sugar, a little milk, rolled into a dough, fried in the frying pan in margarine and served hot with hot jam or stewed fruit. 'I really will try it.'

Mrs Rossiter has been helping in West Ham shelters. She says conditions are dreadful and it took them five days to get out of the LCC a permit forcibly to remove a woman suffering from tuberculosis.*

Thursday, 9 January

We went to the cinema. In the news we saw various pictures of devastation by air bombing. There was one horrible photograph of Japanese bombing an undefended Chinese city. Just hell, because the fires shown were innumerable, smoking blackly side by side to the sky.

Rushed up and down the High Street to get a Hovis brown loaf, but failed. It was rather uncanny going into baker after baker and seeing the shelves entirely bare.

Friday, 10 January

The papers begin to be full of the difficulties of small

* TB is highly infectious, especially in such crowded and enclosed conditions.

businesses in the City with regard to providing roof-spotters. Hundreds of them have written to the British Legion hoping to secure ex-servicemen at £4 a week. But there are not nearly enough old soldiers to go round. Others have offered as much as £1 a night, to unemployed men with no firefighting qualifications. But the majority cannot afford even £4.

A heroic Pole, whose name should be written here, Henry Brun, chairman of the Association of Polish Merchants, and one of the leading business men of Poland, was tortured to death by the Gestapo after consistently refusing to sign an appeal for funds for the benefit of the Volksdeutsche of Warsaw. 'There is no power in the world,' he said, 'which can make me ask my business colleagues to pay a ransom for the benefit of our German enemies.'

Saturday, 11 January

I hear from Muriel that Peter, her army son returning on leave, was obliged to sleep on a floor at Waterloo station in freezing cold.

Sunday, 12 January

In the afternoon to call upon poor, pretty Mrs C.,* who has recently lost her sailor husband. He was knocked down in the blackout in a certain Scottish port, and found with a fractured skull. He died after she got there.

Monday, 13 January

The situation on the kitchen front is precarious. The bit of

* Probably Mrs Coppinger. See previous entries for 28 September and 9 October 1939.

lamb we had given us as a tremendous favour will last out for just four meals of the fourteen we have to put in, because we have a man in the house. With women only, it would do seven. I think I can get enough eggs, owing to a long and staunch friendship with my cook's mother, who sells them, for it to be eggs every night, and we must try for a bunny rabbit, but 'I can't promise' sounds down every phone in Shere. Never a fish in the fishmongers, and 'Not so much as a bone!' hoarsely whispers the melancholy butcher with laryngitis.

Just going to have tea and toast and jam.

Tuesday, 14 January

Started for Barbara's, longing first to hear from Harry of his safe arrival. In the train to Reading I talked with a soldier. He said bread is rationed at tea where he is, just two large doorsteps. In the evening, nothing. So he and a group of pals in his hut subscribe for some loaves, and have a kettle and make themselves cocoa. It saves a lot of money, for going into the town and having supper is expensive.

On to Didcot, where Barbara was waiting for me. It was lovely to be back by her rich fire of wood and coal in the oak-beamed house. Blewbury is full of people who have fled out of London, and Sir William Nicolson, the portrait-painter, is installed in a studio hard by.* He came in after tea. He has painted Winston down in Kent at Chartwell. He says he is a

* William Nicholson, known for his landscapes and still lifes as well as portraits. In his earlier years, together with James Pryde, he had designed posters under the name The Beggarstaff Brothers and, although a commercial failure at the time (the late1890s), their work has since been recognised as a landmark in graphic design and an important influence on artists in both Europe and America.

fine sitter. He does not like them to be too still, or 'they come out wooden in the picture'.

Wednesday, 15 January

Heard that Harry had safely arrived in Cape Town. Oh, the relief! Immediately felt freer and gayer.

Thursday, 16 January

Bey came in to tell us about her time at a Rest Centre. She brought a gay scarf to knit, perching on a tiny chair in her scarlet jersey. She had a week to spare, so presented herself at the LCC hall and asked to help in the raids. They let her go to Southwark Rest Centre, where there is always trouble.

She said there were various conscientious objectors among the staff. At this Robin remarked in a cross, muffled voice, looking up from the *Evening Standard*, that since London Bridge was so near, he thought they might have well been dropped in the river.

Bey said the behaviour of the bombed-out ones was wonderful. One or two nights the blitz was really dreadful. Some women came in tears, but very few. They were offered a wash in warm water immediately, tea, and then other food. One old chap, quite bald, had got soot completely over his pate. He submitted to a child trying to write 'Grandad' on his head with laughter. Wonderful London! They are many of them shaken in nerves after their experiences, but there is not one touch of defeatism, Bey reported. One woman cried a good deal, 'because my little shop has gone, and I was so proud of it, and we were beginning to build up the business ever so nicely. We can never begin again.'

Bey said that one on occasion she was doing office work with two men (they had to check up literally thousands of blankets) when the crumping and Molotov bread-baskets* came so near that between whiles the men ducked under their desks, and she lay flat under a kitchen table. Then out they would crawl, and proceed, till *blast*, *bang* again, and they would once more throw themselves on the floor.

She said that it was an awe-inspiring sight standing on London Bridge after the Jerries had gone one bad night. The flames leaping over some warehouses by the docks were twice the height of the buildings – red and gold – and they were reflected in the dark water of the Thames. Little figures were silhouetted against the dim sky, the firemen rushing out with hoses. One or two air-raid wardens in steel helmets received the fitful gleam of the moon on their tin hats, parading the deserted bridge. I wish I had stood at her side.

Wednesday, 22 January

Biscuits, chocolate and sausages are on British minds just now. The grocer's shop has many slabs of chocolate, but a shilling each for what is worth about fourpence.

Mrs V. said various English people she knew who had not been able to leave Paris had been left free at first, but were now put in concentration camps.

Robin went to the local ARP chiefs this morning with a clear-cut scheme for a Roof-Spotting Centre for the village. This was turned down immediately, and all its ramifications at

* Strictly, the 'Molotov bread basket' was the Soviet RRAB-3 bomb used against Finland, which released a cluster of incendiary bombs as it fell. The name was applied in Britain to similar German incendiary devices.

once dismissed. Robin suggested that ladders and stirrup pumps should be easy of access by night. 'They would be pinched,' was the quick retort. 'Could not the police look after that?' 'Impossible!', etc.

Thursday, 23 January

Tobruk has fallen!* Glorious. I heard it on the eight o'clock wireless.

Picked up at the bus stop by Mrs C. in her car and got a lift to Guildford. There began a long, arduous shopping. I feel sorry for those elderly, dutiful men behind the counter, eternally besieged by questioning matrons. The ration books having to be stamped with tiny stamps, and people all being put in their places: 'Are you registered here? No? Then I can't let you have any biscuits,' etc.

Met Mrs H., who wishes to find two paying guests for two bedrooms and a sitting room, all found and no extras, and even hot milk at night, five guineas each. I waved the ninepenny Woolworths saucepan I had just bought, without wrapping, at her, and she told me she met a woman the day previously bearing a skinned rabbit in her hand.

Robin and I took shilling seats at the Odeon. The news film showed our King decorating airmen. He looked very much older. The Polish General kissing our airmen after giving them medals was amusing. The stolid English airmen did not move reciprocally an inch, and obviously hated it!

Miss Scott came up, and we began to laugh a good deal

* On 21 January the Australian 6th Division captured the port of Tobruk in Libya from the Italians. Some 27,000 Italian prisoners were taken, at the cost of only 49 Australian lives.

over absurd happenings in the day. She has a keen sense of humour. We laughed at my getting a lift in a car which had just conveyed a goat to the railway station. 'It's a little goat-ish; do you mind, Mrs Miles?' The truth is we were tired of the war-stress, and wanted relief, and to gain forgetfulness of what Churchill calls 'the dark and deadly valley'.

Saturday, 25 January

A dull, quiet morning. No air raids. Last night I went down in the dark arm-in-arm with my wealthy, dutiful old neighbour, to the local inn to attend a meeting on Night Watchers for Shere. Our Head Warden, who is dry as the sands of Arabia, was in the chair. A handful of people were there, representing the particular district of the village, about forty-three houses, to be dealt with.

No advice was tendered to us, nor information as to what the rest of the villages were doing. One old inhabitant sprang to his feet, and started talking of the night when we had a shower of incendiaries on the village, explaining how he and a squad of friends had extinguished this and that, 'but have been ignored by the ARP ever since, and not invited to any meeting'.

This grief our pale president did not assuage at all. He looked up gravely and turned it all off, by talking languidly about something else. What a pity! One warm word of apology, a hearty sentence saying they were so glad of his help, would have sent that man away ready for more service.

Resolved to have watchers in shifts. How or where to watch? Undecided. Whether to watch fully dressed or to be allowed to sleep if quiet? Undecided.

Sunday, 26 January

The Sunday papers are as full as ever of remarks about invasion. Certainly things are stirring in the Mediterranean. Malta holds out in the most amazing way.

When one thinks of Dunkirk and the miracle there, when the little ships – *Auntie Gus*, *Bull-Pup*, *Dinky*, *Folkestone Belle*, *Skylark* and the rest – got away with them, one can hope everything. It will always be a big regret to me that Robin was not there, to bring some of our men home in any possible craft he was given, for he happens to be able to handle any.

Tuesday, 28 January

It is terrible to be missing all these joyful weddings of my friends' daughters – Dulcie's in Edinburgh, Phyllis Anne's in the Isle of Wight, now Celia Anne's in the Saltmarket, Glasgow. Then there will take place, I suppose, all among the crocodiles and red kopjes, Harry's wedding, in early spring in Rhodesia. If only Jenny gets her boat from Singapore!

Wednesday, 29 January

Mrs B. rang through to say that her only sister's boy had gone down in the lost submarine *Triton*. She has been up to Rothesay to try to comfort the young widow. There is a baby a year old, a darling. What a good thing! For life will be long for that young girl.*

* HMS *Triton* was lost in the Adriatic. On 6 December she torpedoed the Italian merchant ship *Olimpia*, but never returned from that patrol. In a later note Connie identifies the 'boy' as 'Daredevil' Lt Watkins, commander of the *Triton*.

Thursday, 30 January

Olive has just remarked in the kitchen that some of the soldiers in Aldershot have been caught stealing margarine, to put on the toast they make themselves every night for supper (since they are not given that meal). 'You would think they ought to have butter.'

They haven't a wireless either. 'It isn't fair,' says Olive. 'People subscribe to give the army wireless sets and the officers keep them for their mess.'

At this onslaught I can only feebly murmur: 'Are you sure? It doesn't sound to me like the officers …'

Downstairs our dear old man (over eighty) is agitated because his sister and family, now next door, may move to a house in Worthing, and if they do, they must make him go too. They were bombed out of Folkestone, and the old lady is very nervous indeed after severe bombardments and shivering by night in the garden dug-out. It seems to me rather crazy that they should shift their furniture simply along the shore, to another house by the waves. The little cook, keeping her birthday sorrowfully enough, with a high temperature, says nothing will induce her to move southwards again. We shall see. The old man ought not to have to take any decision at his age.

Friday, 31 January

Muriel sent me a charming letter to read from one of her boys in Africa, homesick for England.

Cis says no potatoes could be got in Glasgow last week. They lived on oatmeal and butter beans.

Monday, 3 February

I went down the village shivering after tea, holding in one hand a bundle of Harry's cast-off clothing, in the other a pudding bowl into which I had put two eggs, some dripping, a shower of sugar from my rapidly declining reserve, all the sultanas I had, and I took it all to the Widow G.

She had already made Robin's birthday cake and accepted what I brought, together with two-and-six.* She said, 'I saw some peel in the shop, and they said, "There'll never be no more", so I took it.

'I heard from my Ted, what's joined up. He says, "It's not too bad, Mum", but he'd never worry me if it was.'

Wednesday, 5 February

To the Valley Hall to see the Ministry of Information films. A group of village boys about eleven stood behind me, exclaiming, 'There's a beauty!' when we had the aeroplane films. A timid young farmer explained later to us that poultry clubs were to be formed everywhere, for those of us who had less than fifty.

Monday, 10 February

Went off to Farnham – a glorious spring day, suddenly. We were all so cheered with the Prime Minister's speech. Every single person I met going down the village spoke of it with admiration. '*Give us the tools and we will finish the job*' was on every lip.†

* Two shillings and sixpence, or half-a-crown.

† Churchill's radio broadcast of 9 February, in which he assured the nation, 'We shall not fail or falter; we shall not weaken or tire.'

Inspectors have called on May's workroom, to see what girls could be taken away to munitions factories. 'Two could be spared,' they said. But you cannot conscript unwilling girls. It is absurd, as every woman knows.

Thursday, 13 February

My idea of earthly Heaven, on this cold and fortunately still February night: a) to talk to Basil *after* armistice, about some happy plans for his work and our moving near him, or b) to walk up the little flight of steps just inside the Hotel du Grand Monarque at Chartres, May Sinclair at my side. We are beginning a long peaceful holiday there, and it is spring, and we have light pretty clothes and laugh together.

Monday, 17 February

Frank Lloyd Wright, one of the world's greatest architects, American, writes of his plans for a reconstructed London.

London should be a motor-car/aeroplane city, 'the spacing all laid out upon a new scale of human movement, set by car and plane'. He advocates elevated railways with continous storage space between the tracks, lorry traffic set low on one side.

'There should be no traffic problem . . . Make broad streets concave instead of convex, with underpasses for foot travellers. No street lights, because roads themselves would be low-lighted ribbons.'

A hideous drawing heads the article, showing the curve of the Thames by Charing Cross with a line of ugly skyscrapers like pillars at intervals all round the bank.

Glamorous Soviet-style artwork exhorted women to contribute to the war effort. Similar posters encouraged them to join the WAAF, the Wrens, the WVS or the ATS.

Photograph © IWM MH4735

Wednesday, 19 February

The old gentleman below has just returned from a trip by car down to Hythe, to see his burgled house. Two really good bottles of claret he had jealously preserved had been found by the intruders and drunk to the dregs. Mr Stevens said he was much struck by the small number of people about in Hythe. One nice little arcade there full of shops had entirely vanished.

Canary seed is to be stopped. What else can they eat but grain? More racing carrier pigeons are wanted to work in the war.

Robin entered after the Red Cross lecture shuddering with cold. The second time this has happened. We have soup always now at night, and he was glad to gulp some down.

It was grand to get a letter from Harry this morning posted in Cape Town. He had been for a walk in the shadow of Table Mountain. He also writes from Salisbury, Rhodesia, where he had been met.

An SOS comes from an old and clever artist in his ninety-sixth year, wishing to sell us two paintings for £4. I fear he is struggling along on very little. What a world this is for the artist and the musician!

Saturday, 22 February

A letter in from Margaret written from New York. It has taken five weeks to come! She says, 'You would be amazed to know how many blind people there are still amongst us who won't see things as they really are, and don't want to. They accuse B. and me of being war-mongers, and still think a negotiated peace is to be desired. But those of us who feel that it is our fight are deeply fortified by all that is now transpiring, and feel more optimistic and less ashamed than in some time.'

I see that you can now buy large metal buttons in New York bearing the words 'To Hell with Hitler' to pin on your coat lapel.

Irving Berlin's new song about Hitler, 'When That Man is Dead and Gone', is selling phenomenally.

A judge in America has given sympathetic consideration to a Mr Ribbentrop in Connecticut who would like to change his name.

Sunday, 23 February

So many buses full of troops went past that I wondered if there was an invasion scare. As I went up the hill with Miss Scott, I said I thought we might each have a knapsack and know what we wished to pack in it. I was pleased to remember that I had a very thin light Jaeger blanket, which went with Robin through the last war and might be squashed into the knapsack.

I am hating very much the thought that the Germans are in Sofia. What next?

Monday, 24 February

Mr Wright, manager of the Curtiss-Wright Corporation, in an interesting article in an American paper, *Aviation*, puts Germany's absolute total of aircraft of all types at 35,000, and British absolute total at 25,000. He estimates that the absolute totals (with American help) will be equal by July.

Friday, 28 February

Rendel, our Ambassador to Bulgaria,* has spoken severely to the Bulgarians. Far too late! He knows that Bulgaria is actively helping the Axis and that the country is flooded with Germans wearing plain clothes for the moment (oh, honourable army!).

The plain truth is that all Europe still feels Germany is winning.

Heard from my Scotch cousin, a minister in Edinburgh. His pretty young daughter is just engaged. He speaks sadly of 'these young people, through no possible fault of their own, cast into the maelstrom. It is we older ones who should be fighting, not they, the mess we've made of things. And quite ready to make another mess of it, once the young ones are all dead again.'

Saturday, 1 March

Basil writes from Kent this morning that he has to teach 1,000 soldiers First Aid and is exhausted with it.

This evening I tried on Robin's old haversack, having packed it with essentials, if compulsory evacuation comes to our village: night clothes, a pair of house shoes, a tube of Horlicks milk tablets, a brandy flask, stamped postcards and a pencil, extra pair of stockings, soap and towel, washing things, aspirin, brush and comb, handkerchiefs. I could not carry more than this, but I have included a beloved, shabby, small fat copy of *Wives and Daughters*.

* Sir George William Rendel, head of the Eastern Division of the Foreign Office from 1933–38 and Ambassador to Bulgaria from 1938 to 1941.

The news is grave: Bulgaria joins the Axis. We lose a destroyer.

Monday, 3 March

In the post office here today I saw a woman who has many loved relations in Jersey. There is absolutely not one line coming through from the Channel Islands.

'I know they are desolate and oppressed,' she said sorrowfully to me, repeating 'desolate and oppressed'.

I took my evacuation haversack to Mrs R. for more strong fastenings to be made. The wild little evacuee boy exhausts that poor, hard-working woman, who is dying for a week's rest.

Tuesday, 4 March

To the kitchen. Soup and potatoes and carrots in it and a host of little suet puddings.

'This is a very nice meal for fourpence,' remarked a big little girl. The babes at their table were busily engaged in trying to scoop up their soup with forks.

Reading a book by Mrs Nicholson, *Norney Rough*. It is all about a real house near Godalming and the struggle of a retired officer and his family to live decently in England.

'Women of every sort,' she writes, 'are learning to live without relaxation. They seem tougher than ever before. How can they enjoy dining out in warmth and comfort when their men face the North Sea's cruel cold?'

Wednesday, 5 March

Walked up the hill in the windy March evening with Mrs M.

She has been given a new pale blue jumper and it is put in the 'bolting box' all ready for hasty evacuation, and kept quite near the front door.

The Germans have fined the town of Hilversum in Holland (gay, geranium-clad, beautifully built town) £350,000 as a punishment for having shot one German soldier.

Friday, 7 March

Went to call on Freda T., who told me that in Folkestone yesterday, when getting into her train for Redhill, a Dornier plane began machine-gunning, and the women porters shut the carriage doors briskly, as spatterings of bullets rained down on the glass roof of the station; and the train moved off, but not before the passengers, hanging out of the windows, saw a Spitfire rise and give chase. The Dornier eventually fell into the sea.

Saturday, 8 March

Basil came about lunch-time, bringing a young RE subaltern (whose people are in Jersey – he hears nothing).

Bertie came to tea, an old, old Scotsman, and I thought again how hard this war is on old people. He never goes anywhere or sees anybody.

The great news of the week is that in the USA the Lease and Lend Bill is passed.*

* Under the Lend-Lease Bill the USA undertook to supply the Allied nations with much-needed materials. Although America had not yet entered the war as a combatant, the signing of the Lend-Lease Bill meant that, in economic terms at least, she could no longer be regarded as neutral.

Will the Germans enter Greece? This seems to be expected. We shall be there, I think, also.

We are on the edge of tremendous events.

Sunday, 9 March

Prices go up. There is an increase of 26 per cent in the cost of living from September 1939 to January 1941. Coal is 41 per cent dearer.

In the *Weekly Dispatch* today, I like this story: 'Please, teacher,' he asked, 'did God make Hitler?' 'Oh yes,' the teacher assured him, 'God made Hitler.' 'Well I *never* did!' exclaimed the little lad, and his face fell as he spoke.

Monday, 10 March

Greece has addressed a spirited open letter to Hitler signed by the editor of the paper *Kathimerini*, Mr Georgios Vlachos. It ends with a reference to Greece as 'a small country but now made great, and which, after teaching the world how to live, must teach the world how to die.'

Tuesday, 11 March

From the *Night Hawk* magazine of the 14th Battalion Home Guard, Hove, Sussex, written by our friend Clive King-George, adjutant:

> Should an attack develop from the air, parachutists and air-borne troops may be expected to be landed on the Downs in large numbers, and these will have to be exterminated. The only way to do this is to shoot them. The training

must, therefore, be concentrated upon musketry, and above all fire control. Remember that to shoot at the enemy at a distance of, say, 1,000 yards is only a waste of ammunition, and will give away your position and probably subject you to artillery fire. So hold your fire until 'you see the whites of their eyes', and make sure of a Hun with every cartridge.

Today Doris and I walked into Albury Park in the sunny March weather, and saw the pigeons on the window-sills under the high red chimneys, and the scatter of purple and white under the trees.

Tonight, looking out of the kitchen window where I had been getting supper ready, I saw on the bank opposite my husband and various villagers vigorously digging a hole and putting sandbags all round it. Will the Germans come?

Thursday, 13 March

Coming home [from Guildford] we picked up an old man poorly dressed. He talked almost incoherently of having been bombed out of his flat near the Elephant and Castle. 'I can't ever tell you, lady, what it was like when the Torpedo bomb came swish, swish, swish down ...' He went on muttering all the way. I could catch 'wasn't going to live in that shelter after a week of it. If I'm took, I'm took.' And again, 'I'm over seventy ... over seventy ... I must pull myself together ...' Poor old fellow: one of the thousands who have been thrown completely off their balance, and thrown out of their homes.

On a bomb-damaged street on the south coast, the local Home Guard train to hold off invaders with Molotov cocktail petrol bombs.
Photograph © IWM H8128

Friday, 14 March

A long cardboard carton appeared, carried round by the post office man as it was so heavy. It came from New York City, and contained a gift of food from my dear Dells.

One *side* of bacon
6 tins evaporated milk
2 slabs chocolate

2 lbs lump sugar
3 sardine tins
1 lb instant coffee
1 lb tea
1 tin guava jelly

This was glorious. I spread them all out except the rich grand bit of bacon which was taken to the cellar.

I am told that many such parcels arrive in our village and some from Canada. I gave the flat below half-a-pound of tea as they found it so hard to manage on rations.

Visited Mrs Pritchard in her cottage and drank vermouth with her. She has been often to Hampstead to see her house there. There are sad gaps everywhere in Hampstead. Her husband goes to London daily, a great fag in the winter specially, and a long pull up the hill through newly ploughed fields.

Saturday, 15 March

Jam is to be rationed. Robin winces over this. Half a pound a month.

Sunday, 16 March

Ernest Bevin is announcing a compulsory registration of women aged twenty and twenty-one in April.* I can see that Olive is all agog to go off to some factory; she is, I think, twenty-seven.

* Both men and women were called up at different times according to their age group: first those in their early twenties, then at a later date those aged up to thirty, and so on. By 1942 all able-bodied men aged 18–51 were liable to be called up, and unmarried women aged 20–30.

A glorious speech from Roosevelt. We are to have ships. But what a strange part his country is playing. To give us weapons and expect our hands to fire the guns while they sit back and feel satisfied. I venture to prophesy that by May America will be all in.*

We have just had the Government's instructions about Invasion read by the BBC. I am convinced that the authorities cannot take the prospect seriously. Coaxing hints only – we are not to send more telegrams than we need and not to use the roads unless we have important reasons, etc. Not a word as to what to get ready in case of compulsory evacuation. We are, if caught in a hostile area, just to stay put. 'If indeed we have a trench, we might get into it.' No need, apparently, to see that trenches are made!

What an amazing war.

Monday, 17 March

A glad surprise in the shape of a letter from Flo Dell announcing her engagement.

She says: 'I realise the uncertainty of the future, as far as all the young men of the world are concerned; but I feel strongly that if you fear what the future has in store there can be no real happiness at all, so I am perfectly willing and happy to take the risk. If I lose I will have been happy and the cause will have been worth the sacrifice.'

Tuesday, 18 March

Phyl says that she could not bear to go to London with me to

* It was not until December 1941 that America entered the war.

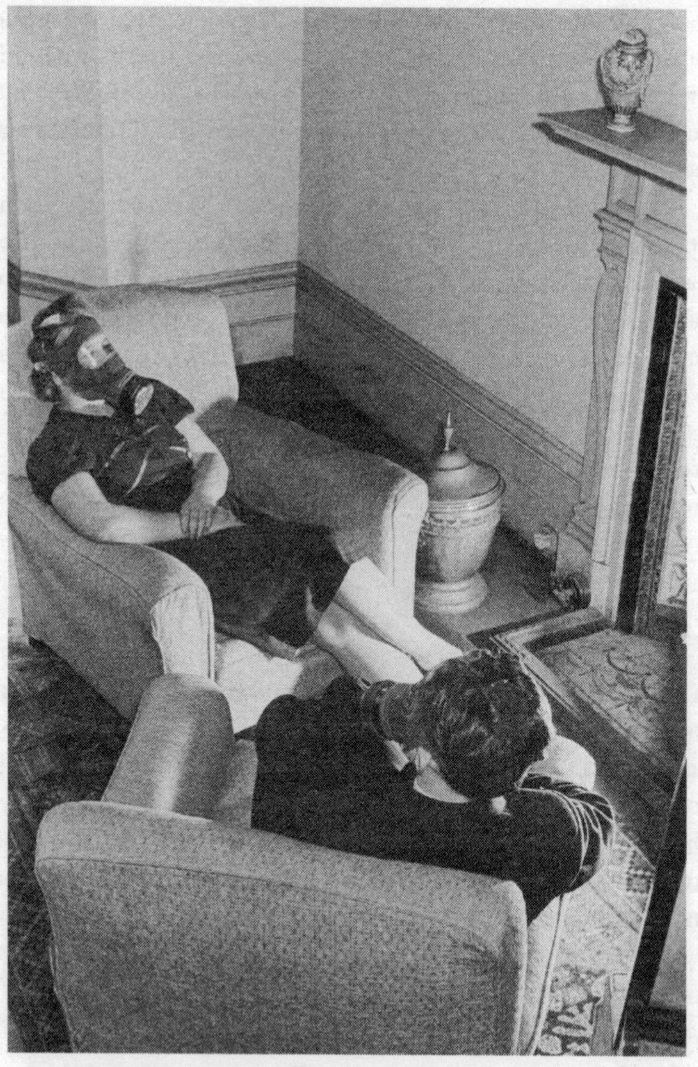

Government anti-gas instructions issued in case of invasion in 1941 encouraged civilians to wear their gas masks for fifteen minutes every day in order to get used to them.
Photograph © IWM D3948

look at Paternoster Row. 'I'd feel just like I would over going to see the corpse of a friend from whom the spirit has gone.'*

She is the proud possessor of a bee hive ('£3. And already I've been offered £6 for it in the village.') She sat up till dawn reading a book on bee lore and listening to Franklin Roosevelt's grand speech.

Emmy W. writes from Princeton University: 'Princeton has just received its new Red Cross quota to be filled by 30 May – 765 knitted garments and 1,700 sewn garments. That's a lot from such a small town, isn't it? We think of you a lot.'

Wednesday, 19 March

Barbara arrives by train from Reading, looking quite ill with cold, and bringing her large bull terrier which howls when she goes out of the room. She distressed me by bringing rations of sugar and butter, but I rejoiced over a pigeon and a jar of apple jelly.

A letter from Alice, who works at an Edinburgh canteen. She says: 'I have a hectic time as there are only three of us to cook and sometimes forty or fifty men at busy times. They can get any amount of women to wait but they avoid cooking, so I have to be very quick turning sausages with one hand and frying eggs with the other. When I come home I take everything off and get into a hot bath and re-dress entirely. All my clothes seem to be scented with chips.'

* Paternoster Row was a centre of the publishing industry before the war, and suffered severely in the Blitz. Hodder and Stoughton, for whom Connie's father William Robertson Nicoll was chief literary advisor, was at No. 27, and it was there that he set up and published his magazine, *The British Weekly*. Phyl's connection to Paternoster Row is uncertain, as Connie does not identify her or what she does in any of the entries in which she appears. She could be Phyllis Twigg, a fellow children's author, who is mentioned once in full in the entry for Wednesday, 17 July 1940.

The Japanese press states today that the landing of the Germans in England is only a matter of time. 'So now we know where we are,' says Robin, peacefully. He is just back from digging a war-like hole in the field, from which bombs may be thrown.

Thursday, 20 March

Barbara thinks she ought to join the WRNS. I wonder if she will. People who have dogs are baking brown bread in the oven, cutting it in squares and pretending it's dog biscuits.

Barbara writes for the BBC, and is glad to hear that the Forces often listen in to her Gummidge tales.* She tells me she thinks her Berkshire village *does* believe in invasion. Our tiny village doesn't, I think.

In the afternoon Robin's aged cousin, Agnes Haycock, came unexpectedly. She lives in a house in Haslemere, all alone because no modern servant will stay with that kind of old person with four prize Pekes. She had pushed on her, in spite of her remonstrations, one grandmother, one mother, one big girl and one tiny boy of two from Portsmouth. The boy behaves like an untrained animal all over her beautiful Turkish carpets.

'When I said, "Oh, don't please push the baby's push-cart into my kitchen walls, and make holes like that," the woman said, "Oh, you'll get compensation in full from the government, *you* needn't worry."'

When she was ill with bronchitis they did not come near her with tea or anything, and she is eighty-four and has to do all her cooking over a small gas ring in her bedroom.

* The *Worzel Gummidge* books were first adapted for radio before the war and continued to be broadcast on BBC Children's Hour for several years.

It seems scandalous, but this vigorous old person has nobody to plead her case, and will not allow Robin to do so.

The war drags on. The attack on Clydeside, Cis writes, 'is the worst we have had yet, there are 4,000 casualties, and 100 buried under rubble quite near us.'*

Cis knew and liked a little Glasgow girl of fourteen, a cashier in a greengrocer's shop. This child, on the night of the raid, was coming home in a tram from the cinema. Nothing has been heard of her since. Blown to pieces? The poor mother is distracted.†

Saturday, 22 March

A light warm rain is falling. The forsythia is thinking of coming out. Letters still delayed from Harry, and I have cabled today.

This war is, as Priestley‡ discerns, and as most men don't, peculiarly hard on women, who loathe it all.

Sunday, 23 March

Walked home with Mrs Foster from London who told me how she had lost all her things in her Kensington flat. All the flats

* The Clydebank raids of 13 and 14 March caused the worst devastation suffered by Scotland in the war, but the figure of 4,000 dead is either a mistake by Cis or a mistranscription of her letter by Connie. There were 4,000 houses completely destroyed, and 35,000 people lost their homes, but the number killed was 528, with another 617 seriously injured.

† Connie adds in a handwritten note that only her handbag was found.

‡ J. B. Priestley, novelist, critic and playwright. On 5 June 1940 Priestley began a regular radio broadcast called *Postscripts* in which he expounded his thoughts on the war and on the future of the country. So successful was it that Graham Greene said of him 'Priestley became in the months after Dunkirk a leader second only in importance to Mr Churchill. And he gave us what our other leaders have always failed to give us: an ideology.'

were blown to smithereens and she could not find one bit of her furniture or one bit of anything else she possessed in it.

'People were blown to bits in Sloane Square,' said Mrs F. 'Bits of bodies were put into dustbins; a naked woman was caught on a cable, her clothes blown off by the blast. England truly is at war.'

At supper of salad of shredded cabbage and carrots, Robin and I discussed the mystery of the great London air raids – the endurance and indifference to them displayed by so many people we know, who we should have imagined would have simply crumpled up and fled through repeated *crises des nerfs*.* Yet they stick it week after week, and hardly mention it.

Monday, 24 March

Tried to buy something for our lunch tomorrow, but failed. The cooked meat shop had its shutters up. The fish was *very* dear. The cakes had vanished entirely from the shops by midday, the glass shelves in Nuttall's windows stripped clean as always now.

Tuesday, 25 March

I see that eagle feathers, a gift to the RAF from the Indian Council Fire, an Indian Society of Chicago, have been awarded to a small group of British pilots who have distinguished themselves. I should love to see one!

Yugoslavia has caved in, I am afraid.

* Literally, crisis of nerves.

Wednesday, 26 March

America quite likes our slogan, 'Britain can take it', but would prefer, 'Britain can dish it out'.*

Thursday, 27 March

Felt very low-spirited about the war. I was just saying in a melancholy voice to Robin at lunch that we did not seem to be doing very well, when the one o'clock news came on, and we were electrified with joy to hear that there had been a revolution in Yugoslavia, and that the government who signed the Axis had been arrested.

Now what? Will the Germans rush in to the rebellious country?

Grand news tonight. We have captured Keren and Harar.†

Friday, 28 March

The good news has cheered us up. The sky is blue, the buds on the lilac swell: there are a fair number of daffodils, and opposite, Scratch is heaving sacks of carrots and potatoes destined for the army on to a lorry bound for Dorking.

Joan told us an interesting true story. A friend of hers, a woman living in Sussex, was suddenly told that a German

* *Britain Can Take It* was a shortened version of the public information film *London Can Take It,* which showed how ordinary Londoners were coping with the Blitz. Distributed in the United States, the film was nominated for an Academy Award in 1941 as Best Live Action Short Film. The expression 'we can take it' was adopted as a catchphrase in Britain, especially in London.

† Both key acquisitions in the East African campaign, Keren giving the British forces access to the Eritrean capital Asmara, and Harar opening the route to the Abyssinian (Ethiopian) capital Adis Ababa.

aeroplane had been shot down in one of her fields. Would she come out with some brandy and rugs: a German was dying.

'No,' she said, 'I can't. I simply can't. Let him get on with his dying – the brute.'

They returned. 'Do come. He is suffering so much.'

'Oh well, I suppose I must,' said she, and she went to the field. All her resentment and hatred vanished at the sight of the suffering youth, with his face of utter anguish. He died in her arms, and his last words were 'Heil Hitler!'

The young English aviator who shot him down stood near by and was terribly affected, saying, 'I didn't think it could be half as bad as this!'

Saturday, 29 March

Mrs Hazeldine writes from Coniston on the Lakes: 'This is an awful place to get food. Although it's right in the country, vegetables are just like gold, you simply can't get them at any price . . . I can't think what it will be like to live next year. I have been without a kettle for three months, and at last, in desperation bought a copper one for twenty-five shillings – the last to be procured anywhere for miles.'

This has been a wonderful week. Yugoslavia's sudden resistance has stirred sad hearts all over the world. 'A brave choice of the hard way,' says the Australian, Mr Fadden.*

I should like to have written more about the battle of Keren, among its thick clouds of sand and smoke. Our British soldiers toiled up steep slopes in a temperature of over 100 degrees.

* Arthur William Fadden, later Sir Arthur, Australian politician. He was leader of the Country Party from 1940 and of the UAP/Country coalition in 1941, serving briefly as Prime Minister from 26 August to 7 October 1941, when the coalition broke apart.

Moslem and Indian troops surged along and smashed their way through a whole colonial brigade and a regiment of Carabinieri. The Italians held out for six weeks. We have, of course, heard nothing about our casualties.

Sunday, 30 March

What an amazing world it is! The Jews in Poland now may not go by train without a special permit, and *never* by express.

In Germany, baptism should be postponed until twenty, say the Nazis. The German youth are growing up in a pagan air.

Monday, 31 March

No letter from Rhodesia yet. What a pause! In which ship's hold is it lying?

Tuesday, 1 April

The morning paper continues to be most interesting.

'Laxfield, Suffolk, looks like becoming a village of young Winstons. To help the War Savings Campaign, a resident has promised to present a Savings Certificate to every baby who is named after the Prime Minister.'

Again:

'A refugee from Holland was admitted to the London Homeopathic Hospital with a packet of diamonds worth thousands of pounds sewn into the seat of his trousers, besides 3,000 American dollars and £100 in Bank of England notes.'

And in an article on the conditions in Belgium:

'Passive sabotage is almost universal, and sometimes more positive acts are committed, which call forth savage reprisals.

When someone cut a telephone wire in Ypres the whole town was left without bread and meat for a fortnight.'

Thursday, 3 April

I notice that our food situation is such that when on the screen any food is shown, the audience begins to exclaim softly. In one film, somebody ate a grapefruit in a glass – and Betty groaned with longing.* 'What is the worst thing about this war?' I asked Sibyl. 'Having no chocolate,' she said promptly.

Saturday, 5 April

Virginia Woolf, our greatest living woman writer, has drowned herself! She had been bombed out of her Bloomsbury home: the lovely mural paintings there, done by her sister Vanessa Bell, and the man Mrs Woolf considered our finest living artist, Duncan Grant, were destroyed. 'Every beautiful thing will be gone soon,' she said. She felt it most acutely.

Sunday, 6 April

Woke to the news that Germany and Yugoslavia were at war.

Wednesday, 9 April

Death rides abroad in the Balkans as I write, and brave men are falling before the immense German divisions. Churchill's speech, as reported by the BBC just now, is sombre.

* Connie was staying in the New Forest when this entry was written. From references to her elsewhere in Connie's journal, Betty was probably Muriel Andrews' daughter.

Everybody is talking about national re-planning after the war. (Poor country, it's no use trying to rebuild you for a time, you were bombed last night by the devilish young men who were breathing in English air, under a divinely moonlit sky.)

Felt exceedingly depressed over the heavy new income tax. Where can we economise?

'Heaven defend us,' says witty John Betjeman in tonight's *Evening Standard*, 'from pompous Civic Centres with memorial fountains, paid for out of the rates, from chaste shopping arcades among municipal flower beds, and miles from the workers' flats in unfriendly districts. Heaven preserve us from one big garden city with communal this and communal that.'

The Pope has cancelled his Peace talk and has rewritten his speech since Yugoslavia entered the war. 'The Nazis,' says the Vatican, 'are sowing a seed that will ripen to a terrible harvest for the German people.'

Thursday, 10 April

I read aloud to Robin Churchill's long speech about the abandonment of Benghazi, with the regrettable acquisition by the Hun of useful airfields.* Of our obligation to move troops to help Greece.

Winston was very serious, and spoke of 'this sudden darkening of the scene.' There is a threat to Egypt.

We seem to be doing much better, however, and getting down Hun bombers in the moonlight.

I fear Coventry has been badly damaged once more.

* On 3 April the retreating British forces had pulled out of Benghazi, a major port and Libya's second-largest city, and on 4 April the Germans and Italians entered the city unopposed.

It is a cold evening. The BBC announces that Harry's General once at Singapore – Gambier-Perry – is missing in Libya. A very charming person, Harry used to say. I can imagine how sorry Harry will be sitting by his Rhodesian fireplace, to hear it.*

Easter Saturday

The news is bad and there have been many appalling raids. But we have great resources and America stands behind us, very nearly awake.

Easter Monday

I have tried to think how I could cut down expenses, owing to this fresh income tax, and all our extra repair bills. I have decided that I had better close the journal at the end of the week.

Tonight we hear that the British have withdrawn in Greece, that Turkey is very depressed, that German propagandists there are boasting of their victories in Libya. Turkey is nervous about this.

'This war,' remarks Robin from his chair by the fire, 'is come upon us when we have too highly organised a civilisation, yet without increased wisdom. Still all the old faults are at work.'

Wednesday, 16 April

To Guildford to lunch. The usual wistful glances into crowded

* Major General Michael Gambier-Perry, commander of 2nd Armoured Division in North Africa, was captured at Mechili in Libya and imprisoned in Italy, successfully escaping in 1943.

bare shops. Petronelle and I went to see the film *All This and Heaven Too*. Wept a very little at the end. Petronelle cheerfully owned that she wept a lot. I got her the last plate of cakes to be had at the Astolat tea shop after, where a weary, hot-looking little waitress tore about doing the best she could.

The news tonight is shattering: Yugoslavia is broken up, disintegrated. Let us hope they will continue to conduct guerilla warfare.

Our carrier told me yesterday he had looked through a pair of field glasses yesterday, and perceived that some planes had written 'Adolf' in the sky!

Cis writes from Tweedmouth to say that an old Scotsman whose cottage was badly damaged in a raid replied, when asked what time the bomb fell, 'Twelve o'clock, but a didna' get up till eight.' 'So wise,' adds Cis.

Thursday, 17 April

Home from a day in London.

The city had the previous day experienced the sharpest and longest assault of the war.

The damage to the Kingston by-pass was not so bad as I had imagined, but a great many of the confident little villas had boards over their broken windows, and one or two houses were down. The bus conductor urged passengers to assemble in Cavendish Square in good time for the return buses, as there were great crowds.

Not till we drove past the outlying suburbs did I understand how many people had left London. Road after road showed deserted, empty houses, silent, forsaken, often shuttered.

My first journey on arriving was on foot to Harley Street. London had gone through the most ghastly ordeal. You could see it in the people's faces: the women looked sleepless and worried, and the demolition squads hurtling along in their lorries with ladders and tools held crews of grimy-faced and weary men.

A chauffeur hung about outside a house. I asked him if it had been very bad the night before.

'Down in my little place, lady, you couldn't get a wink of sleep. There must have been thousands of them over. It was terrible, the worst of any night I've ever known.'

I saw his face was haggard. 'Well, we can take it,' I ventured.

'Yes, but we want to dish it out,' he replied.

Harley Street has lowered its proud flag. Gone are the rows of brightly enamelled front doors – at least the doors are there, but they are no longer cherished. Dirty and gloomy and faded, and the little silver plates all dim and rusty.

A great cavity, too, showed the entire departure of at least two houses.

I went down the Oxford Street tube. The bunks on the platform were most hygenic I thought, steel and wire, and numbers were written on the wall behind them. Coming back, I saw that bundles of bedding and shabby, broken suitcases were already placed there.

Children play on the space at the bottom of the moving staircase, and canteens come out with tea.

I got very weary, toiling about. Every major street seemed to have a barricade across it with 'No Entry'. St Thomas's Hospital had a pile of rubble still alight and smoking, near the Terrace.

Depressing and agitating to see the fantastic holes made in the rows of windows in County Hall. One poor little shop near the cab stand, a cobblers, had its shop window blown out, and I saw the old shoemaker on his knees in the hall, nailing up a box. God! What is going to happen to these people whose living and occupation has gone?

Then on to Leicester Square. Here men were digging at a pile of debris; a shelter had received a direct hit. I wondered if there were any bodies remaining. At one of the very worst moments of this day I found myself passing the Haymarket Theatre, outside which was written up

'No Time for Comedy'

Very true. With mind and heart oppressed by the fearful damage, the name of the play (I'd like to see it) rang through my soul.

Up Kingsway and into Holborn tube. A tall house next to it had a big bit of roof in a pendant position; it looked most dangerous and about to hurl itself down. I saw Paternoster Row, which was my main object. The opening of the Row and its name plate are still intact, and miraculously enough Nicolson's shop (showing pretty linen teacloths and little napkins) is intact. You go for a few yards and then – a barrier, and a shambles that was the Row, extending far back into a kind of square: all rubbish, planks leaning on bricks, dust, ruin. Where are the lost manuscripts, where the writers' broken hopes?*

In Cavendish Square I lined up in a queue and studied the square intently. I should imagine quite half the inhabitants had gone. An old man played the fiddle for us, 'To cheer you all up,' he said, collecting our pennies as the Green Line buses for Hertford and Gerrards Cross started up.

A woman, very pretty and smart, passed with a blue coat and skirt, a maroon pill-box hat and mauve gloves. This did me good.

* An estimated 5 million books were destroyed in the firestorms of 29–30 December 1940.

The wreckage of Paternoster Square. The dome in the background is the Old Bailey, which somehow survived the devastation, although the streets around it were almost entirely destroyed.
Photograph © IWM HU108965

But in a few minutes we were moving by Langham Place, and a perfect inferno of a fire showed itself behind the BBC. There was a high curtain of smoke. In Portland Place, where many houses seemed to have crashed, I saw red flames leaping and firemen with hoses. All down this broad, once luxurious street I saw flats with windows blown out. Oh, what havoc there has been here!

Friday, 18 April

And now on this chilly spring afternoon, I take leave of the journal which it has given me such joy to write. Things in Europe are serious, the Greek war does not go well, we are being pushed back, and are very much outnumbered, and the poor Yugoslavs have given in. We trust Wavell,* but the Germans are giving us trouble in the desert.

Not too much to eat; our income tax about to drain our pockets; life docked of happy travel and happy meetings, the necessary machinery of a million households cracking. Girls of twenty conscripted – what a chaotic business, its humorous side apparent to every woman, and to no man.

*

Editor's Note: in the eight months before Connie resumed the journal on 17 December 1941, the complexion of the war changed considerably.

The German invasion of Russia began on 22 June, ending the non-aggression pact and bringing Russia into the war on the Allied side.

Japan, which had been at war with China since 1937, was threatening US and European territories in the Far East, aiming to gain full control of the Western Pacific.

America entered the war on 8 December, following the Japanese attack on Pearl Harbour on 7 December.

Also, during the intervening period, Basil got his wish and was posted to North Africa.

* General Archibald Wavell was Commander in Chief of the British Army in the Middle East in 1941, where he was successful against the Italians but was pushed back by the Germans. Transferred to the Far East as Commander in Chief of the Allied forces, he was promoted to Field Marshal in 1943 and was Viceroy of India from 1943–7.

PART TWO

December 1941 to April 1943

Connie and Elystan (Robin) at Springfield, 1947.

1941

Wednesday, 17 December

Resumed 17 December, 1941 for, I hope, a year. This is for Harry and Jenny, in their far Rhodesian home with its lovely rose-garden, so remote from war-torn Europe.

The news is, as I begin again, quite bad; Singapore and Hong Kong are threatened. 'We have not won the war by a long shot. It is going to go on for a long time.' They must do 'unheard of things' in production. (They will!)

America has, in the first ten days of their entry into hostilities, lost seven per cent of the number killed in 1917 and 1918.

Hong Kong has been bombarded quite eight times a day. Mount Davis fort, which Robin knew so well, has been heavily shelled.

I wish I could give some idea of this Xmas of 1941 in a Surrey village. If you go into the grocers, you almost despair of being served, the crowd of strangers is so extensive. The basis of our housekeeping is American bacon, which we can get without coupons. I keep on telling people this: they don't know it.

I am sitting by the fire; the boys of the Home Guard are coming in for their lesson in signalling. We have some lovely preserved fruit from Harry and Jenny, and I am eating some ginger which is heavenly and pre-war.

We are delighted with the Libyan and the Russian front, but

anxious, very anxious, about Hong Kong and even more about Singapore.

The spirit of the people, as I find it in my little circle (stretching from the north of Scotland to the west of England) is calm and patient and unmoved. Yes, the outlook is hopeful, in spite of everything.

7.30 p.m.: Not so good. The Japanese claim tonight that part of Hong Kong is in flames, and that the resistance of the Governor General is destroyed.

Friday, 19 December

Walked arm-in-arm across the frozen December fields, and saw the raw cold grey mists floating around the old church spire. We had been depressed by the news of the Japanese landing in Hong Kong. Robin keeps on talking about his pleasant years there, and the water picnics attended by the young officers. He was as gay as a lark then, in his twenties. Now he sits by the fire, sixty-three, apprehensively reading the news, while Mozart's heavenly music is being played. Einstein said recently that we could not despair of a world that had produced the man Mozart, or something to that effect.

Christmas is indeed subdued. I never remember a Christmas so sombre, and with so slight an air of festivity.

Met Mrs Bray,* who has a good deal to do with the local Land Girls. She says several have had to give up as they get rheumatism. Her own girl gets wet through twice a day, and is none the worse.

* The Bray family have been Lords of the Manor of Shere since 1487, when it was gifted to Sir Reginald Bray, a leading figure at the court of Henry VII.

A delightful event at breakfast; another airgraph* from Basil. 'Apart from the Greys I look after some of the local soldiers who keep on saying, "I am dead". It is useless to argue. The other day I was able to buy Pop a 5lb package of various foods and two pairs of silk stockings for you.'

Sunday, 21 December

Last night came Bey who told me some touching details of the house full of Czech refugees she looks after. There are some small children who attend school and already have acquired more English than their parents. One child wrote a letter to Santa Claus, asking for certain delectable expensive toys. The poor father, unable to buy them, wrote a letter back from Santa, explaining that there was a war on. The child read it thoughtfully, accepted the reply and only said, 'Santa Claus has made a mistake in his English.'

Bey says that the Czechs often write on long paper streamers the words, 'We shall be home next Christmas' and pin it on the mantelpiece. Poor things!

She said that whereas only a few children at the High School where she works used to stay to lunch, now 200 do!

Monday, 22 December

Mrs F. was very jubilant over having found a fifty-year-old chintz dust-sheet which she had made into two overalls – it saves coupons. At the hairdressers I was told that the one and

* Airgraphs were designed to reduce the weight of mail going overseas to and from the troops. Letters written on standard forms were photographed and transported on film and printed out at the receiving mail stations for delivery.

only assistant was going into the WAAFs. The proprietress owned that she could not earn enough working alone to pay her rent, and her advertisements for elderly assistants have not yet been successful. And all her money is in it. Tragedy lurks everywhere.

'Shall be glad when it is all over,' exclaimed two women separately to me this afternoon when I went round with the last parcels for Christmas day: soap for Isobel, a book for Bey, a little woollen quilt for Rachel's cot.

I am feeling so happy now that I am going away for a few days. I shall adore seeing the flat brown and purple stretches of the New Forest again.

Tuesday, 23 December

The New Forest is specially lovely in winter with the bare oaks and the glistening holly trees. There was a warm welcome at Picket Post, and a room filled with Christmas cards, many from the Forces. Muriel's eldest son is in Burma, the second is flying in South Africa, the third arrived from Aldershot on sick leave. Peter is very thin and tall in his khaki. What a hideous colour it is, especially for women.

Thursday, 25 December

Rose joyfully, and gave and received gifts.

Later. We heard with dismay that Sir Mark Young, Governor of Hong Kong, had been told by his naval and military advisors that it was of no use to defend the place any longer. The Japanese had destroyed the water system.

To bed in great gloom. I considered the miserable case of my great friends the Eustaces. Every penny they had was invested in Hong Kong and Shanghai. He is white-haired, but will have to find a job.

At tea today, a Colonel said, knowing Hong Kong well, that it was never anticipated that we should be able to keep it: the defence, he surmised, was made to delay attack on Singapore.

Saturday, 27 December

Received with wrath and indignation, all sitting round Arthur's comfortable fire, the news that the Japanese had bombed Manila, the *open town*, for two and a half hours.

Monday, 29 December

Very busy trying to get straight after the blessed and restful holiday. Various women I know listened enviously to my account of my trip. 'I have not slept out of the house for over two years; one gets so *stale* . . .'

Tuesday, 30 December

Petronelle, my god-daughter of seventeen, has arrived to stay. She is longing for February, when she will join the Wrens. News about the Philippines is bad. Winston has made a long speech to the Canadians.

Wednesday, 31 December

Sad and restless today. What is happening to Hong Kong and to Manila?

1942

New Year's Day

To tea with the Hopgoods. Marna is now an officer in the ATS. 'Will you girls miss it all when peace comes?' I asked. 'Yes – but we all want six months' fun at the end of it.' Grace and I shivered, as we thought of the confused period directly after the peace.

Today came a parcel from Harry and Jenny – sugar and chocolate and dried figs.

What will this year bring? Final victory in Libya, at any rate. But how can we regain Hong Kong? Perhaps only at the Council table. I hope Sir Mark Young is being considerately treated.*

Friday, 2 January

Medical supplies weighing more than 100 tons, including surgical gloves, sterilisers, hypodermic needles, amputation knives, syringes, hot water bottles, and 695 lbs of agar-agar (a

* He was not. He survived a series of Japanese prisoner of war camps until his liberation in 1945, eventually resuming the governorship of Hong Kong in 1946 after several months' recuperation.

type of seaweed to be used for bacteriological work) were yesterday loaded in London ready for dispatch to Russia.

This morning I had letters from Tickie in Boston, from Nancy in Canada, from Jenny in Rhodesia. Tickie, who is engaged, says her fiancé is volunteering for the Navy: they can't be married for ages. 'But why should our affairs go well, when the world is upside down?'

Saturday, 3 January

Rachel says in her letter this morning: 'As I listened to Winston's firm promises of ultimate victory, I thought, yes, but what of all those we lose by the way? I'm afraid I don't even feel any delight in thousands of Germans being done in. We can only drift on, just snatching at passing happiness, and doing any kindness we can along the way.'

Sunday, 4 January

Cyril Thompson, able seaman, was fined £6 at Hull yesterday for neglecting to proceed to sea after he had been lawfully engaged to serve on a vessel.

Thompson said he found his two brothers were in the same ship, and he did not think there should be three from one family on board. He had been twice torpedoed already.

The Stipendiary, Mr J. R. MacDonald, asked Thompson to visualise the position in the Mediterranean if Admiral Cunningham had said he did not like his brother, General Cunningham, to be be fighting in Libya at the same time.

Thompson replied that two were all right, but not three. Mr MacDonald told Thompson not to be so superstitious.

It was a great privilege to hear Robert Nicols, the poet,

speak of Japan on the wireless last night. He was urgently concerned that we should understand that we and the Americans were up against a formidable foe. Behind an iron self-control, there lurked an underlying hysteria. The Japanese are not encouraged to be individuals. If they lose, there will, he thinks, be a most terrible internal revolution in Japan.

I finished *Pepys and Wife Go To It*, a diary of this present war, by R. M. Freeman. I laughed at this passage:

Mr P: 'Late last night, just before going to bedd, we heard a weird, piercing noise, that I did instantly identify for a screaming bomb, my wife likewise. Whereat she hurriedly to dive under the bedd and I under the table. And there we lay, holding our breaths, and awaiting the explosion, when lo! through the party wall the clearly audible voice of neighbour Lee, saying, "Poor old Babbs!" (being the name of their catt), "Did I tread on him, then?" Never did I enjoy a laugh against myself soe heartily.'

Monday, 5 January

Can we hold Singapore? This question is in all our minds, on this very cold evening, with mists hanging over Newlands Corner.

Saw the film of our Commandos' attack on Vaasgo:* the snow-covered hills, the dark water, the black outline of our ships, the humble houses, the sturdy figures of our men dashing hither and thither; the German prisoners looking impassive as they hurried along with upstretched hands.

* Properly Vågsoy, an island in the Nordfjord district of Norway, which housed a German garrison.

Tuesday, 6 January

The Russians have issued a statement about the price Germany must pay when the war ends with the Allies' victory. Here is an extract:

'For all eternity, Russia declares that for all the German brutalities, Russia will call down on Germany the most solemn curse, and the most sacred vengeance. Russia will pay back a hundredfold every crime committed by Germany.'

I have always been persuaded that the Germans in Germany are still hugging themselves with delight over their victories, but surely any thoughtful Hun must be disturbed by the simple fact that *America has come in*.

Today Roosevelt has promised 45,000 fighters, bombers and dive bombers in 1942 and 100,000 next year.

Robin had a talk over the Russian manifesto with L., our local builder. He was all for the manifesto, and wished 'to exterminate them all.' Truly the tide of hatred towards Germany is running at the flood in Britain now.

L. said to Robin in wrath, 'What, you'd let the Germans come in here again after the war?' Robin replied gently, 'I hope that will be possible.' 'I never did like your ideas,' was the wrathful reply.

I see that Mr Ernest Bevin will now excuse domestic servants from leaving old and infirm people. How late in the day! Many tragedies have occurred already, in houses all over the country. But perhaps it is a good thing for old people to die during this war.

Friday, 9 January

The Japanese are drawing nearer to Kuala Lumpur. The

Australians are said to be rushing fighter planes to help General MacArthur* in the threatened Philippines.

Mrs Rayne to tea – her boy is flying over Germany. He writes to her about the cloud effects and the moon and the islands lying far below. No word of bombs.

Sunday, 11 January

Bitterly cold. Now four o'clock, Robin is teaching map-reading to some NCOs in the clear frosty air and enjoying it fully.

Monday, 12 January

Woke to find bitter cold, and pipes frozen. Robin worked very hard from eight-thirty. It was three before we heard the welcome sound of running water. Poor Robin did not even cast a glance at the newspaper. Kuala Lumpur has fallen, and where is Lilian of the bright hair? I hope she got away in time. The lights have now fused, to add to the entertainment.

Tuesday, 13 January

I was aghast at being asked on the telephone this morning to become Billeting Officer – I am considering it; as there are 8–900 children in the village it would be no sinecure.

Went to London. Coming down in a crowded carriage with two men standing, a Canadian soldier turned on his small wireless set and the whole packed carriage listened gravely to a fairy story from the Children's Hour about Grimalkin. So

* General Douglas MacArthur, commander of the US Army Forces in the Far East.

English were we, we made no sort of response or comment, or thanked the Canadian. But I suspect we all enjoyed it, jogging through snow-covered fields. Returned much elated, and gave Robin the gift of an apricot tart. Tried not to think about Malaya and the increasing danger there.

Thursday, 15 January

A. writes from Edinburgh. She has taken a job as a domestic servant, and finds herself living in a tiny back bedroom in a tall house, with a hard chair and a broken radiator, in spite of the promise of a nice comfortable bed-sitting room. There is a steep stone staircase and there are three coal fires to light (apparently no electricity); and the old lady, who is sole occupant, and A. between them have half a pint of milk every second day. I think the old woman is living in a dream and should be rudely awakened. Such monstrous houses must either be torn down, or made into flats.

Friday, 16 January

Great fear is expressed about the possible fall of Singapore. Articles on this appear everywhere. Japanese submarines based in Singapore would be able to interfere seriously with the British supply routes to and from Australia.

The papers are calling for Winston's return,* and say it is high time to 'knock a few heads together and put some order into a disordered situation.'

* Churchill had been in the United States for meetings with President Roosevelt following America's entry into the war. He had in fact set out on the home voyage on 14 January.

Parcel just in from America. Honey, chocolate and bacon. What a help!

In the bank today Mr F. was very bitter about the approach of Warship Week,* of which he is secretary: 'I never knew such a village. The same set of people do everything again and again.'

Afterwards I rang through and offered to type any letters for him. 'No, there would be no need.' 'Very well, then, I'm ready to do anything else.' 'Thank you, I'll bear it in mind.'

Robin received a communication from the Labour Exchange at Guildford this morning, calling up our maid, Mrs Olive Sutton. Could she not go to make munitions? He answered by pointing out that she was a soldier's wife, her husband did not wish her to leave home, and so on. Compulsion cannot, very rightly, be applied to married women.

Sunday, 18 January

Snow still lying thickly over Shere. The lonely soldier arrived for tea,† and we enjoyed his conversation as usual. He spoke of the beautiful carved stone mantlepieces in the country house where he is stationed, and of the thoughtless way some of the troops idly carve circles on them.

The papers are exceedingly interesting, as usual. I should like to know the name of the Belgian woman who found a

* Warship Weeks were fundraising drives to raise set amounts of money towards the cost of building a naval ship. Cities, towns and villages were given different targets to raise, according to their level of population, and when the target was achieved the community would adopt the ship they had funded. Quite apart from the money raised, these and similar schemes had the benefit of making people feel that they had made vital contributions to the war effort.

† Connie does not explain who the lonely soldier was, or refer to him by name, but he was a frequent visitor during 1942.

German soldier pointing a rifle at her when, the other day, she was proceeding to lay flowers on a dead British airman's grave. She went on with her task in spite of it. When the Germans marched down the cemetery path, the assembled Belgians just turned their backs on them.

Tuesday, 20 January

An awful day, snow and cold and frost. Everything looks very quiet and very unfriendly in the garden. The paths are hidden in snow, and the elms hold up their branches as if saying, 'We are dead and gone, and will never have green leaves again.'

There are some stories of the capture of Halfaya Pass* that are interesting. An orderly of the RAMC said in an interview: 'I operated with a penknife and amputated a German's arm, after he had been hit by a British bomb splinter. It saved his life, and the German commander sent down a packet of cigarettes as a reward.'

Wednesday, 21 January

Basil writes from the desert. His nearest hospital is at Nazareth: how strange.

Florrie writes that the Air Ministry has told Iris that her husband is undoubtedly dead, and buried at Dunkirk. He was last seen diving in his plane into the sea. Poor Iris.

Mr Churchill has a cold, and is obviously feeling rather touchy.

* On 17 January 5,000 Axis troops surrendered to the South African 6th Infantry Brigade. Halfaya Pass in Egypt was the main route into Libya, and hence a key part of the campaign in North Africa. The fierce fighting that took place there earned it the nickname 'Hellfire Pass'.

Thursday, 22 January

Feel sick with anxiety about Malaya. The authorities there are ordering many rubber plantations to become scorched earth. The rubber tree takes years to cultivate; tens of thousands of trees must now be charred and burned. It is pitiful.

I shall write on a postcard, 'America is In', and put it on the mantlepiece to remind me of Hope.

Sunday, 25 January

The lonely soldier, who again came to tea, said, 'I should go potty if I couldn't come here.' He brought back *Wuthering Heights*, which he has read for the first time, and remarked that he would not like anybody dear to him to go through such sorrow as that.

Monday, 26 January

Distressed to find that my firm friend and hairdresser in Guildford was left alone to cope with her work: the last maiden has gone off to the Forces. Nora has a heavy Guildford rent to pay, and I fear she *cannot* make things go as they should if she can't get help. She can't get anybody, and has advertised twelve times in vain. I cannot think what she can do: expenses mount every day, and she has only two hands; and she deserves to succeed. Many people have left the town, going back to London, so in any case business is not as good.

Thursday, 29 January

The debate last night seems to have been bitter and unpleasant.

Lord Chatfield in the Lords and Sir Archibald Southby both accuse Winston of having denied an aircraft carrier escort for *Repulse* and the *Prince of Wales*: they allege that he manages and controls naval strategy. This is all very wretched, and I hope it may be denied.*

I am sitting by the fire. Robin looks up and says the Japs are only thirty-one miles from Singapore.

Saturday, 31 January

Came an army chaplain to tea, who said that he surmised that the government did not compel the lads of fifteen, sixteen and seventeen to join some organisation because there were not sufficient people ready and trained to deal with them. Sagacious comment.

The lonely soldier came and left a small chocolate offering on the mantlepiece.

Monday, 2 February

Today is the birthday of my nieces, Pam and Prue, to whom the brand new world is going to belong. I have written to Gorringes for two brocade bags for them to take to parties: one geranium red, one green.

* HMS *Prince of Wales* and HMS *Repulse* were sunk by Japanese long-range bombers off the Malayan coast on 10 December, after they had sailed without any air support. They were the first large warships to be sunk by air attack alone. Churchill later wrote that 'in all the war, I never received a more direct shock ... over all this vast expanse of waters Japan was supreme.' Conservative MP Sir John Wardlaw-Milne raised the fate of the ships in the debate of 27–29 January. He also questioned why troops from India had not been sent to support the defence of Singapore, concluding: 'It seems incredible in the circumstance that we should have been left with such a meagre force to stand against the attack of an active, powerful enemy like Japan.' Despite his critics, Churchill won a vote of confidence by a large majority.

Tuesday, 3 February

Awful weather again. Interesting letter from May Sinclair. She is in charge of a 'crisis' department at the BBC.

'When you get a News Editor with a broken knee-cap from a fall on ice – three typists sick, a fourth (new) found to be hopelessly incompetent. The head clerk had two broken ribs (fell on ice). All in one department. But the news must go out to the Empire! I have to get replacements.

'I dined with Ted Morris* last week ... heard some really amusing stories about Stalin. He said at one of those dreadful Kremlin feasts to the British Mission, 'Do your Marshals drink much?' The horrified Englishman said, 'No, very little.' Stalin cried, 'What a pity! The better the drinker, the better the Marshal. My Marshals are great drinkers.'

Friday, 6 February

So dismal a day, with the snow lying thick and cold everywhere, that I did not go out. I feel restless: I wish we could go off and do some war work, and let the flat, which gets shabbier and shabbier.

Dean Inge† is now writing to suggest that the depleted middle classes should form communities after the war and occupy country houses that nobody wants, 'to save what can be saved of the cultural tradition of the shattered Empire'.

It is very surprising, since the Socialist idea is so rampant in our midst, that the community idea does not take surer hold: it

* General Sir Edwin Morris, who shortly after this dinner was appointed Chief of the General Staff in India.

† William Ralph Inge, author, newspaper columnist and Dean of St Paul's Cathedral.

Many women who could not work full time did part-time war work. This group are sorting rivets at a converted private house in Northchapel, Surrey.
Photograph © IWM D14147

is not popular. The small shops are at the moment being urgently advised to amalgamate and save themselves from bankruptcy, what with the growing scarcity of goods to sell, and the depletion of their small but important staffs. But many will not hear of it. Mrs James, for instance, who has a suburban baby-clothes shop fairly near another one, said to an interviewer in the

Daily Mail, 'I'd rather go on Poor Law Relief* than merge with another. I am temperamentally unsuited to working with another woman.' So said others all round her.

Saturday, 7 February

To Guildford again. Readers standing four deep in Boots' Library to have their books changed, and about eight deep at Lyons where I drank a hot lemonade in the freezing cold and talked with a dark-eyed young man at the same table. He has made a study of Russia, and admires her very much, and thinks Socialism is *the* thing. I said I did not think it was, which he accepted with gentle resignation.

Heard from Picket Post – still no cook, no scullery maid, and the mistress of the house washing up for the great school household, and her daughter (fain to be off to the Wrens) gallantly cooking for forty or so. What will be the end of this?

Muriel has had a cable from Eudo in the East Surreys in Malaya saying he is safe. The rumour is that they were cornered by the Japs and cut off and heavily punished.†

Sunday, 8 February

Abominably cold. Snow still lying. I talk with a young WAAF

* Poor Law Relief provided support for the destitute or for those unable to work. First instituted in 1597, it was replaced on the creation of the welfare state in 1948 by the National Assistance Act.

† The 2nd Battalion, The East Surrey Regiment had lost so many men in Malaya that it was no longer viable as a fighting unit. On 20 December 1941 it was amalgamated with the 1st Battalion, The Leicestershire Regiment to form the British Battalion, under which name it fought until the surrender of Singapore on 15 February. Out of an intial complement of 786 men, only 265 were left, and a further 149 were to die in Japanese POW camps.

who is staying here. She longs to fly – her face lights up with delight at the very thought. She told me that the postal arrangements of all the Services are very inefficient. When girls are suddenly despatched all over England, and their mail arrives at the stations from which they have departed, many of the letters don't get sent on. The postal people just burn them. 'What, burn unread, unopened letters?' I said incredulously. 'Yes, I had all mine registered when I was at Gloucester; that was a bit better.'

She added that many tough, cynical women, who abuse their authority, are in charge. She described queueing up for breakfast on an ice-cold morning at seven, having been up for ages, only to be told there was none. 'What did you do?' 'Drilled half the morning, and then had a cup of tea in the NAAFI, you know, one tea leaf and gallons of water.'*

She loves the life, however.

Monday, 9 February

Robin's birthday. He is sixty-four. He had four gifts:

A tin of anchovies from me. A twopenny slab of chocolate from a WAAF. Two fresh eggs from our neighbour, who said while putting them in my hands, 'It is as if I gave him a pearl and a diamond.' A pot of jam from Rosemary Murray, I fear almost the last she has.

The soap rationing is a real trial. I had bought a hat-box full of tablets at the beginning of the war, and am thankful. The ration is sure to be reduced.

Woke to hear that the Japanese had effected a landing on Singapore. Very distressing.

* The NAAFI provided retail and recreational facilities – stores, bars, canteens, restaurants, etc. – to all branches of the British armed forces.

E. writes: 'I have got to know some Canadian officers, thank God; it makes life less dreary. Am actually being taken to a dance by one of them, in a lorry. I expect it will be the death of me.'

A beautiful parcel came from New Jersey today: a tongue, a cake in a tin, and two boxes of Swiss cheese. They say the war has, as yet, affected the Americans so slightly that sugar and motor tyres are the only things that can't be procured.

The WAAF was a hospital nurse, it turns out, on an ambulance river boat during the worst of the Blitz. She told of the awful night when the cadet training ship near the Tower of London was hit,* and the water was full of bodies. They picked up seven, one of them without an arm (he took it so bravely), gave them hot coffee at once and the doctor on board ordered a shot of morphia. They took them up the Thames to Bermondsey hospital, and they all recovered! She spoke of the blaze in the sky; of the tramp ship which struck a mine in the river and blew up in half.

It is jolly to think that this little woman is going to be happy this evening. She is meeting her RASC fiancé in town and they are dining at the Café Anglais and going together to *Dumbo*.

Very much troubled about Singapore. It seems as if it is going to be taken.

Thursday, 12 February

There is hand to hand fighting in the city of Singapore; the air

* HMS *Wellesley*, a 74-gun ship of the line first launched in 1815, was serving as the naval training ship TS *Cornwall* when she was bombed and sunk on 24 September 1940 at her moorings at Purfleet (not near the Tower of London as Connie records it). Her figurehead is now at Chatham Historic Dockyard.

is dark with Japanese bombers, and our lads go up in ancient planes which go slowly. It is all ghastly.

A Home Guard died in A.'s hospital in Dorking the other day. He had been bombed by mistake at practice, and had both legs amputated. After that, lying in bed, he said brightly to the nurse, 'I am so glad my feet feel warm again.' Later he realised suddenly what had happened, fell silent and quietly passed away.

Friday, 13 February

News of the great naval battle. At the time of writing it seems as if it were another setback for us, but we may get more cheerful news later. What a fearful thing a sea battle must be, with all those planes!*

I go to see about a dozen three-year-olds at a local war home. Where the mothers are, I don't know. I believe they are making munitions.

I meet a corporal coming up the hill, obviously on leave. There are four children. He has the one next to the youngest on his shoulder, and makes him laugh, and then glances at me, and I laugh, and the corporal laughs, and the child laughs. I can't help saying to the wife, 'It's good to have him home, isn't it?'

* The battle known as the Channel Dash. On 11 February a German naval squadron successfully ran a British blockade in the English Channel en route from Brest in Brittany to their German bases. Beyond the Straits of Dover they were attacked by the RAF and the Fleet Air Arm, and defended by the Luftwaffe. Two German ships were damaged, but none was sunk. Accounts of the aircraft losses differ, but the Naval Situation Report delivered to the War Cabinet records 37 British planes destroyed and 17 German.

Tuesday, 17 February

Singapore has fallen, and all is lost.* I feel physically ill when I think what the suspense must be for Muriel, who has her boy there with the East Surreys. Harry's regiment, the Loyals, are there also; dead, wounded, prisoners, those men and officers he knew so well. I have much to be thankful for, that he is out of it.

There seems a great cry going up in the House (not the country) against Churchill – the old familiar way of making a scapegoat of somebody. I feel terrified he will resign in a temper. Then what?

Robin has mended Mrs Murray's kettle. You can't buy one in Guildford. She is so grateful, but as she gave him a pot of jam the other day, he feels very friendly towards her.

Wednesday, 18 February

Cold, unflinching cold, perfectly sunless and bitter. A brave letter in from Muriel about Eudo in Singapore. The East Surreys' colonel got 'a packet in the leg' and was safely evacuated. But what of the Major?

Friday, 20 February

Much cheered by a letter from Harry, written before Christmas. This had taken sixty days to come.

In the House of Lords yesterday, Lord Atkin said that the figures of juvenile offenders had increased alarmingly

* Churchill called the fall of Singapore on 15 February 1942 'the worst disaster and largest capitulation in British history'.

during the war. From January to August 1940 they increased by 41 per cent among children under fourteen and by 22 per cent among those between fourteen and seventeen. There are many waiting to be taken into special schools.

No news yet from Japan about our Singapore prisoners.

I place it on record calmly and gravely that this stage of the war is the worst that we have gone through. Suspense, death and cruelty. Silence between those that love one another. All this sorrow intensified by the bitter, stormy grey weather with no sun.

I go to sleep thinking of Eudo, gallant Major, East Surreys, whose very laugh I hear in my ear, young and infectious. Where is he? Alive or prisoner?

Sunday, 22 February

The dining room is full of Home Guards learning map reading. Robin is very much excited.

An old woman of eighty says, 'I always bake some little cakes every Saturday in case one of the boys (in Libya) comes in.'

The news seems terribly bad.

Monday, 23 February

Received an arresting letter from a great friend, in whose thoughts I am always most interested. She says: 'Do you have a horrible feeling that nothing will ever be the same again? One will never just be quite pleased with life – a lovely sunny day in the country perhaps. Just as you are going to enjoy it, a memory of this horror will come like a cloud over the sun. More and more I feel I'd like to go and live, afterwards, somewhere that doesn't remind me of post-war England. Somewhere where one can work and build up from the beginning – not merely to patch up . . .'*

Went to tea with Baby Lisa, the seven-month-old daughter of an airman who died before she was born. It was very touching, sitting by the bright wood fire watching the fatherless baby drink her orange juice – obtained, said the pale young mother, from America, under the Lend-Lease Bill. She talked a lot about her husband, and how he loved flying above the beautiful Scottish hills, and would come home and tell her about it. I came away so thankful that she had a child. All the difference between heaven and hell for her.

Tuesday, 24 February

Nothing more about our men in Singapore.

I discover an advertisement in today's *Times* about a job I think I am able to fill. If only I could! They want gentlewomen for portresses at University College Hospital, London; no manual work, but answering enquiries, phones, etc.

Robin throws cold water on it firmly. 'You would always be ill,' etc. I can do nothing, of course, as my duty lies at home. A nuisance.

Thursday, 26 February

Cissy writes today that her mother-in-law's estate cannot be settled until her daughter M. comes out of captivity –

* It is apparent from the context of this letter, which later mentions being at the BBC, that the writer is May Sinclair.

she is interned in Jersey. Everything is held up till – when? That seems appallingly stupid. I hope they can make a fuss.

The thought of our prisoners in Singapore and the lack of any news is more and more intolerable. Poor Henry, whose son is there, I hear strides about the countryside for hours to try and forget it.

Friday, 27 February

To Guildford. Shopping was difficult. Waited for twenty minutes in a grocer's for some loose mustard. Also waited a long time for four meat patties (fourpence-halfpenny each) at Lyons. A large indignant woman pushed me back.

Everybody looks worn and anxious. But the sun has actually come out and cheered us a little today.

We hear that spring has come to Libya and now soldiers tread through fields of asphodel.

Tuesday, 3 March

There is to be an official enquiry as to what stocks of coffee remain in England. I see rationing coming. I have two tins from America, in my sadly depleted store cupboard.

At the Ministry of Information films today in the village hall, there was a clever film of Hitler and his soldiers doing the Lambeth Walk. Adolf would be furious if he had heard the peals of laughter that greeted his frantic appearance. England has never been impressed by the Führer: his ways do not suit us.

Bad news about brave Java.* The Japanese Navy is ruling the waves.

Thursday, 5 March

I forgot to copy this poem by Mildred, sent me some time ago.

To the Pianist

Don't play 'Auf Wiedersehn'
Not while the rain is dropping from the eaves,
Nor while I think of ghosts …
Recall again
Vienna of the dropping golden leaves.
And don't play 'Balalaika'
Not again
While down the Nevski Prospect pour the troops,
Not in the dazzling colours that I knew
But drab and sombre as the Volga's hue.
Play something light and cold,
Something quite new;
I must forget
These cities drowned in pain.
Stop 'Madeleine',
That's France and Quatorze.
God! How one grows old.

Rangoon will go next, then Java. Then India? Then certainly,

* On 27 February in a battle lasting seven hours a combined Allied naval force had failed to prevent a Japanese invasion fleet from reaching Java. The Allied commander, the Dutch Rear-Admiral Karel Doorman, was killed and the USS *Houston*, the largest US warship in the Far East, was among those sunk.

I fear, Australia. What agonising times! Appalling hours dragging on, with the news ever worsening . . .

Saturday, 7 March

Barbara writes of her office work in a Ministry. She says: 'I am rather horrified to note the awe in which the women hold the men. My co-mate, married to an Eton master, talks about being afraid of forgetting her pass, and "getting into a row" as if she were a schoolchild.'

To my great joy I have discovered a woman who will come and work for me when Olive goes. Thank God, I say, most sincerely.

Heard from Cousin Jo this morning. Their younger boy, a fine, gallant, upstanding fellow, went into the army, and wrote confidently just before Christmas. Now no news, and the poor father is stunned, and works all day long so as not to think.

Robin reads out an odd article in the *Daily Mail*, which surely should know better, saying that the American fleet is sailing towards Java, poor, falling Java! If only it was true!

Sunday, 8 March

What an amazing feature of this war is the way the Germans transplant whole populations. Now it is announced that they think they will move a Polish town, called Katowice, *entirely*, because there are rich seams of coal under it.*

* Katowice is the largest city in the industrial region of Silesia, in southern Poland. Following the German invasion in 1939 it became Kattowitz, and from 1941 to 1945 was capital of the German province of Upper Silesia. Around 40,000 Poles were expelled from Upper Silesia, and ethnic Germans were settled in their place.

One Maria Goralezcka has been shot in Poland, for hitting a Labour Exchange official in the face. How I sympathise with dark-eyed, world-fatigued Maria! God rest her.

Surely this dark tide of misfortune must turn soon?

Tuesday, 10 March

Went to the village kitchen to help. Met Freda on the way, who said: 'There is no food in the village. I can't get Jack any fish, or any meat. Women alone are all right. It's the men . . .'

True.

Later. Horrified to listen to Mr Eden's speech on the Japanese treatment of our people in Hong Kong. Words fail me utterly. Felt *desperate*, and suggested to Robin that we should both give up our home at once, and get war work. We *must* win! Robin dissented. To bed, thoroughly wretched, and took a sleeping draught, to help me to forget it all.

Thursday, 12 March

The wireless has just announced that private motor cars must go off the road. Alas!

The Japanese armada which went to Java consisted of more than 200 warships and sixty troop carriers, and the Allied fleet that tackled it was less than a third in size.

How long will this continue? At the present moment there seems no real opposition.

Friday, 13 March

Went to sleep last night thinking of what the loss of the car will mean to us. Of course there's not the slightest feeling that we should be allowed to keep it. I like to think of our happy trips – it brought me to the gates of many friends. To a gate by a walnut tree in a Berkshire village, to a loved gate in the New Forest, to a green gate and quiet home in Highcliffe where there was always a warm welcome and a prospect of happy talks. This war is certainly forbidding meetings and discouraging all travels.

Saturday, 14 March

May S. came, looking terribly exhausted, full of talk about the BBC. She knows the governor of the prison which houses Hess.* Mrs Pakenham amused May and me by telling us this true story: 'Hess is here,' announced the housemaid, bringing Mrs P. her morning tea in a Scottish country house last year. 'Mrs Bailey asked me to tell you.' 'Oh,' said Mrs P., quite baffled. 'Well, please tell Mrs Bailey from me that Hitler is standing just outside my window!' 'Yes, m'am,' and the girl went off, convinced that this was so.

Tuesday, 17 March

Today *The Times* says that Greek officials predict that half the entire Greek population of 7,000,000 will be dead before the war ends.

Barbara is worried about her garden. She thinks it more important to cultivate that, possibly, than to work at a Ministry.†

* Following his flight to Scotland on 10 May 1941, ostensibly to broker a peace deal between Germany and Britain, Rudolf Hess was held until June 1942 at Camp Z, Mytchett Place, on the Surrey/Hampshire border.

† The Dig For Victory campaign encouraged everyone in Britain to grow their own food in allotments or turn their gardens over to food production, keeping chickens, goats or pigs if space allowed and digging up lawns and flower beds to grow vegetables.

Wednesday, 18 March

Olive left today, much to my sorrow.

The other Olive has been here, telling me about life in a factory. 'It's the money I must have. It's very monotonous; I would rather do housework. But my husband, who has left the Dorchester and is in the army, only gets seven-and-six a week to spend, and I get twenty-five shillings army allowance, so we can't pay our house instalment, unless I make about three pounds, which I do. Ever so nice the forewoman is, and you can talk if you like. The afternoon's the worst, about three o'clock, so tiring, and you go on till six doing the same thing over and over. I'd like to change my machine, but if you get good at your work, they won't move you!'

Australia is said to be at zero hour, awaiting an invasion. If only we could get some success!

From the Bundles for Britain League* last week came 12,000 garments. A hundred Afghans, 280 pairs of shoes. From New Zealand, 9,900 garments. From the Kinsman's Club of Canada, 40,000 pounds of milk powder. We are not (though it almost seems as if we are) alone.

Thursday, 19 March

Mr Bracken says we are about to hear more bad news. It must be Burma that we are to lose.

The Americans are having a great welcome in Australia; 'the

* Bundles for Britain began as a New York knitting circle set up by Natalie Wales Latham in 1940. By mid-1941 it had 975 branches and more than a million contributors, and as well as clothing it also shipped medical supplies, up to and including ambulances. Mrs Latham was awarded an honorary CBE by the grateful British government after the war.

men swing through the streets to billets and camps with a splended, careless swagger,' and towns declared an unofficial holiday.

Leaving this country for the Malaya front last year, a soldier called Ayres said to his wife, 'If anything happens to me, don't take up the struggle alone. Follow me every mile of the way. We love each other too much to be parted. Bring the baby with you.' The poor wife, hearing her husband had died of wounds at Singapore, drowned the baby and tried to drown herself, but was rescued. The judge told her this: 'You are the victim of the lusts of the warlords of the world.' She was recommended to mercy, poor soul.

Friday, 20 March

From May Sinclair's letter:

'I got into a railway carriage (after leaving you) with three soldiers. Two cursing Churchill, and saying they wouldn't trust him farther than they could see him, etc. Making the most astounding statements about our politicians *selling* us to Germany. First they said Ramsay MacDonald made his pile and then cleared out, then Baldwin made a fortune by selling steel to Germany, and then he resigned when things got too hot for him. I couldn't contain myself when they started on poor old Chamberlain, and enquired in an icily polite voice, "Would you tell me where you got these astounding facts? Because I suppose you are quite sure you are speaking the truth?" They stopped and looked amazed, then went off into that good old speech that we know by heart: "In Russia, it's different, there they don't do this and that." The end of the story was (so typically British) they both recounted with relish all the battles they had fought in – one had 27 years' service – and so pleased was he with Comrade May Sinclair that he insisted upon carrying my suitcase off the station. As we parted, I said in a very schoolmistressy way, "Now remember what I've told you about Russia – I've been there – and about making wild and wicked statements about public people," and he said, "Very good, m'am." No other country could possibly understand us!'

Saturday, 21 March

Ten p.m. The Home Guard have been ordered to stand to. We were drinking coffee with Captain and Mrs Pakenham below when an excited fifteen-year-old appeared to summon Robin. He has gone down the street in uniform – unarmed.

We went over to the Rawlinsons, our last car expedition till the end of the war. Also, I suppose, I drank my last cocktail of the war, in the Wentworth Club, with our kind host and hostess.

Thursday, 26 March

The news is bad. The Japanese have landed on the Andaman Islands. (I can't help remembering the Andamans in Conan Doyle's wonderful story, *The Sign of Four*.)

Should Russia conclude a separate peace, what then? They cannot last for ever. Alexander Werth, the war correspondent, told May Sinclair that the Russians were very short of food. No doubt they think us fools over our neglect at Singapore. A storm seems to be blowing up over this matter of Singapore. Sir John Wardlaw-Milne, MP, who seems to be true hardheaded son of the Manse, asked in Parliament if it was true that immediately before our surrender, some British reinforcements were landed, and almost at once marched into a prison camp.

As I write, the news is pouring into the room. MacArthur is pledging American blood to the cause. The Japanese are surely at their peak of power, they are pressing us hard in Burma, and so on. It is difficult to convey the war atmosphere of today. We know that the Japanese are triumphant, rushing here and there. There is silence from our men and women in Hong Kong, and silence about our dear ones in Singapore, and the Germans are pressing the Russians with new vehement efforts. Libya is watchful: but quiet. I have so much extra housework that the day goes more quickly, I'm glad to say.

Sunday, 29 March

To church this morning, for the Day of Prayer service. It was a long, extremely intense service, far too long to follow: one's emotion was running dry during the first half-hour. Why does not some vicar or rector perceive that people are feeling the strain of this war, and a brief service would much better serve their needs.

Monday, 30 March

The papers are full of news of our great commando attack at St Nazaire.

'The story of their amazing exploits is one of the most stirring that this country has had during the whole course of the war. They went ashore in the early hours of the morning and systematically wrecked harbour installations, lock gates, and power houses. They were met by strong opposition, but this they overcame with the utmost determination.'*

Wednesday, 1 April

To the Women's Institute. Mrs T. spoke of her idea of getting up a communal kitchen for grown-ups. In the discussion that followed there was no enthusiasm at all, and the village women were unconcerned. The relief of having a British Restaurant† near at hand, when cookless, was not even mentioned, but great stress was laid by a couple of speakers on the saving in gas and electricity.

Wednesday, 8 April

To tea with the Rogers. Miss Margery Perham, of the Nuffield Foundation, was there.‡ She spoke of the visit of the Russians to our factories, and said they were horrified to find that women workers in them were not paid the same as men.

Friday, 10 April

News very bad. The Japs are masters of Batavia. We have

* Led by Commander R. E. D. ('Red') Ryder, the raid took place on 28 March and put the dry dock at St Nazaire out of action for the rest of the war, depriving German warships of any means of repair on the Atlantic coast. Among the 89 decorations awarded to the raiding party were five Victoria Crosses.

† A Ministry of Food initiative, British Restaurants served basic nutritious meals at minimum prices. By the end of 1943 more than 2,000 had been set up.

‡ Margery Perham, Oxford don and a renowned authority on Africa, was the sister of Connie's near neighbour, Ethel Rayne. She was awarded a CBE in 1948 and in 1961 became the first woman to deliver the Reith Lectures on BBC Radio.

lost two valuable cruisers. *Hermes*, an aircraft carrier, has been sunk.*

Monday, 13 April

From Lady Adams' Californian letter this morning, about the outbreak of war in America:

'The nation was dumb with surprise, and I was dumb with surprise too, because the nation was dumb with surprise. Didn't they know what was going to happen? You see the USA had always watched dreadful things happening to the people next door, and they just could not believe that Pearl Harbour had crashed about them. I was lunching in Pasadena the day of Pearl Harbour, and an acquaintance said to me, "Are you anxious?" "I have been anxious night and day," I said, "for two years and three months," and she seemed surprised.'

Tuesday, 14 April

I shook hands with Tony Dodds today, on survivors' leave. He looks much older. His ship, a fine destroyer, was sunk. 'She went down in three minutes,' said Tony. There appears to have been a ship full of ammunition near the destroyer in Valetta harbour. Most of the crew of Tony's ship had gone ashore when German bombers appeared. Eleven were killed on board by the Germans. 'There were so many planes,'

* Batavia was the Dutch colonial name for what is now Jakarta, capital city of Indonesia. Both the *Hermes* and her destroyer escort were sunk by Japanese bombers. Many survivors were rescued, but 302 were lost.

Tony said rather sadly. 'And you watched it?' 'Oh, I went to try and pick some of them out.'*

Monday, 20 April

The raid by daylight over Augsburg seems to have been very wonderful. The Prime Minister has sent the following message to Air Marshal A. T. Harris, C-in-C Bomber Command:

'We must plainly regard the attack of the Lancasters on the U-boat engine factory at Augsburg as an outstanding achievement of the Royal Air Force. Undeterred by heavy losses at the outset, the bombers pierced in broad daylight into the heart of Germany and struck a vital point with deadly precision.'

I wrote to Mrs Winston Churchill today to ask her to beg her husband to say one sentence to women in Britain in his next speech. One sentence to brace the anxious wives and mothers, the tired workers. Oh, I hope it will be answered, and I shall watch for it, but I don't think it likely. Winston must be behind such a very thick wall of business.

To Guildford. The windows of the bakers' shops looked stripped and bare. A few doubtful looking little rissoles at Lyons.

Tuesday, 21 April

Lord Haw-Haw has just broadcast and says the British fleet has retired from the Pacific and gone to Durban, thus presenting the Japanese with Ceylon and India.

* Connie writes elsewhere that Robin met Mr Dodds in the village, who told him that Tony had walked in saying, 'Daddy, I've only brought my body with me, I've lost everything else.'

The familiar voice rasped away and I left it to go to the kitchen and wash up.

Muriel and Sibyl both write of sharp raids on Southampton and the New Forest.

Thursday, 23 April

I have just cut out a charming picture of Princess Elizabeth, one day to be Queen of England, shaking hands with one of the officers of her regiment – the Grenadier Guards. His head is bowed in shyness and she is smiling up at him. The Colonel looks on, half smiling, half anxious. All this, her first public ceremony, will remain with her, even after years of public life.

The Americans' sugar ration has gone from one pound a head a week to half a pound, so no more sugar will cross the Atlantic for us. Nor tea.

Later: I have been remembering our happy visits to beautiful Rouen. And here in the paper, I see this:

'Rouen, where 80 more hostages are due to be executed on Friday or Saturday for the attack on a troop train, is in mourning. All women are in black, and all men have black armbands or a piece of crepe in their buttonhole. When the first 30 hostages were executed last Saturday, the Dean of the Cathedral held a solemn requiem mass, which was attended by thousands of people. The night before, a crepe-decorated wreath was placed by unknown hands at the gates of the courtyard of La Nouvelle Prison, where the executions were to take place at dawn.'

Saturday, 25 April

The papers are full of hints as to an Allied offensive. I wonder. Our air raids are becoming even more intensive.

Monday, 27 April

A great day – the opening of the grown-ups' communal kitchen. The ugly, dusty faded village hall looked so much better, as, having paid out ninepence each to the First Lady of the village at the door, we advanced to the table.

The Three Graces, who so kindly have undertaken this, looked rather anxious, as they directed us to bring up our plates and take our forks and spoons. There was corned beef, lettuce, nicely mashed potato, and a divine pudding with dates and sauce. We much enjoyed our meal. The Graces looked so pretty, Molly of the very blue eyes, kind upstanding Helen whose face speaks generosity, and Dorothy, so picturesque, with her curls and gaily striped overall. A whole posse of Forrest Stores employees came in at once, about ten of them. I feel this kitchen (the first in Surrey) will presently be crowded.

In the evening Miss Davey, formerly the Principal of a Physical Training College for girls in Kensington, came to see us. She described the terrible adventures she had trying to evacuate her thirty pupils when war came. The government commandeered her premises almost immediately. She was down in her little Cornish cottage and despairingly tried to evacuate there. She stuffed girls into various farmhouses – distances were great, staff disgruntled, there was no proper hockey field, etc. Finally she secured premises at Bournemouth. And after two pleasant terms came the Blitz, the cry of the parents, 'Why choose the coast?' And the enterprise is broken up. Her money was all in it. Now it is vanished, and she finds she is just too old to get a job (I think she is forty-five). It is a sad case. I hope she will turn to the domestic side. I expect she could get into a hotel.

Tuesday, 28 April

We bomb Rostock and they bomb Bath – lovely grey old Bath! The churches and domes are smashed in Malta, and every single building of the Knights of St John is destroyed. This system of tit for tat between us and them terrifies me. Is the whole world to become a mass of rubble?

Last night it was Norwich. I hope they did not get the cathedral.

Thursday, 30 April

During these brilliant spring days we are experiencing big nightly raids. These are all reprisals. We have done so much damage at Rostock that it is a closed town. Firemen and troops are still pouring water on it. The casualties at Lübeck are officially stated to be 500.*

Falling asleep, one wonders where the terror will next begin. Who will die, who will be wounded, who will feel their hearts beat madly?

Friday, 1 May

Washed up sixty plates at the children's kichen. Later walked with Robin among fresh green hawthorns in the Park. But

* Rostock and its port quarter of Warnemünde on the Baltic coast housed important aircraft factories, including the Heinkel works where the first jet plane was tested in 1939. The historic Hanseatic port city of Lübeck had been devastated by firestorms on 28 March, when 400 tons of bombs were dropped by RAF Bomber Command. Retaliatory raids by the Luftwaffe on the comparable historic cities of Exeter, Bath, Norwich, York and Canterbury were dubbed 'the Baedeker raids' after the well-known series of travellers' guides.

much time was occupied by my soldier waving his hand to show just where the Hun invading could bring his tanks, here and there, quite easily avoiding the road and using the pastoral slopes all round us.

Part of the GHQ Stop Line which roughly followed the base of the North Downs in Surrey, this anti-tank ditch dug in July 1940 was near Farnham.
Photograph © IWM H2473

It is exciting to hear that the French have got a message through to us at last. It is from their Trade Unions to the world on May Day.

'We do not ask for pity,' it says, 'we ask you only to keep your confidence in us. We have had no part in the betrayal. It is by force, and by the threat of starvation, that our people are driven to work for Germany. Think a little of us: a great deal if you can, and remember you are working for comrades in danger of their lives.'

Sunday, 3 May

We are slowly and surely losing Burma.

The Japs are still refusing to give lists of the prisoners in Hong Kong and Singapore, so Muriel still waits in agony of mind, as do a thousand other mothers.

Monday, 4 May

Today, the question of carrying dinner from the communal kitchen across the street to the bank manager, who must not leave his bank, came up, and I offered to take it, and had quite a thrill of pleasure at the idea. The New Order, of course, is a world in which we will all do more, infinitely more, for each other.

Sara writes telling me of a terrible accident at Pembroke Dock. One Garrett, a great friend of hers, was lecturing on bombs. One exploded, and the nineteen troops listening were all killed, as was Garrett. Terrible.

Our troops in Burma seem to be very hard pressed.

Tuesday, 5 May

The eight o'clock news gave the information that we had occupied Madagascar. This is good.

'The Burma campaign was a long, grim, delaying battle, to exact from the Japs the highest possible price in casualties for each mile yielded.'

'Ernest von Kugel, claiming to be one of the German pilots

who bombed Exeter on Sunday, broadcast to the German people yesterday in these terms: "It was a night of horror for the people of Exeter. When I approached this town, the bright reflection of fires on the horizon guided me. Over the town itself I saw whole streets of houses on fire, flames bursting out of windows and doors, devouring the roofs. People were running everywhere . . .

"We thought of the thousands of men, women and children, victims of our deadly visit. But we thought, too, of the Führer, and the word of command he gave. He had said, 'Revenge!' With cool calcuation, we carried out our orders."'

Thirty-four people lunched at the Communal Kitchen today. Helen begged me not to write to the local paper about this enterprise, in case people all over the place should leap into buses and come to Shere.

Wednesday, 6 May

This afternoon, hearing a big explosion and numerous explosions overhead, I went into the garden shelter, which was full of dead leaves. I felt very safe. The noise of the planes, and the firebells ringing, was not very good for our invalid below, who had recourse to brandy.

Friday, 8 May

I hear from Muriel that a letter – a kind of farewell – written 14 January by Eudo in Singapore has come. He sends me his greetings, among others. I have felt like tears all day.

Alice writes that her son-in-law is, after eight months, still flying over Germany, somewhat nerve-wracked, but unable to get relief, 'for lack of trained pilots'.

Sunday, 10 May

I have just been sitting, Robin opposite me, listening to Churchill's long talk. To my great disappointment, there was no special message to women.

Churchill spoke with much vim, and did not sound tired. His account of the future bombing of German cities was terrible. (Robin interrupts and says Adolf will have no appetite for his breakfast.)

Monday, 11 May

Sad news this morning. Dulcie has got a telegram saying her young husband is missing.

We must hope he is a prisoner. I'm so sorry for the pretty fair-haired girl, crying her heart out in an Edinburgh flat, 'and thinking of him,' writes her mother, 'as coming down in flames.'

I *cannot* forget this: will her life be shadowed for always, or but for a time?

Tuesday, 12 May

Came to tea today Charlotte R. – an officer in the ATS. She was in charge of a religious weekly newspaper, and now she is in a new world, in an Ack-Ack* battery where the girls work and eat with men. Charlotte is ten times brighter than she was, uses lipstick, and looks nice in her khaki kit. 'Tis a big adventure indeed.

* Anti-aircraft fire. 'Ack-Ack' comes from a First World War phonetic alphabet used in signalling.

Sunday, 17 May

In this most dismal war, letters from friends are the greatest joy. In Holland, the Nazis have sent the Dutch army officers and men into concentration camps – the old, loyal Regulars. Also four hundred hostages, important folk – not, I hope, my friend Ada – have been seized.

Monday, 18 May

The country shines with blossom. Thousands of white candles are on the tall tree in the lane. Letter from Cis about the missing Jim Cameron. Apparently the Squadron Leader wrote to Dulcie, and said that on this flight – to Warnemünde – Jim was acting as wireless operator. The customary signal to say they were over the Channel did not arrive. They have just vanished, that crew.

Grace says that her boy was flying over Rostock and Warnemünde, and for once was completely exhausted, slept for hours after, and wrote admitting that the flak sent up against them was 'about as bad as I shall ever see'.

Many are saying that our airmen are often overworked and fly too long.

Sunday, 24 May

In spite of having the very barest of necessities from the grocer and other tradesmen, I find my weekly bills are pre-war, or slightly more.

I hear on the wireless that a crowd paraded in Trafalgar Square today, calling out for another front: a second front.

This seems to me quite impossible at present.

Met Mr W., the vice president of the Stock Exchange today. We waited together in the leafy churchyard while the Rector became more and more oblivious of the time within.

Mr W. said that business was not so bad as one might have expected on the Stock Exchange. He says eleven souls are on fire-watching duty in his office; he himself takes his turn and has a Lilo mattress.

He advised me to go to Moorgate when next in London, and look at the ruins in Fore Street. The City consists of 650 acres of which, he told me, 300 acres were blitzed.

Monday 25 May

The usual bank holiday depression is hanging over the village, which is enveloped in rain. General Stilwell says we were pushed out of Burma in a most humiliating way and must reconquer it.*

Who can do this but America? And, oh Lord, how long?

Nothing has been heard of Jim Cameron, or the crew of his bomber. I keep thinking of the fair-haired young wife, who sits for hours distraught.

Tuesday, 26 May

The charwoman arrived in misery; her husband has sudden orders for abroad – and no embarkation leave, as he has just had leave. 'I told little Jimmy he would not see his daddy for ages

* US Army General Joseph W. Stillwell, whose abrasive manner earned him the sobriquet 'Vinegar Joe' and whose command was characterised by difficult relations both with the Chinese leader Chiang Kai Shek and with the British Commander in the Far East, General Archibald Wavell, whom he considered overly cautious.

and ages.' Her eyes filled with tears. 'And my husband isn't really as strong as I am.' Difficult to say just the right thing to her.

Wednesday, 27 May

Tonight I hear that the offensive may have begun in Libya. And it is so hot! Poor Basil.

Sunday, 31 May

Robin has just rushed in at 8.15 to say the martins have arrived again, and are once more hovering above our bedroom window. Amazing the way they return every year to our yellow wall.

Yesterday, apparently, more than 1,000 bombers set forth for Cologne, and bombed it for an hour and a half. One thousand! 'Enough to send people mad,' Robin said soberly.

The stern announcement from Churchill that this vengeance shall extend from city to city must disturb the Germans. One thinks of the bombers being wheeled out of the hangars, of the young men climbing in, all over Britain.

Tuesday, 2 June

Troubled again by my visit to Nora to have my hair done. She can't pay her rent, and the landlord of the shop won't meet her, 'so I just don't send the money'.

Saturday, 6 June

May Sinclair has been here since Wednesday. She spoke of her trip to Russia in the garden yesterday evening, while fifteen friends of mine sat round and were fascinated by her account of her adventures.

The evening before, we had had a session with Bey. She worships Russia (and hasn't been there). Bey became very defiant whenever May said such things as that 'police control was universal', 'the people looked shabby and depressed', etc.

May received a telegram saying that her boy Jack, RAF, was just leaving for training overseas. The war presses on her heavily: 'I sometimes feel almost insane about it.' We agreed that our waking hours were most depressed nowadays. I feel so much better for her visit.

Robin is out on a Home Guard exercise in his hot khaki uniform.

I am *always* thinking of Basil in the battle.

Monday, 8 June

A lovely drive down to Picket Post. We went in the Royal Blue bus. At Southampton I again gazed sorrowfully at the once hospitable little hotel opposite the bus stop. It is now an ugly ruin.

The Forest is unusually quiet. People have given up their cars, and only military traffic goes by.

News had just come from Peter that three officers of the East Surreys had been seen safe and well in Singapore, two days before the surrender. That is really good news, though the poor mother is still despondent. I lay awake looking at Peter's fishing library, and was so thankful to be here, away from my own sink.

Tuesday, 9 June

To Bournemouth. They had bombs four days ago, and there were two huge craters in the gardens and many dilapidated houses.

In a private garden, three ladies sat last Saturday afternoon, tranquilly drinking tea. The bomb fell, and they were all killed.

Thursday, 11 June

I ought to copy a paragraph from May's letter:

'Tell Robin it would do him good to see the BBC working on their allotments in Regents Park, all most beautifully done – fair maids and talented announcers all gardening away for all they're worth.'

Saturday, 13 June

Practical work is what is wanted and asked for from women of sixty like me. Just washing up old dingy forks and spoons at the children's kitchen and dipping countless greasy plates into greasy water. It's all. It's all. No thought, no anxious mental consideration, no reading of poetry, no comment on the war or anything else, no account of what is being read is needed – just the soap and the water and the tea towel!

Lunch news was that our army is locked fast with the German army in the desert. God help our side!

Monday, 15 June

This evening on the wireless there were grave hints about a big reverse for us in Libya.*

* 'Black Saturday' 13 June, was a decisive moment in the Battle of Gazala, which lasted from 26 May to 21 June. In a major push beginning on 11 June, Rommel forced the withdrawal of the Guards Brigade and destroyed or disabled more than 220 British tanks. Further withdrawals over the next few days laid Tobruk open to the German advance.

Inventive posters encouraged people from all walks of life to 'Dig for Victory'.
Photograph © IWM PST2893

I felt suddenly very hot, and then cold, shivering, as the idea that Basil might be prisoner came to me. I felt suddenly as if I were dying, and dissolving into thin air. A stiff drink, which I immediately fetched, pulled me round sufficiently to go through the evening. I have never had this feeling before. Slept very badly, and was very cold all night. We were warned by a great manly voice, very severe, that we must prepare for 'disturbing news'. Of course I do not know if Basil is in the line or not.

Wednesday, 17 June

Was very angry with two little village lads when I saw them this evening, watching a really lovely tame pigeon strutting by the churchyard wall in the clear mild evening. The bird was ringed. It showed great confidence. One boy took up a large stone, and was going to throw it at it. I stopped him in time. He said, 'I want it for my dinner!' I had to speak very sharply to him.

Rommel has now the initiative in Libya. Basil may be in it all. It is impossible to think much of details – too ghastly.

Thursday, 18 June

From a letter in today, Sara writes: 'Weymouth was dreadful when I visited it the other day. Except for the blue sea, and even that is not so good, seen through line after line of wire entanglement. Then half our terrace is flat on the ground and the sight gave me a shock from the distant train.'

Friday, 19 June

Basil's airgraph this morning was *so* welcome – but dated 29 May.

Now where is he? The Germans claim a great many prisoners. We have evidently had a severe setback and Tobruk is again surrounded. I think of Basil all the time, and wonder what he is doing. He would be very calm and sensible whatever happened.

To Guildford, and went to a film. George Formby, quite funny, and there was a good Blitz film. How the Blitz lends itself to filming – the crashings and the zoomings! There were some amazing pictures of the tube stations full of people sheltering.

Saturday, 20 June

To see my doctor. He told me his partner (already rushed to death) might be called up. 'At any rate he would get a rest.'

Anybody wanting to know the condition of England in June 1942 might remember that people are still drifting out of all sorts of jobs, and of houses, and out of partnerships. I heard of a sad case today. A very old public-spirited lawyer and his wife are losing their housemaid, and the cook threatens to leave also. 'I,' says he, 'could go and live at the Working Men's Club, I suppose, as I am its President. But you, my dear?'

News from Libya is all bad.

Sunday, 21 June

After a bad night, thinking how horrid would be the sight of a telegraph boy, the bell pealed, and there was a man on the step, but the message he held was gold, and I knew it to be a birthday greeting.

I haven't enjoyed being sixty at all. Life's now all jobs I don't like, and don't do well, but the worst of it is the continual background of England's defeats, in spite of our bombastic speeches. Very thankful that Harry is out of Singapore, and Jenny. And that Robin and I are together and that he has splendid health.

I have just been in the heat to the village to post some letters. All morning the ARP, complete with helmets, worked a pump under my window, for a practice. When I walked up the hill, six Spitfires flew over me, and as I write, another drones outside.

Later: To our intense surprise and dismay, on the six o'clock wireless comes the news that Tobruk has already fallen.*

The Hun claims 25,000 prisoners, including several Generals.

I think Basil is not there. But this will affect all his future – the struggle will be longer, the endurance will be greater – one simply cannot understand it yet.

Tuesday, 23 June

To Wentworth. Dickie told us that a Hun plane, anxious to drop a mine in Portsmouth harbour, had been chased inland, so he let it drop on the land. Two whole streets of the city were destroyed.

Thursday, 25 June

Went up to London for the first time in many months. It cheered me to find my young sister so smart and attractive in

* Rommel took Tobruk in a surprise attack on 21 June. The Allies did not retake it again until 11 November.

her Glengarry hat of scarlet straw. We lunched at Marshall's, with a brief side-glance at the horror of what *was* John Lewis. Then, resolved on a pious pilgrimage to the office in Paternoster Row, where the *British Weekly* was first started, we leapt on a bus and went down to St Paul's.

The desolation at the back of the great cathedral is truly frightful. Yes, it frightened me, as I stood looking across the great space full of ruins. A solitary tower, a tiny bit of a house with a curtain at the ghostly window, then – nothing as far as the eye could see.

I felt that if I poked my shoe under some of the rubble by my feet, I should come upon a lock of hair or a baby's rattle. If it had not been Mildred with me, I think I should have wept. What hopes have sunk upon this ground! What loved possessions have been burned! What kind and gentle people have been killed, what tidy office arrangements have been blasted, what valuable papers destroyed! What feelings of fear and indignation hang round these lost acres, what emotions of terror and despairing farewell. Yet St Paul's stands intact, proud and glorious.

Later, gazing at the ruins of Paternoster Row, we thought of our young and ambitious and delicate father, mounting the office stairs at No. 27 (entirely vanished now as if it had never been!).

Determined to have a good tea after our sorrow, we asked the Oxford Street bus conductor to put us down near Buzzards. 'It's blown to hell, lady!' was the cheerful remark. And we presently passed by a dreadful hole.

So we went to Barballion's in Bond Street, and had good cakes, and felt refreshed. As we hurried for a bus again, and read two very discouraging placards scrawled on boards, one about the raid on London which Mildred had heard in the night, her customary light-hearted manner broke, and she shuddered and said, 'It is all horrible.'

Tuesday, 30 June

How do we bear ourselves in these days of dreadful crisis? Sebastopol seems about to fall,* the Rommel campaign seems to go in Axis favour. The news is exceedingly grave.

I sit writing this; the sky outside (9.30) is very pensive and grey, after a brisk thunderstorm. Robin, in his dark grey coat and grey flannel trousers, looks very tired. Perhaps it is the heat.

From Joan K's Hove letter this morning: 'Down here we are living in the shadow of a horrible bogey of compulsory evacuation.† It's too grim for words, and would mean just leaving the flat *unlocked* and just as it is – so even if it was still standing on one's possible return, you can bet it will be well looted.'

Wednesday, 1 July

The papers say that children are to be kept at school all holidays, so that the mothers may go on with their war work.

This great edict must be the work of a purely male mind. Village school children at any rate only go to school for so many hours a day, and their mothers are kept at home keeping house, all of them here, unless there is an aunt or young grannie to supervise. Very bad, too, for the tired teachers. The youngsters

* The Black Sea port of Sebastopol (now Sevastopol) in the Crimea had been under siege since the end of October 1941. The Russian forces surrendered on 4 July.

† Compulsory evacuation was considered for South Coast towns which would be in the front line of a cross-Channel invasion, but was never implemented.

are quite conscious that something unusual is on, and take advantage of it. They are as wild and naughty as they can be, eating together at the school kitchen in the village hall, instead of sitting quietly having lunch in their cottages. I imagine the teachers would refuse.

And from today's paper:

'Police were called to keep order in Nottingham Street, Melton Mowbray's main thoroughfare, yesterday, when women in a crowd estimated at 4,000 fought for strawberries sold from two stalls.'

Thursday, 2 July

Surely one of the blackest days of the war. Sebastopol has fallen after an epic defence. Auchinleck has issued a manifesto to his men, the tone of which strikes fear to the heart. (Backs to the wall once more.)*

Lyttelton's speech of defence seems very feeble.† We have been making Crusader tanks, which are no use; we have not yet put a big anti-tank gun into production. Nor have we dive-bombers. The muddle seems ghastly. And our men are fighting what may be a decisive battle now in the Egyptian heat, under a sultry sky, out-gunned, out-tanked.

I cannot think, taking it all in – the fall of Sebastopol, and the fact that we are fighting against heavy odds in Libya – that we can *ever* have so black a day again.

* General (later Field Marshal) Claude Auchinleck, Commander in Chief in the Middle East from July 1941 to August 1942, when he was relieved of his command. He had greater success as CiC India, from January to May 1941 and again from June 1943 until 1947.

† Oliver Lyttelton, 1st Viscount Chandos, Minister of State for the Middle East in 1941–2 and Minister of Production 1942–5.

Friday, 3 July

Rather better news, thank God, this afternoon. Rommel has not got through yet, anyway, and has even retired a few miles, and our planes seem to be superior to theirs. I feel slightly comforted.

The scope of this war indeed is so vast that the average person, busy all day, *cannot* take it in. I should have liked to have written more about the siege of Sebastopol here, but have had no time.

Sunday, 5 July

News from Egypt is still tense. I suppose the strain will snap this week. Strange to think that when my airgraphs reach Basil (as God please they may) he will know the result.

Tuesday, 7 July

Watched the pandemonium in the children's kitchen from my seat at the money table. Grown-ups flying about in the greatest haste; children holding out plates in a desperate manner, as if to say, 'Don't forget *me*.' I grow very severe these days and insist on 'please' before I take their orders. Thirty-two to lunch (grown-ups).

Letters in from Princeton. Margaret writes, 'Now that we are in the war, we are certainly taking it seriously, and it is quite amazing to see how many people feel inspired to co-operate, and how few are upset and indignant about restrictions and rationing.

'We have just started on the gasoline rationing and are aware of how spoiled we have been in the past. When we lived at

Meadow Gardens we used gasoline at the rate of 250 gallons a month. The card for which we applied last month entitled us to 21 gallons from now to 30 June.'

Saturday, 11 July

A cable in. When a voice on the telephone said this, I felt very faint, supposing it was bad news. But they would not telephone that, would they? News was joyful – from Basil in the desert: 'I am well and safe.'

Lovely. Of course I don't know on what date it was sent. But lovely. Now the fighting is starting again. It was a pity, the *Times* military correspondent says, that we had to pause, as Rommel and Co were so fatigued. But possibly we were too.

Sunday, 12 July

D. said that many Wren officers cry themselves to sleep. Being in the Women's Services is not all joy. A lot of loneliness and hard work.

We are greatly amused by extracts (given in today's *Sunday Dispatch*) from the handbook given to the American troops coming to Britain. Warnings are given about the deadly damp climate, of the reserve and silence and soft deceiving manner of the Briton (but we are tough). 'The English language,' says the clever writer, 'did not spread across oceans and over the mountains and jungles and swamps of the world because these people were pantywaists ... You will not be able to tell the British much about "taking it". They are not particularly interested in taking it now.'

Strong warnings are given against boasting. 'If somebody looks in your direction and says, "He's chucking his weight about", you can be pretty sure you are off base. That is time to pull in your ears.'

Tuesday, 14 July

Mr Dodds told me a story. In Aldershot an American soldier entered a pub and said: 'Some iced beer, please. And fetch it as quick as you can. As quick as you got out of Tobruk the other day!'

As soon as the sentence crossed his lips a hefty labourer standing by felled him across the counter.

'A very good thing!' cried Mr Dodds' wife as we motored along the Merrow road. 'Excellent, I'm glad,' I replied from the back of the car.

One million and a half Americans or possibly two million are expected over here in due course, and Mr Dodds is coping with the hut question. They will not accept our standard of hutment. They want superior washing facilities, more room, better beds, and huts not placed so close together.

To see Aunt Gerty at Woking. Here is a true story of her today.

An old lady of seventy-four or so looks out of her window and espies on her quiet road a car containing six men, followed by men with a lorry. One man comes to her front door with a government permit. They had come (without any preliminary warning) to take away the railings that edged the path and the tradesman's entrance.

The old lady is not annoyed. 'If it will help to win the war I am glad,' she murmurs and as they are working away with a blow torch, she causes the cook to take out cups of tea.

Strange world; she had gazed at the iron railings placidly that morning, then by noon they had been masterfully removed. (What next?).

I almost forgot to record my impressions, standing on Guildford Station platform today, and watching a number of passengers walking from the London train to the ticket office and exit.

These faces, it was clear, did not belong to persons who *made wars*. On them was no fiery resolution, no concentrated thought.

I saw the English after a hot hour's journey from town on a July morning – Hitler's War 1942; and the adjectives to apply to their countenances were 'humble, worried, deprecating, gentle, plain, modest'. There was nobody, as far as I could see, who held himself upright in a military fashion. The majority of faces were very tired, and many had a bad colour, and almost all were everyday and homely. The mass of our people are not interested in war, unless they have to be, and then it only fatigues and upsets them. At the same time, behind these nondescript faces, I *know* there lurks a silent resolve to fight the thing through.

Thursday, 16 July

From Phyllis Hazeldine's letter this morning. 'I have been in awful trouble since last I wrote, having lost my beloved little sergeant-pilot son. He and the whole four boys of his crew never returned from air operations over Emden on the night of 26 June, and nothing has been heard of them since. It nearly killed me, all the more as the suspense was terrible, waiting and hoping against hope.'

Basil's last airgraph, 29 June, runs thus: 'I hope you have not been worrying about me. There has been no need, but it has been difficult to write. I am well, but rather tired, as we have had a fairly sleepless time ... You ask me about the heat. I don't seem to mind it.'

The Russian news is very grave. 'They are pushing towards Stalingrad,* the solar plexus of our country,' writes a Russian paper, putting the crisis clearly.

Saturday, 18 July

No real news of the battle in Egypt yet. This is a great strain on us and I felt suddenly sick with fear yesterday about 6.30; really shivering with vague, sharp apprehension.

Monday, 20 July

The eight o'clock news was appallingly serious about Russia. They are yielding town after town. I heard it as I hastily tidied the library. Sibyl's bedroom door was open, and she heard it mournfully, too.†

Tuesday, 21 July

I don't think I convey enough in these pages my belief that We Shall Win.

Friday, 24 July

Petronelle, aged eighteen, is doing land work. From her letter:

'We sleep on the ground on straw palliases. Isn't it surprising how quickly we become accustomed to things? Whereas ten days ago I would have screamed if I saw an earwig, I now nonchalantly pluck black beetles from my sponge, earwigs

* Known as Tsaritsyn until 1925, and as Volgograd since 1961.
† Robin's sister Sibyl was visitng them at the time.

In order to free men for the armed forces, women worked not just on farms and in factories but in heavy industry too, as in this shipyard.
Photograph © IWM HU36242

from my pockets and spiders from my pillow. We go out to work for farmers in gangs. I have now risen to be forewoman of a gang.'

Girls are the gainers in this war.

Saturday, 25 July

The Soviet communiques speak this morning of 'fierce, bloody battles' before Rostov. The Germans say they have got it.*

Sunday, 26 July

The paper is full of horrors:

'The Germans have just decreed in Belgium, where there has never been a Jewish question, and where equality of race and religious opinion is established by law, a series of new measures against the Jews. In the province of Antwerp Jews are forbidden to enter a theatre or a cinema, to attend concerts or lectures, or appear in any public meeting place.'

And this: 'Children over eight years of age are among thousands of refugees from Axis-conquered countries in Europe who have been rounded up in France during the past week and sent to concentration camps. They are to be sent eventually to Upper Silesia. It is the biggest round-up since the Blackshirts took over the policing of France, and was made by French police and German occupation and Blackshirt troops.'

How optimistic we are! Take this advertisement in today's *Observer*:

* Rostov, on the River Don, had been taken by the Germans on 21 November 1941 and retaken by the Russians six days later. On 23 July Germany captured the city for the second time, and held it until 14 Feburary 1943.

> CHANNEL ISLANDS. In response to numerous applications, Jersey and Guernsey Airways Ltd have opened a waiting list for those desirous of returning to the Channel Islands by air as soon as the Islands are free of enemy occupation. Applications should be sent to Jersey Airways, Ltd.

All the same I am never pessimistic as to the result.

I have enjoyed, in spite of the Russian news, this quiet Sunday. But it is quite impossible to picture the Russian battle: the look of the terrain, the width and breadth of the Don, the faces of the furious combatants.

My Don in Aberdeenshire I love better.

Monday, 27 July

A postcard from the Scots Greys' Adjutant's wife. She says her husband has cabled to her: 'All merry and bright. Leading a gypsy life. Lovely weather. Little cause for worry.'

That is good, and there comes an airgraph from Basil, 3 July. 'You would be surprised how early I get up nowadays, so the days are very long. The great times during the day are the "brew-up"; when a halt is called we all leap from the truck, get out an old perforated petrol can half full of sand, and soak the sand with petrol. This makes a first-class fire – better than a primus, which lasts for twenty minutes or so; then we put on the other half of the petrol can full of water, and when it boils, put in the milk, tea and sugar, and then dip in your pint mug – it is a most refreshing drink. Personally, I'm very confident about the final outcome of this battle. We seem to have a considerable numerical advantage in the air, among other things.'

Thursday, 30 July

Just sending Jenny a letter from *The Times* by a Mrs Spooner, who was in Singapore at the time of its agony. It is about the brave ladies of Malaya, who showed courage and endurance. Many British women were 'killed at the last, attempting to escape when the Japanese were on their doorstep.'

Barbara writes from her home in Blewbury: 'Have now got first part of vast equipment for First Aid Party – gas-suit, service respirator, tin hat.' She adds, 'My life is a strange mixture; when not putting dried blood on tomatoes, I'm making a compost heap or new chicken run, or mattocking, or digging, or weeding or nettle cutting. It never ends. I suppose harvesting begins on Sunday, if fine.'

Goebbels says: 'We still consider a British-American invasion on the Continent a crazy enterprise, which would be accompanied by the most disastrous consequences for Britain and the United States . . .

'We offer the British a cordial welcome. We hope they will bring some Americans with them. The German soldiers are looking forward with pleasure to making it clear to the Yankees that for them, too, Europe is forbidden territory.'

Friday, 31 July

To see my good neighbour of eighty odd. She said she had been awake all night thinking about the Russian battles. When first married she lived in Russia: 'It was very nice then.'

Mrs F. said it was impossible to be happy. I agreed, and remarked that the war hung like a burden on all our backs, and was never lifted off for a single second.

Saturday, 1 August

Rachel writes from the Links Hotel, Thurlestone:

'We strolled out on the cliffs last night and saw an amazing panorama, a very flamboyant sunset over Plymouth all sprinkled with their balloon barrage, as big as London, I was told. To the left the tiny Eddystone Lighthouse, and a microscopic destroyer in the sea.'

Cissy has been to Inverness, and there she met a Norwegian officer, who showed her snapshots of his wife and four fair-haired children, and described his escape from the hands of the Gestapo. He said the spirit in Norway is wonderful, even the children turn their backs on the Germans. 'This coldness is our only weapon, and the Germans hate it.'

Monday, Bank Holiday

I hear from Mildred that Rosemary, who arrived in Derby the Sunday before last, discovered that there had been a bad raid the night before, and twenty-five workers in the Rolls Royce works (where she is now attached) had been killed. There was another raid that night, and one the next night. Rosemary has to stand up at her work all day long. Personally I doubt whether her health will stand it.

Jack, fresh from Malta, talked a little about it. 'Will they give in?' 'Never, unless supplies fail.' 'Are the Hun pilot prisoners truculent?' 'No. Many are mere boys, not sure what they are fighting for.'

Wednesday, 5 August

I went to Haslemere by bus, a lovely journey. Such gracious red houses at Chiddingfold, such golden harvest fields, such leafy ways, such a merry girlish air about the happy bus conductress, singing to herself.

Found Kitty in the kitchen, putting the last touches to her lunch. The table was set for nine: four little children under six were coming, their fathers two naval officers.

Looking at the children, three little girls, I wondered what world they would live in.

Kitty looked exhausted. Two naval officers are billeted on her. And she finished washing up the dinner dishes at 9.20, and her feet just ache and ache. She is sixty, and has angina pectoris, and she is game for anything.

Thursday, 6 August

The sunset is radiant pure gold. The garden is full of heavy green trees, and I can see some pale green apples on one of them. Robin is at the D—s, explaining his ideas of having rockets by the wayside for – well, I'd better not write about that here.

Tuesday, 11 August

Last night I was sitting peacefully opposite Bey Hyde, about 8.30, hearing all about her temporary postman's job, when the bell rang.

Opening the front door I was faced by no less than five men. Colonel B., Mr Leager, head of the Home Guard, and two other NCOs, local Home Guards, and also Major R.*

He spoke. 'We want to see your flat. We want an office and a place where the picket can sleep.'

* Probably Major Rayne.

I suppose my face showed my perplexity, for Major R., straightening his pleasant mouth, added, 'We've got to be very FIRM.'

I was quick enough to mention that our garage, now stuffed with furniture, was made originally as a bedroom.

Then they liked the ping-pong attic and will take that too.

It quite shook me up, feeling that they were going to insist on the ground floor flat. In that case I think we should have had to leave.

Where should we go? The sisters-in-law are too near the coast. The men would inevitably ruin our house. I could not sleep very well. I should hate to leave home, and my pretty cream and blue bedroom, and all the photographs and books in it.

Colonel B. said rapidly that they would, in a case of invasion, enter the lower flat. And that in any case they might want our garage. And also might require us to clear the luggage loft. (Where should we put our stuff? There is little warehouse room.)

I am feeling sad about Russia, and about the bad news which we seem to have all the time. I feel the war will go on for another eight or nine years at least, and I feel I may reach my seventieth year before it is over.

Wednesday, 12 August

Joan King-George of Hove came to tea and told us that hundreds of invasion barges are lying in the creeks and harbours of the south coast. She described them as painted grey, with seats for the troops round the sides, and room for a tank and gun inside. She said she saw a line of these invasion barges from a hill the other day, and it stretched along the sea as far as the eye could reach. From each barge floated a balloon.

This is real NEWS to me, and thrilling.

Joan's husband is in a high position in the Home Guard. He thinks that the Mayor of Brighton will be unable to fix up the evacuation of the quarter of a million people that dwell in his group – Worthing, Shoreham, Hove and Brighton. The mothers and young children, yes, they can be arranged for – but the whole question of a million – no, it seems impossible. The idea, of course, is to clear the coast of civilians; it is bound to be shelled. Also the soldiers might easily be sheltered in the houses if necessary. Joan, who was looking very ill, can't make up her mind whether to go away now or to stay. Her son-in-law has flown back from America, and the bomber went up to the sub-stratosphere and the passengers were all in oxygen masks.

Friday, 14 August

What a wonderful country is England! Edna writes that she is going to the Federal Union Summer School at Dartington Hall in Devon. In spite of government entreaties that we should not travel – in spite of the crowded trains, in spite of rationing trouble, in spite of the fact that nearly everybody is working from morning to night – the Summer School will be held!

Two conversations in the bus today:

The wife of the Angel of the Catholic Apostolic Church: 'The war is all over the world now. It is Armageddon – it is the judgement. But people don't realise it.'

Then: 'I had nothing in the house to give my husband for dinner yesterday, so he had vegetables. And do you know, in the evening, he was quite limp! Hadn't had his proper dinner, you see.'

Sunday, 16 August

The lonely soldier came – he had some of Barbara's honey for tea. He thinks the Second Front will open soon. I wonder.

The effect of hearing of Russia's slow retreat morning after morning has spoiled this lovely part of the summer for me, and already Netley Woods show faint hints of autumn gold.

Monday, 17 August

I went to see Mrs Rayne, who has two sons missing. She said she had been in Swansea, and that was the most blitzed place of the many bombed towns she had seen. She described it very well. She said, 'It's like a film.'

Her missing airman son had told her that if they land in occupied territory they have full instructions as to how to proceed. Robert seemed to know that there is a set of people in France who work to help the English and to get them back.

I returned down the sunny hill, but first of all my hostess took me over the golden harvest field, and began to talk of her lost boys. Wilfred – supposed to be drowned. Robert – where? Had he come down in 'the drink'? She explained, poor thing, with haunted dark eyes, that she was not going to allow herself to hope, only perhaps to be disappointed. Far better not. She was glad she had all these land girls, one from a big draper's shop, one an heiress. One fair-haired girl I saw reading on the terrace was studying *Othello*, hoping to go up to see the Czech who takes the part. All the girl workers are conscientious and tireless. ('Would you like me to go out again and help you? Shall I? What field do we cut tomorrow?')

Robin told me that he had just heard over the wireless that

Churchill had been to see Stalin in Moscow and was just back. *Mirabile dictu*. What did they say to one another?*

The Germans tonight claim the whole of the Don bend.

Tuesday, 18 August

Mayo writes: 'Yesterday had a horrid experience in Salisbury. I was quite near the bomb and in the street and saw the smoke from what they hit. People were very calm, but I didn't feel at all so. I saw the girls fire-watching on Woolworths' roof, as cool as cucumbers during the raid.'

Irene came to tea. She and Robin disputed the idea of the Second Front; Irene thinks it is all bunkum, but that we and the Yankees will bomb Germany to blazes and stop the war.

Robin *au contraire* says in prophetic mood that the Second Front will open in early September: we shall land in Brittany, the Americans will land at Bordeaux.†

Wednesday, 19 August

Much excited by news of our commando raid on Dieppe.‡ With what light hearts did Robin and I motor out of the town, towards the south, in the winter of 1938!

* Stalin was pressing Churchill to open a second front by invading occupied France, thereby diverting German resources away from the Eastern Front. Roosevelt had promised Stalin that this would happen in 1942, although it would not in fact take place until June 1944.This meeting was the first time Churchill and Stalin had spoken face to face.

* Robin was wrong on both counts. He was a year and nine months out regarding the timing, and the D-Day landings would be in Normandy, not in Brittany or Bordeaux.

‡ In fact the raid was a failure. The likelihood is that Connie heard the BBC early morning news which announced it was taking place, but was unaware of what had actually happened. One unit, No. 4 Commando, achieved its objective and neutralised the gun battery at Varengeville; but elsewhere 3,367 Canadian landing troops and 257 British commandos were killed, wounded or captured, with further losses at sea and in the air.

Thursday, 20 August

The Home Guard has seized our garage now. Inside is our car jacked up for the duration, and a stock of winter logs. The car may find room next door, the logs will go – where?

What is happening to certain old people in this war? I heard today of two very dear to me who are grown shaky and very old and feeble and do housework as well as they can, often walking from the room hand in hand to fetch the dishes for their meal. To my horror I am told that the old darlings stand in queues for their provisions.

They have an invincible dislike of the idea of going to a hotel. Were they but established here in our local guest house all would be peace and they could live a little. It is tragic.

Sunday, 23 August

Spent much of the day hotly criticising the government's fuel plan.* Gazed at the elaborate target advertisement. Robin declared it was the work of a 'robot in an office who knows nothing of practical facts.' He kindly wished to find him, execute him and throw him on an ant heap!

Monday, 24 August

The Germans have got across the Don at last, and are nearer to Stalingrad.

* The Fuel Saving Scheme was introduced in July 1942 and encouraged people to use less coal by limiting heating and hot water use in the home. Most houses had coal-fired boilers and each household had a weekly target amount of fuel which it was supposed not to exceed.

This is very terrible. Every day during this summer we have listened to doubtful news about the Russians, but I hope against hope.

Tuesday, 25 August

From Cis's letter: 'My dear Connie, Christine (18) is looking so pretty now, why oh why can't she be living a normal life, and meeting men of her own class? But I suppose we must forget all about class now, and our girls must work as hard as men and fight too and still with the feminine handicap. Let us hope it will be a more settled world for Baby Gillian.'

From May Sinclair's letter this morning: 'This last week I have never left the office (Bush House, European Broadcasting) before 10.30 and have been there before 9.30 in the mornings ... I have taken Luminal every night to ensure sleep, and to stop the stupid dreaming which attacks me when I am tired.'*

This is surely the most amazing thing we shall ever see in print (consider its implications):

'By a special decree issued in Berlin yesterday, Hitler has appointed Thierack to be Minister of Justice, *with power to set aside all written law*.'

Thursday, 27 August

Feel very pleased to see Mother yesterday.† It was like old days, and she looked so pretty and alert for seventy-nine. The war has not really touched her.

* A trade name for phenobarbital, a barbiturate in common use as a sedative until the 1960s.

† Connie's stepmother had come down from Scotland and was staying in London.

Saturday, 29 August

We have awakened from the nightmare of feeling our flat below might have to be cleared for the Home Guard. Maurice's letter tells how *his* delightful furniture was treated by the troops who entered his Essex house. It was commandeered by the army early in the war. The men smashed up the chairs and tables for firewood.*

Bey called later, and told me the harrowing story of Hazel Hill, where troops were billeted. They smashed the linen cupboard open, and sent the sheets and towels home to their wives. The CO discovering that told the men to ask their womenkind to post back the stuff, and no questions would be asked. I spent the evening gazing at my precious things and imagining them broken and stolen by a band of brigands.

Sunday, 30 August

We read of Mr Henry Kaiser claiming a world record for speedy shipbuilding with the launching of a 10,000-ton Liberty cargo vessel twenty-four days after the keel was laid.† The harvest in Holland is bad because the Dutch farmers know that the Germans will take it. The poor little French Jewish children are being herded off into camps, and their identity cards are being got rid of. Some little things will perhaps never know who they are. This seems diabolical cruelty.

* Maurice was Connie's brother. A psychiatrist and author, he was a leading authority on the esoteric thinkers Gurdjieff and Ouspensky.

† Liberty Ships were cargo ships mass-produced in the United States. Their standardised simple design meant that they could be built as fast as the German U-boats could sink them. In November 1942 a Kaiser shipyard produced one as a publicity stunt in less than 5 days.

Monday, 31 August

Today I've been to London. I happened to have to wait for May for some time and to study the faces of the crowds was very absorbing. Oh for a paintbrush! To record the anxious downcast looks, the strained glance, the hurried step. What thousands of dowdily dressed men and women. What inadequate-looking boys with mild faces, for officers.

I liked the rude health which exuded from the Mercantile Marine, standing drinking tea at a very ramshackle counter.

Wednesday, 2 September

Walked up in the evening to see the Raynes, as I had heard the night before that a prisoner of war postcard had come from the despaired-of son, Pilot Officer Robert, lost in the dark night as they flew over Hamburg.

What joy, after the deepest despair. There has been a six week pause. All Robert's squadron felt he was gone! 'He will organise and cheer the whole camp and will get up classes,' said his fond mother to me (he was a schoolmaster). 'He does not care for external things, so will be as content as he can in Germany.'

The joy of this family would be now complete if their second missing son was accounted for, but we think Wilfred (last seen leaping from the deck of a torpedoed ship) is drowned.

Saturday, 5 September

Joy came and told me Basil has sent her from Cairo some turquoise stuff for a house coat.

Negley Farson writes warningly in the *Mail* about Russia. It is in a very serious situation. They are so *hungry*.

Monday, 7 September

Yesterday I saw the most appalling thing about the Germans that I've yet read. In Paris they hounded the Jews even out of the hospitals. The police waited while one poor woman had her baby and then turned her out. God punish them fully, as they deserve!

Tuesday, 8 September

There is much talk in the press about a State Medical Service.*

From Mrs Hopgood's talk at a tea party here yesterday: 'I don't believe men take the faintest interest in what we women talk about.'

Marna, her daughter, is very much overworked in the ATS. She is the only officer in a remote country paratroop camp, and has seventy girls to look after.

Thursday, 10 September

Mrs Rayne came to tea. She had a prisoner of war postcard from Robert in Germany telling her all his crew were killed. They were three. She had to tell the mother of one and the fiancée of another the sad truth.

She mentioned in her first letter to him that Lord Haw-Haw (of whom we are very tired) had mentioned his name among those of British prisoners. Her letter was returned by

* What was to become, in 1948, the National Health Service.

the censor's office after ten days, with a note gently pointing out that we did not want the Huns to *know* that we listen in to the German broadcasts.

Alice writes that Dulcie heard, through a friend of her husband's, that he was almost sure he saw Jim's plane flying below his, that fatal night of the raid, but not flying out of control. Dulcie wrote back to ask more questions – but by that time, alas! the airman was himself missing. It is horribly sad.

A glorious evening sunset glow beams over the green lawn, and the mauve daisies are all shining in the light. I wish every day was like this as regards weather. Mother has arrived safely in Aberdeen; I'm so thankful.

Thursday, 17 September

A letter-card from Basil written 4 September, speaking of the recent battle in Egypt. He says we had a real victory.* He is unhurt, 'but had several near misses'. The regiment did well and Montgomery himself came to congratulate a sergeant (anti-tank) who shot four tanks.

No extra sugar is to be allowed for jam-making. The countryside is thick with blackberries.

Monday, 21 September

This afternoon to the film *The First of the Few*, about R. J. Mitchell, designer of the Spitfire. Admirable.

Women and children have left Stalingrad. All must be over soon.

* The Battle of Alam el Halfa, a major reversal for Rommel and the Afrika Korps, who were forced to withdraw.

Tuesday, 22 September

To the kitchen. The faithful workers are all present; little Mollie B. with her neat golden head, and W. H. with an air of desperate energy. At the door, at a card table with a money box sits C. M.,* rather distracted and feeling the cold. At long tables, friends instinctively cluster together: the garage hands in their dungarees (who May said looked exactly like Russians); the stores assistants, pretty, fair girls, looking rather impudent; a Jewish woman and her grandchild. At one table sits the Squire's sister, very determined and ruthless under a blue hat, who kisses no-one, but does kiss her clever old black poodle; at another an exhausted mother of three, without help, begins to shake her head slightly, which shows how real is the strain on her nerves.

When the kitchen, which is in the Scouts' Hut, is left empty, it is like a battlefield.

Thursday, 24 September

Petronelle, a newly joined Wren, writes: 'We are already steeped in naval terms and traditions. This building is HMS *Pembroke III*. I belong to Effingham division and sleep in No. 20 bunk, Cabin 3, Suffolk deck. It's fun.'

From an airman's mother – he is lost: 'I am still,' she writes, 'in the depths of misery over my little baby son, and time seems to make it worse. The Air Ministry is simply ghastly about everything, absolutely no system, and half of all their letters to me appear to have been lost. They even told me he had gone to Dunkirk, when they meant Emden,

* i.e. Connie herself.

and I should never have found out the mistake, had I not, after the greatest difficulty, got in touch with the rest of the crew's parents. Now I find half his things have been stolen. His expensive Leica camera, and about £20 in cash. His brand new bicycle was returned, minus all the gadgets, and bent and broken to pieces. I have not yet succeeded in obtaining any of his private papers, so I don't know if he left behind any letters or last wishes.

'He flew on the most appalling night, as regards weather, of the whole year.'

Florence writes: 'Bournemouth is full of Americans, looking very bored. They look too well-dressed, have well-fitting uniforms, too tight, I should think, to be practical. They won't take houses unless they have got central heating, which does not say much for their toughness.'

Sunday, 27 September

Lord Hankey,* whose opinion I think very valuable, writes in today's paper:

'The prospect of a few more years of war should not dismay us. We have powerful allies, and vast reserves of strength well advanced towards development. We are already dealing our enemies heavy blows, the weight of which will increase. Above all, we have those unlimited reserves of spiritual strength ...'

The prospect of a few more years of war should not dismay us. Alas! I want to see my children!

* Maurice Hankey had been a key member of the War Cabinet during the Great War and a member of Neville Chamberlain's War Cabinet from September 1939 to May 1940.

Monday, 28 September

The Belgians seem to be half starving. They never see a potato. Thus says the *News Chronicle*. And we have sacks, a bumper crop.

Tuesday, 29 September

To the film *Mrs Miniver*. Just before the first Blitz scene, the lights in the cinema went out, and a voice from the stage said that there was an air-raid warning, and anyone who wished could leave the building. Nobody stirred, so far as I could see. It made the picture much more thrilling. An 'all clear' was sounded about ten minutes later.

The sun is shining bravely in the autumn garden, and we are listening to the six o'clock news, which announces that the Hun panzer divisions are pressing into *the* city. The Volga crossings are under fire.

Saturday, 3 October

May S. came down by tea-time, and we sat on the lawn in the mild sunshine. I asked her what was the prevailing mood of the many people she meets, and she said it was cheerful, and that Stalingrad was a long way off, and so people rather forgot it.

Sunday, 4 October

Mr Brook arrived from Exeter.* He could not get even a cup of tea at Salisbury Station, nor at Woking. 'People are not supposed to be hungry on a Sunday,' he said.

* Mr Brook was the new downstairs tenant.

At tea there was a very bright interlude indeed. Somebody mentioned Sark,* and May and Brook and I all broke out in warmest praise. Mr B. has camped out with his son (now dead, killed in the air) at the Silver Mines, a gorgeous bit of shore. We all love the steep cliffs of the island, and the quiet out-of-doors days we spent there. Brook declared he would never, never forget them, so long as he lived. He has kind eyes and a little pointed beard and a very great mass of luggage.

He told us that on the occasion of the Exeter raid ('We were six miles away and the city was lit up like a fine palace') some Home Guards captured three German airmen who had crashed. Their manner was extremely arrogant. All spoke English. One said eagerly, 'Oh, have we hit the cathedral?' The other two young men rubbed their hands together and said gleefully, 'At any rate, it's been a good raid, we've done a lot of damage.' All this so incensed the Englishmen that they killed all three there and then with their bayonets.

Wednesday, 7 October

'Have you worked out your fuel target?' was the question put in the latest Gallup Poll. Eighty-four per cent of those questioned replied 'No'.

Stalingrad holds out. More and more Romanians are pushed into the battle, and rearward troops have been pushed by the Hun into the front line.

* Sark had been much in the news, owing to a commando raid on the island which led to a series of escalating recriminations with Germany over the treatment of prisoners. Connie and Robin both felt strongly that in shackling German prisoners in retaliation for Germany having done so to those captured in the raid, Britain was losing the moral high ground over the issue. Mrs Rayne had urged Connie to write to their MP in protest about it.

To the Women's Institute. I was vexed by the lecturer's failure to mention any brave actions of our sailors, so impulsively offered our President a lecture on 'Brave Deeds of the War'. I hope I can do it.

From Edna's letter from Haywards Heath:

'When I hear of other women who have to pay £4 10/– a week in these boarding houses where there is no comfort, where they make their own beds and do their own fireless rooms, I think we are very lucky. I have a pathetic picture of an elderly worker of mine, who was dragging a skirt from shop to shop to get it ironed, as she wasn't allowed to use an iron in her boarding house, where she is perfectly wretched, with no other place to go to. Everything is full up and the landladies all arch tyrants.'

Friday, 9 October

The scene at the communal kitchen today was really very nice. Five strong soldiers were eating the meal of mince and mashed potato. Robin talked quietly to the local stores assistants opposite him and the land girls in their breeches ate with relish. 'The brotherhood of men,' I thought to myself, for the children there were actually being quiet, and not spitting out damson stones, or chucking the cutlery at each other and screaming.

Tuesday, 13 October

Curiously enough I received this morning two letters from two very old friends of my girlhood. I think women tend to cling together and to avoid any sort of estrangement in these difficult days.

I question myself closely and ask, 'What is the difference

this afternoon in our little village from days of peace? What do I see that has changed?

(1) I see many army lorries packed with soldiers. Many army waggons. Often a tank and many motor cycles.

(2) I am pleased when I see a pile of scones in the tea shops (they both tend to close constantly).

(3) I receive a tiny bit of bacon for boiling with enthusiasm at the grocer's. It is a battle to get it, and one takes what one is given.

(4) Many more ladies with shopping baskets.

(5) Dull, dismal blackout curtains at every window and no new paint – every house almost shabby.

But the antique shop shows old ivory chessmen and champagne glasses, and even a lovely green and fawn dessert service in its brave windows.

In the greengrocer's there are cauliflowers tenpence each, pears 1/– a pound and tomatoes 1/– a pound.

Friday, 16 October

Again impressed by the difficulty in going away from home. Accomplished a million chores before breakfast of porridge and coffee. Robin woke up to the fact that I was going away, and asked when I would be back.

I am writing as dusk falls gently over Mayo's garden. The high screaming note of a bomber may be heard (possibly a Liberator), but the machine is wrapped in cloud. The brightening moon is looking in through the panes.

May is putting the pony to bed, and Sibyl is exercising the red setters; enormous Barney with the noble head, large Nonie.

Saturday, 17 October

As I write (2.45) there is an alert, and great activity in the air. Walking among the bright-berried holly in the Forest today, we saw a lovely white-winged Liberator storming along the grey sky.

Sunday, 18 October

I have just been across the heath to post a card to Robin. Autumn's intense stillness was in the air, only broken by the hum of many bombers above the trees.

Yesterday the big armament works at Le Creuzot was attacked, the greatest daylight raid of the war. Lancaster crews went over and bombed for twenty minutes, very successfully: only one machine was lost.

We walked again and in the afternoon strode across the bracken and grassy slopes to look at the new aerodrome at Bransgore.*

May assured me that many nice houses – 'as nice as mine' – had been pulled down to make room for it. 'And the carefully kept gardens all trodden down.'

It looked *enormous*.

The C—s came to tea. This Colonel and his frail, bright, active little lady are doing without baths four days a week. This is a great, true sacrifice. They laugh gently about it.

The large Colonel is not so certain as he used to be that the war will soon be over.

* This was the three-runway Holmsley South airfield from which USAAF B-17 Flying Fortress heavy bombers operated, along with RAF Wellingtons and Halifaxes. RAF Typhoons and Mustangs, Royal Canadian Air Force Spitfires and Mosquitos and USAAF B-26 fighters also flew from Holmlsey on missions over occupied France.

A peaceful Sunday evening, Sibyl cooking a good supper, great wafts of country silence muffling the house, which like Noah's Ark stands in its lawn among apple trees. In daylight, beyond the hedge, riders go by, but not so many as in peace-time.

Monday, 19 October

May drives me in the trap across the flaming golden Forest to Picket Post. First I say goodbye to her friendly stable tenant, Mr Mossop.

Mr M. is gloomy. He has two proud, lovely cart horses in May's stable, Tom and Prince, and has a contract to load timber.

He can't get a single man to help him. No labour. And he can't heave the great logs himself. So he is at a standstill.

He tells me the New Forest trees will be entirely cut down very soon, if the war goes on. And he says the war is only just beginning.

He lends me the *New Statesman*; brings it up specially. Returning it, I say mildly that it's rather red in politics. Mossop says it is only pink. I wish him well.

We drive past the large new saw-mills. In the distance I can see two Italian prisoners, one each end of a long saw, working away at a tree trunk. Nearer us some Forestry maidens are marking lengths on bits of wood, and measuring with great confidence.

Sunday, 25 October

A lovely autumn day, crisp and cold. Thinking of the great offensive in Egypt. Will the war change Basil and the rest very much? It can't leave them the same.

Monday, 26 October

A day raid over Godalming this morning. John H., bomber pilot, was at our communal lunch. He was over Le Creuzot in a Lancaster the other day. He nearly got blown up as they flew low over a power station and there was such a tremendous explosion that the plane was knocked edgeways and he had difficulty in getting it back.

Wednesday, 28 October

Rosamond told me one of her three precious hens, for which she has just paid one guinea each, has been stolen at night. She can see the manly footsteps up to the hen house. A shame.

There has never been such scrounging as there is today in Britain.

Thursday, 29 October

Robin has gone into Guildford, desperately resolved to buy a really good pair of shoes, come what may.

Grace says that she simply couldn't get her airman son to talk of his experiences this time. He was awfully tired, went to bed early on his leave, and slept till ten-thirty.

Old Mrs K. to tea. She says her son, a West End physician, finds patients strained by the war and difficult to treat. 'People are beginning to lose their grip, and to let their friends go without an effort. Bills are not paid by very many. The doctor can wait.'

Monday, 2 November

Mrs Lutyens came to tea. She has been working at factories for the Ministry of Information, observing conditions for women's labour. She reports that the girls are working much too long. The lavatories in one works she was at were full of girls sleeping on the floor. She says the health of these women will be much worse than the returning troops.

Tuesday, 3 November

It is 6.05. The light is on, the fire is burning brightly. The wireless is speaking of an advance in Egypt. The news is good. What is Basil doing? I picture him in a little tent giving blood transfusions far from the battlefield.

'It is an extraordinary sight,' says the BBC observer. 'Shells by the thousand are going over to the enemy – the Eighth Army in its might.'

7.15 p.m. A bell rang: I answered it and was handed a wire for Robin. 'I fear it is bad news,' said the man who brought it.

It said: 'Regret to report that Capt. B. E. Miles RAMC is wounded and is placed on the seriously ill list. Oct 28th. Letter follows shortly.'

Wednesday, 4 November

I feel I must try in the middle of this anxiety to go on writing this. But I don't know if I shall be able to do it.

Captain Basil Miles, taken during his service in North Africa.
Photograph courtesy of Mary Wetherell

Thursday, 5 November

We hear that Basil sustained a gunshot wound in the chest. He is at No. 19 General Hospital and *if so desired*, we may write.

It is an un-understanding piece of work. 'If so desired', indeed! Also, we are told that all gunshot wounds are classed as 'serious'.

We went down through the rain to the post office together and sent him a cable for 7/3* sending our love and hopes. If only he is alive to get it!

We are chasing the enemy in a great rout. Thus: 'The Axis forces in the Western Desert, after twelve days and nights of ceaseless attacks by our land and air forces, are now in full retreat.'†

'This, Mrs Miles,' says Mr Brook, our tenant, kneeling over an old oil stove and tinkering at it, 'This is the turning of the tide.'

Saturday, 7 November

Very glorious news. American troops have landed at Algiers, Oran, Saafi, Casablanca. And Montgomery is pressing on. Truly this *is* the turning point.

I did not see any flags hanging out, on gazing at the roof-tops of Shere out of my window. We have had such a trouncing we can hardly believe in success.

*

* Seven shillings and three pence: about £17.50 today.

† This was Montgomery's famous victory of El Alamein, of which Churchill said: '... this is not the end. It is not even the beginning of the end. But it is, perhaps, the end of the beginning.'

Later: To Mrs Rayne's to tea at Pond Farm. I read an account of how her brave son perished when the *Clan Campbell* was torpedoed off Malta.

Wilfred was busy helping to launch the boats till the very end; he was in charge of the troops and did his full duty. 'We were like lovers,' said his mother sadly, as we came back over the autumn bracken. 'We liked all the same things. His idea was to settle down on the farm: what is the use of it all now?'

Miss Perham is going by and by to Abyssinia, on a hush-hush job.

Later: A policeman called to bring us a War Office wire to say Basil was dangerously ill. October 29th. Very much shocked. Robin took a determined optimistic view, basing it on the cheery wire Basil himself sent, on which is the date October 30th. I do intensely desire not to give way to tears: but to keep quiet.

Wednesday, 11 November

No news.

Thursday, 12 November

At 5.30 this afternoon Joy rang up from the BBC to say that Otto had sent on a cable from Basil to say – November 4th – 'Health improving. Please don't worry.'

It was like passing from night into day. I cannot write much about this.

Friday, 13 November

Very much exhausted. The news goes on being excellent. Resumed work at the kitchen.

Sunday, 15 November

This journal is extremely desultory these days, as one is thinking half the time of Basil, and much is left out.

Robin was against the ringing of the bells for the Victory of Egypt, but I tried to convince him that it was lovely. And they rang out, sweet and clear, at 10.30. I went to church, and we sang 'Now Thank We All Our God' and 'Praise, My Soul' with great gentleness and timidity. There was no swagger or arrogance: it was evident that everybody was conscious of how long a way we had to travel before real victory comes.

Monday, 16 November

Philip Jordan, the war correspondent, is in Rangoon. He says it is a terrible doomed city. 'Such is Rangoon today: streets of great and unnatural peace and full of unnatural horror: a lily festering in sunlight. The abiding memory will always be of great bravery against great odds.'

Violets are sixpence a flower now, but there was sunshine today and our brave irises are coming up in the garden.

Rosamond came to tea, with a tiny basket containing a tiny bottle half full of milk. Luckily I had not to accept it. Her milkman gives her a much smaller milk ration than we get.

Robin is sitting making a fresh set of tickets for the communal kitchen. Bits of cardboard elegantly marked with figures are all round him on the old hearthrug.

A week ago the telegram about Basil being on the danger list arrived, and froze our hearts. We are hanging on to the hope of a letter with better news from the authorities this week.

Tuesday, 17 November

Still no more about Basil.

May Sinclair writes: 'My niece Didi, a Wren officer, is now at Gibraltar. Popsy says her daughter's tropical kit is charming. White pique dresses, with naval buttons very well cut. Didi is loving Gib., and every week the Wren officers have to dine at Government House. What a charming scene it must be!'

'Petronelle says the American troops have such good manners. After their Halloween party at Oxford, to which were invited American and British troops, the American CO wrote the very next day on behalf of his men to thank them, saying that his men had decided that the Wrens were the most beautiful and charming girls they had met in England.

'Our British Intelligence Corps also wrote a week afterwards to say thank you, but the Air Force did not see fit to do so.'

A great victory has taken place in the Solomons, the Americans smashing the Japs.*

Wednesday, 18 November

Greatly delighted by the news that Major Mavor cables from Cairo, that Basil's improvement is satisfactory. I can hardly force myself to believe it.

We keep on thinking about the great Battle of Egypt – for

* The Naval Battle of Guadalcanal, which took place over four days from 12–15 November.

ever specially important to us because Basil was there. I quote this from today's paper:

'It is possible now to get a fairly clear picture of the Allied Commander's tactics. It looks simple on paper. An enormous number of guns pelted the enemy and his guns; the Air Force blasted more of the enemy's guns and his supply lines; the infantry went in and cleared up what was left.'

Thursday, 19 November

It is beginning to dawn on us that the War Office does not mean to send us anything more about Basil but tranquilly leaves him as 'dangerously ill. Oct. 29th.'

I am writing a letter of one sentence to *The Times* suggesting that mothers should be employed at Casualty offices.

Dr Johnson said the great point of keeping a journal was to describe one's state of mind. Here goes, then:

I am restless, and not entirely happy about Basil. I want so much to know where he is, to have a line from him. This shadow makes me stupid and vague.

Friday, 20 November

The War Office writes that they cannot tell me where No. 19 General Hospital is, but it is not either at Cairo or Alexandria (I had said in my letter that we had friends at both places).

Saturday, 21 November

Robin is very cross about the news that men of the Observer Corps over fifty are to be retired. All through the morning, he came to and fro saying, 'I only wish I could write a play, and show how absurd it is.'

So ends another painful week. We hope to have more news by next Saturday of Basil in his Egyptian dwelling.

Sunday, 22 November

Here is the story of a drastic punishment:

'An Aldershot court martial has sentenced Driver Peter Singleton, aged 28, of the Royal Army Service Corps, to two years imprisonment with hard labour for spreading reports calculated to create unnecessary despondency, and for absence without leave.

'Witnesses at the trial stated that Singleton visited a Service canteen at Darlington on October 6, and said in the hearing of two voluntary women helpers, "The British will never drive Rommel out of Egypt, as our equipment is inferior. There is no British general to compare with Rommel."

'Singleton told the court he had been drinking, and did not remember having any conversation.'

We are listening spellbound to a German singing, on the wireless, a heavenly song.

Tuesday, 24 November

In the evening I read W. J. Brown's *I Meet America*. I skipped most of the tiresome politics, but extracted some honey.

Coming home, after incredible delays by sea, Brown was rather nervous, but he says he argued this way:

(1) The Convoy will either be attacked or it won't.
(2) If it isn't, there's no need to worry.

(3) If it is, it will either sink or it won't.
(4) If it doesn't, there's no need to worry.
(5) If it does, we shall either be picked up or we shan't.
(6) If we are, there's no need to worry.
(7) If we're not, well, after a few hours in this arctic cold, we shall go to sleep, and all worry about this life will be over anyway.

Wednesday, 25 November

Electrified with joy to get an airgraph from Basil this morning written Nov. 7 from his hospital, which he says is in the Canal Zone. He rather thinks that he will be sent to South Africa to convalesce.

The Russians are doing marvellously.*

Friday, 27 November

News continues to be excellent. Am wondering if Basil is up yet.

Saturday, 28 November

May Sinclair arrived just when I was feeling like death, with a most horrible cold. I thought my dearest old friend looked very tired indeed, but Robin saw no difference. She can now leave her desk at Bush House about 7 to 7.30 p.m.

* After three months' tenacious defence of Stalingrad, on 19 November the Russians launched a counter-offensive which cut off the invading forces outside the city, giving the defenders the upper hand for the first time since the battle began at the end of August. For the next three months the now beleaguered German Army, unable to be supplied by land or air, slowly starved through the depths of the Russian winter.

She has been talking to one Sandberg of Orange Radio who is at present broadcasting in the Dutch section. He is a nice little man, she says.

Sandberg is Head of the Socialist Party in Holland (but has always directed it from Paris). He told May that Holland was riddled by Fifth Columnists.*

His own father was an important man and a keen Nazi, before the Huns arrived. Then the father had been given a good job, and naturally enough all the Dutch Nazis have been well looked after by the Germans.

He pulled out a letter and showed it to May. 'This has just come,' he cried, 'from my father. In it he begs me to bury our differences. "I have a tolerance for your creed and you should have a tolerance for mine."

'But that is impossible, and I am unable to answer this letter,' he concluded.

Wednesday, 2 December

Nine women gathered together in my library to hear Mrs Lutyens speak on 'Women in Industry'. Three of the five married ladies had lost sons in the war.

Naomi Lutyens,† slim and fair in blue, sat on a tiny chair in front of a big log fire, and gave us some of her experiences in factories in the north.

All is by no means well with the women in industry.

* Despite the strength of Dutch anti-Nazi feeling, the number of active Dutch Nazi Party members was quite substantial.

† Naomi Lutyens was the daugher of Henry Devenish Harben, a noted philanthropist and supporter of the women's suffrage movement. This corner of Surrey was home to several generations of the Lutyens family, the best known of whom was the architect Sir Edwin Lutyens.

Factories vary very much. Some are airy and modern and convenient. Many are old and gloomy and inconvenient.

Night shifts should last more than a fortnight at a time. Like hospital nurses, the women should be allowed time to settle in to night work. She told us she felt terrible about four o'clock in the morning, and a girl next to her machine turned to her at that ghastly hour and said, 'Eh, luv, I feel like ten men, and all of them dead.'

A twelve-hour day is being worked by women in many factories up and down the land.

In spite of the representations of the British Medical Association.

In spite of the findings of tried psychologists, who tell us that people work better with reasonable hours.

We all, I think, felt shocked and sorry.

'And the workers,' she continued, 'have no faith in the future. They just don't believe they will get work after the war or that anything will be done about it.'

Later: the Beveridge Plan* is today published with the unintentionally misleading title, 'Two pounds a week for all.' It is to be nothing of the sort. One pound to the man, one to the wife. After many years!

Mussolini has just reproached Churchill ('drunk with tobacco and alcohol') for calling him, in 'an ungentlemanlike way', a hyena.

Musso then proceeded to say that Roosevelt was a hyena!

* The economist and social policy reformer Sir William Beveridge chaired the Interdepartmental Committee on Social Insurance and Allied Services. Their findings came to be known as the Beveridge Report, and formed the basis of the post-war Welfare State.

Friday, 4 December

Nothing more from Basil. Mr Struben cables from Pretoria that he cannot locate No. 19 General Hospital.

Field Marshal Mannerheim* today informed the International Red Cross that 20,000 Russian prisoners of war have died of starvation in Finland.

What a world! How can we sleep, laugh, dream, go out and eat? Twenty thousand men feeling worse and worse.

Saturday, 5 December

About seven o'clock the phone rang. A girl said that she had an important wire for Major Miles and wished to give it to him personally, 'For it's important, you see.'

I said faintly, 'Is it bad news?' and she replied, 'No, I don't think so.'

Robin came to the phone and the wire was about Basil. He has been taken off the dangerously ill list, and put onto the seriously ill list.

So the iron silence has been broken, thank God. I had hoped for even better news. I had been feeling very sad and rather frightened before it came, about the possible consequences and length of the war. We went to bed comforted and thankful.

Sunday, 6 December

Fine weather. Robin contending with difficult and elusive Home Guard. He looks very fair and Saxon in colouring in his

* Carl Gustav Emil Mannerheim, Commander in Chief of the Finnish Defence Forces during the war, and President of Finland from 1944–6.

little forage cap and khaki battle-dress (which he thinks most clumsily designed).

Monday, 7 December

Discouraged rather by a letter from the Matron of Basil's hospital who writes on 11 November, a grave and guarded letter. It seems he has bouts of pain over the hepatic region, and fluid is drawn off his chest when necessary. Poor Basil. Thank God we have the War Office wire about 30 November.

Both at the little village post office and in the large post office in Guildford today, women were eagerly buying letter-cards just issued for writing to the troops. I got one and wrote it to Basil, wrote an airgraph to the Matron, and also framed a cable to Mrs Dell on Nantucket Island about Basil.

Mother sent a really glorious gift of suet and Mrs Rapson is going to make me a Christmas pudding, and I have given her a little tot of rum to put in it.

Again, the sense that it's to be a very long war comes over me; we seem to be hung up in Tunis, awaiting reinforcements. Peter Andrews must be there – may he be kept safe!

Sir William Beveridge has been making a speech in Oxford, and says this very significant thing: 'I simply will not believe it is impossible to abolish mass unemployment, but I do not know how it is to be done, and I do not know whether anybody else knows.'

Thursday, 10 December

The 1942 Red Cross Jewel Sale at Christie's included a diamond brooch given by Viscountess Swinton which realised

£680. From the Canadian Red Cross last week we got among other gifts 44 quilts and 3,012 lbs of jam.

The papers make sad reading. Young Belgian children are sick, listless and dying through hunger.

It was quite dark when I got up, and threw back the household curtains and turned on the light. I was rebuked for this at the kitchen by one of the Russians,* and must tidy the flat henceforth in the dark, and I shall miss watching the dawn.

Had a letter-card from Basil this morning dated 12 November, explaining that his wound had taken a turn for the worse, that the fluid on his chest was infected, and that it would be many months before he was well. Would I be patient?

However, I think the operation, two days after he wrote must have relieved his condition very much, and I hang on to the fact that the very latest news is that he is *off* the danger list as of 30 November.

Saturday, 12 December

A very glorious day of happiness. About seven o'clock this evening came a wire from the War Office. Basil, to put it briefly, is off the seriously ill list as of 6 December.

My heart is too full to comment on this.

Then a greetings wire awaited us when we came in from tea at the Theobalds, to say Eudo was a prisoner of war at Singapore. Thank God! After all his mother's desperate fears! Also in the wire came the news that John has a son; Michael Andrews has arrived safely.

Shall slumber soundly tonight.

* Presumably one of the garage hands in their boiler suits, whom Connie describes earlier as looking like Russians.

Monday, 14 December

Rommel has not given battle, it seems; that is tonight's news.

Audrey says on the telephone that her sister's three sons are flying (all the family), and though the mother 'quakes when they are away, when they are home they laugh about it all, and I feel there is no danger'.

'Very gallant, these boys,' was their aunt's comment. 'They know perfectly well what the risks are.'

Later: Rommel seems to be hurrying away from us. Good.

Thursday, 17 December

Perfectly glorious news this evening at six o'clock. Our Eighth Army has cut the Afrika Korps in two. Germans are not being told the truth.*

I wish Basil could have shared in all this victorious advance. I daresay the Scots Greys are fully in it.

Yesterday the Huns machine-gunned the Girls' High School in Guildford, but the pupils were not in the classrooms. They also machine-gunned a train at Bramley; two were killed, and twenty were taken to hospital. And one house was demolished on Bramley Common. 'All their pictures and belongings are lying on the grass this morning.'

Splendid news came by post today. The Matron of 19 General Hospital wrote that Basil was getting up for a little time every day now.

* The remnants of the Afrika Korps had retreated to the town El Agheila, from which they withdrew on 17 December.

Friday, 18 December

I go to Weymouth Mews to lunch in May Sinclair's beautiful, brightly-gleaming little flat. All is lightness, light rugs, light walls, cream painted chairs with elegant flowers, light round dinner table.

John talks a little about his work at the Ministry of Supply. He is liaison officer for the BBC to that Ministry. He is arranging for ten broadcast programmes suitable for broadcasts in America about our British war effort. He has £50 to spend on each. He says they will be recorded on gramophone discs and sent over to the States. It is not easy to get the right scripts.

Wednesday, 23 December

Robin has begun *War in the Sun* by J. L. Hodson. Here are some extracts:

> A major on a sinking ship said to a sergeant, 'Can you swim?' He said 'Yes'. The major went on, 'I can't. My wife's going to be peeved,' and he waded into the sea and went straight down.

> A South African soldier has written home: 'Dear Mother, they say there are 200 miles of desert. About 100 miles of it blew past me today, and we expect the other 100 miles of it tomorrow.'

> In a destroyer on the way to Tobruk, an air raid was developing. Just then a neighbouring destroyer winked a message, and they were all agog to know what it was. Had she spotted

a submarine or something? The signaller read out the message: '"Salt-caked smoke stacks" – is it Kipling or Masefield?'[*]

Later: an amazing sight. We heard the buzz and hum and thunder of passing planes, so rushed out. It was about two o'clock, and the sun shone brightly in a pale blue December sky. High, high up there was a flock of planes – Flying Fortresses leaving behind them a skein of white cloud looping round the sky. In another direction came a second lot, tiny in the height of the blue dome. There seemed to be an enormous number of them. One could not help being thrilled to think that human beings so master the elements.

What must it feel like to soar so far away from earth?

Christmas Day

Out in the dark to go to Early Service holding Robin's torch and stumbling on the stony lane under a dark sky. Very dark also in church, and the candles not lit; many forms could be seen outlined in the dusk and a few torches were shining over hymn books. Mr Isherwood improvised beautifully: 'While Shepherds Watch' while we flocked up to the altar, and the light came at last flickering through the glass.

Came back and heard that Darlan had been assassinated.[†]

Dinner at Towerhill Manor. A turkey, red and silver table decorations, crackers, a pudding on fire and licked for a long time by a blue flame and brandy butter. Our host observed

* The line is from 'Cargoes' by John Masefield.

† Admiral Francois Darlan, Commander of the Vichy French Forces and deputy leader of the Vichy government from February 1941 until April 1942. On 24 December Darlan was assassinated by a member of the French Resistance in Algiers.

Lord Woolton's request, and made a little grave speech of thanks for the Merchant Service, ere we sat down.*

Joy looked very pretty and fragile in a pale blue frock, and the three men wore dinner jackets, including Otto, the brave, once-interned Austrian authority on Byzantine Art.

Sunday, 27 December

Otto at tea said he decidedly preferred to live in England rather than any other land, even America, if he could not be in his native Austria, 'because you are so quiet and restful and one feels so safe in England, and nobody beguiles you into conversation in a train as they always do in Austria, where they talk all the way and tell you their excitable life-stories.'

Wednesday, 30 December

Gentle Sara says in her letter: 'I gave thanks on Xmas morning for the murder of Darlan.'

Thursday, 31 December

So the year dies! Basil seems to be going on well, but has lost two stones and is very weak. But alive! How thankful we are can't be expressed.

The Russian news is fine. Robin and I feel soberly hopeful. We think peace may come in 1944.

* The Merchant Navy kept Britain supplied at a heavy cost in ships and men. By the end of the war some 4,700 British-flagged merchant vessels had been sunk, and 30,000 merchant seamen lost their lives.

1943

Monday, 4 January

The local paper is full of accounts of village and town parties. In spite of war, in spite of great difficulty in obtaining Xmas trees, toys, decorations, cakes of any kind; it all goes to show that England remains stubbornly England.

Am listening to some German jazz, beautifully played. No news from Basil. I wrote and thanked his specialist today for his care of him.

Very cold. Robin wears three vests and three pairs of socks, and Mr Brook wears a terra-cotta smoking cap such as I used to embroider for J. M. Barrie as a little girl of twelve or so.*

Most interesting today to read the description of those in the News Year's Honours List. For example, taken at random from the long columns of awards we have:

T. D. Dunn, quarry foreman
C. Edgecombe, electrical fitter
A. V. Evans, chief butcher
E. Chadwick, boatswain

* The author of *Peter Pan* had been a friend of the Nicoll family during Connie's childhood.

A. S. Cromarty, skilled workman
Miss E. Cox, greaser
J. Craig, lamp trimmer and AB Merchant Navy

Wednesday, 6 January

Our feelings are mixed. Sometimes at this stage of the conflict (though I have heard twice the joyous news of the Russian advance pealing through the house today), one is overwhelmed by the thought of all the suffering to come, when armies are locked together in Europe, and also overshadowed by the terrible feeling that peace may not come in one's lifetime. I'm sixty-one, you see, and Robin sixty-five next month.

Friday, 8 January

Basil has seen his Field Medical Card. As he is a doctor, they allowed it.

He says, directly after he was wounded, he suffered from shock. He had no pulse. He was put on the front of a tank and rushed to the Regimental Aid Post of the Rifle Brigade where transfusion took place. He had four pints of blood given to him. I fancy this saved his life. All the arrangements for evacuation to base hospital, were, he says, excellent. (This is good to hear.)

From Sibyl's letter on the Italian prisoners down at New Milton at mass. 'They sang marvellously on Sunday, so harmoniously. At the end they all trooped up to kneel at the crib in a side chapel which was lit up. From where I sat it would have made a perfect picture: forty or fifty of them in brown, kneeling. They all have very well-oiled black hair, and are nearly all very handsome, fine-looking men, and the lighting showed up their colouring. They seem most cheery, and the woods resound with axes and hammers and song.

From Muriel's letter of Eudo, being with the other prisoners in Jap hands, short of food: 'Oh, how much better to have died fighting! Diptheria and dysentery rage. I expect they have bad water to drink.'

Later: An agitated talk with Rosamond over the events of yesterday: the arrival of over 100 Canadian soldiers to billet in our Village Hall, while the Women's Institute party was going on. Instead of abandoning the party instantly, the WI actually sent out to ask if they might keep the hall as arranged till 7.30. No. But instead of welcoming in the soldiers who had come overseas to fight for us, the women apparently lingered on and had their tea and the soldiers who were shoved into the school (some sat on the icy surface of the playground) did not get in till 5.30.

I should have thought the members would have loved to be hostesses. As it was, they did leave some of the cakes for the men. Robin visited the troops today and they were cooking stew merrily.

Did my accounts, and found them very unhealthy. Expenses are quite heavy, and dividends shrink.

Sunday, 10 January

To church. Astonished to hear the name of Basil Miles, seriously wounded, prayed for. Thanked the Rector coming out. The more prayer the better.

Thursday, 14 January

Grace rang in the afternoon, and asked me if I had a copy of *The Times* of yesterday, in which there was a memoir of her cousin, one Fison, RAF, who had just been killed.

She said she had gone to his funeral yesterday at Seaford. She was very sad. He apparently was a very fine man of forty-seven who leaves a widow and two little girls.

Friday, 15 January

Went to Guildford. A caretaker on the bus with me was distressed that the village school has no black-out, and the soldiers who are sleeping there must not, consequently, even light a fire, though they bring their own coal.

In the evening Robin fetched in one of these Canadians, whom he met wandering in the square. A nice fair-haired modest young miner, from a place called Donkin, Nova Scotia. His regiment is The Cape Breton Highlanders; his father was a Fergusson, his mother is a MacDonald: both lived on the isle of Lewis, and he is hoping to get enough leave to go and see their island.

He appreciated a warm bath and a drink (cider) and a smoke. I offered to write to his mother and tell her he was well and bright (certainly he was enjoying soldiering).

He accepted eagerly, and put down her address, printing it very slowly, so today I've written to Mrs Minnie Fergusson, Cape Breton Island.

Later, by the fire, the phone rang, and I was much upset to hear a cable: 'Second operation yesterday, tenth January, too early to say how successful.' Had a disturbed night. We had imagined Basil quite out of the woods.

Sunday, 17 January

About 8.40 there came a noise of guns. Some planes tore past our windows at a great speed. Remembering we had bombed Berlin the night before, I said to Robin, 'Where are they off to tonight?' But it soon became clear that it was the Hun, as bombs began to explode. We went down, and Robin went out into the bright, moonlit garden: shrapnel was falling.

The planes, it appeared, came back about five o'clock, but we did not wake.

Our Eighth Army has advanced again. Bravo, Montgomery!

Monday, 18 January

We hear the terrific news that the siege of Leningrad* is raised.

Tuesday, 19 January

A kind cable in from Harry saying he had heard that Basil's convalescence would not take place for some time. I felt very nervous listening at the phone, and at first believed it was from Basil himself.

The BBC is just telling us that the cheese ration is to be reduced to four ounces.

Ethel Rayne had been to London yesterday, and heard that the Sunday raid was mostly at Peckham (where a big store was cut in half) and Tooting. On the raid to Berlin, the air crews

* Begun on 8 September 1941, in fact the siege was not finally ended until 27 January, 1944. Lasting 872 days, it was among the longest sieges in history. The news that Connie refers to was that the Russians succeeded in opening a land corridor on 18 January 1943, breaking the blockade for the first time and enabling some supplies to reach the city.

sang coming home. The girls of the Ack-Ack gun crew sang, also, as they took part in the defence of London during the raid.

South London suffered substantial bomb damage.
This wrecked bus in a crater where the road once ran is in Balham.
Photograph © IWM HU36188

Thursday, 21 January

Our sub-tenant below is incensed because Mr Isherwood has called to inform him that in case of invasion, his flat will be requisitioned by the Home Guard, so that he must make arrangements to take his wife (a stout, helpless invalid) elsewhere.

I ring up Mr Isherwood later, and ask if I shall inform Madge the tenant in Aberdeen.

He says airily I must please myself and it is no good for Mr Brook to be angry with him, 'as I didn't start the war'.

Nothing more from Basil. Very trying.

There is a rumour flying round the village much concerned with the children killed at a school near London – the latest casualty figures are: killed forty-five, injured and detained in hospital fifty; fifteen children still feared buried in the wreckage.

Mr Reginald Armour, Managing Director of Walt Disney films in Hollywood, has arrived at the Savoy Hotel, London, to investigate the Gremlin.

Mr Armour has only got hold of a few facts as yet: 'Gremlins are about six inches high, they wear red and green and can ride on aeroplane wings even in the roughest weather.' Of course the plot of a film which will make many people's fortunes will be the impish Gremlins playing naughty tricks at first, but rallying round when the RAF is in trouble.*

Friday, 22 January

No news from Basil or Harry. Mrs Hall tells me that the school bombed just lately was at Catford. The papers are full of pictures of helpers digging feverishly away. It must have been dreadful.†

* Connie adds two handwritten notes, one explaining that the gremlin is 'an RAF imp of mischief'; the other, written in 1947, saying that the film had not yet materialised.

† Thirty-eight pupils and six staff members were killed on 20 January when a Luftwaffe pilot released a bomb at close quarters on Sandford Road School, Catford.

Saturday, 23 January

Still no news of Basil or Harry. I am always so sad when I examine the envelopes thrown in at the front door.

Later: At lunch-time today with the sunshine streaming in at the open window the glad news has come at last – Tripoli has fallen!

Monday, 25 January

Shocked to hear that dear John Andrews has crashed and been killed in his Halifax.

'Bad news, sir,' said Mr Ponsford again at the door with the yellow envelope. Luckily for me Robin received it, as I was on the phone.

I can't begin to write of John, tall, clear-eyed, broad-shouldered, devoted to country life, connoisseur of butterflies. He was flying, curiously enough, in the New Forest, near Picket Post, the school he hoped after the war to take over.

Thank God he saw his baby. The poor young mother, and his own poor devoted mother. I was sad all day.

Tuesday, 26 January

Have heard nothing of the funeral arrangements for John. I suppose I ought to go down. I dread it very much.

Nothing from Basil.

Nothing from Harry.

Stayed in, and let Robin go to the canteen lunch, as I wanted to be near the phone. It did not ring.

Wednesday, 3 February

No wire about the date and place of John Andrews' funeral. In any case I decide not to leave, as I am not satisfied at all about Basil's condition.

Wednesday, 17 February

I have been in bed a wretched fortnight with tonsilitis and a bad reaction to M and B,* which made me feel as ill as I have ever been. Thank God a reassuring cable 'Much improved' came at last from Basil. It had been held up seventeen days (the last cable took three!). No wonder I thought the operation had been a failure, as there was this long silence.

Dr Lankster told me my heart was going far too fast, and he was going to give me digitalis.

While I have been in bed, the Russians have taken Rostov and Kharkov.†

Thursday, 18 February

So February goes by, and I feel better and the lines under my eyes are not so black, and I have crumpled up the cables I have just found in my pocket on dressing again, saying that 'John has crashed and been killed'.

* M&B 693 (Sulphapryidine) was an early sulphonamide antibiotic and the first effective treatment for pneumonia. Produced by May & Baker in 1938, it was also used extensively to prevent gangrene and septicaemia throughout the Second World War.

† Connie also missed recording the German defeat at Stalingrad, which, even more so than El Alamein, turned the tide of the war. On 2 February, the day before she fell ill, the Axis forces under General Paulus surrendered, in contravention of Hitler's order that they should fight on to the last. The German 6th Army had been almost completely destroyed.

The House of Commons seems to have behaved very absurdly indeed over the Beveridge Report. Labour member after Labour member demanding it in full, and having no sympathy for fat, true, tedious Kingsley Wood when he said we really must examine our finances to see what we could do, and also that that was hard, as we did not know how much more the war would cost us.

Nobody grasps how magnificent these proposals are – they actually mean to tackle the medical profession about universal free medical service. This point alone is worth many columns in our press, but is ignored entirely.

Saturday, 20 February

'According to returns compiled by Ley's German Labour Front and by the great insurance companies, the total losses of the German Armed Forces up to December 31, 1942, in killed, permanently disabled, and prisoners, amounted to about 4,800,000. To this figure must be added the losses suffered during January, including those at Stalingrad, which were about 600,000 or 700,000.

How terrible it is for any woman to read this!

There was a dreadful tragedy at Farnham last week. At a Home Guard meeting in the Drill Hall, a demonstration of loading a trench mortar was being given. A dummy bomb was being used, but the fact that there was a live cartridge in the mortar was overlooked. A sergeant pulled the trigger to explain to his class how it worked, and the bomb shot straight out, and killed the Manager of Lloyds Bank. He was such a nice man and universally popular. Everyone was feeling very shocked and sad.

Wednesday, 24 February

Out again, thank goodness, after a weary month indoors.

The twins are learning to plough.

Tuesday, 2 March

Have been too tired and occupied to write. Today, to our enormous relief, Basil writes (17 February) that he really is very much better, and hopeful of being sent to Pietermaritzburg or Johannesburg; he hopes the latter. We are to write care of Harry for a time. He will cable when he arrives. What bliss if he really does get away this month. I feel so happy, nothing else seems to matter.

Robin is gazing at the map of South Africa, seeing where Johannesburg and Pietermartizburg are. Two tiny pies from the Co-op are rapidly being heated in the oven for dinner, supported by heraldic leeks, and tiny potatoes in brown skins.

The Home Guard has tiresomely requisitioned our two garages and apple loft, after many weeks of dithering.

Friday, 5 March

To the communal kitchen. Miss B. back from town very mysterious about the shocking tube disaster in London. She knew quite well where it took place, but would not say.*

A much more normal letter from Basil, all impatient to get a boat: 'It may be two days or may be six weeks'.

Robin is convinced that there will be a big push very soon.

* On 3 March 173 people were crushed to death on the stairs leading down into Bethnal Green tube station when two people fell and the crowd packing in to the shelter fell over them. It was the worst single wartime civilian disaster in Britain.

Saturday, 6 March

Into Guildford after many, many weeks.

I made friends in the bus with a teacher in the East End of London. She informed me that it was at Bethnal Green, the tube acccident. (I knew I should hear by today: why withhold it?)

She said she lived near Elstree, and had to come in to work by tube, and was quite terrified in the dark winter mornings very often, of the crowds plunging down the very ill-lit staircases, barging together with suitcases and bundles. She perfectly understood what had happened on those steps in the darkness with the awesome barrage of London thundering outside. 'If anyone called "Hold back!" you couldn't have heard, you see.'

Monday, 8 March

Last night Mr Brook banged on the bedroom door and said, 'There are bombs falling!'

Today we hear this was at Haslemere.

I rang up Kitty Eustace and found she was staying in a different part of Haslemere, with her daughter, Betsy, who has two little children, Rosamond and Mary Rose, five and three.

In order not to frighten the children, Betsy woke them and told them that guns were firing and planes flying about on practice, and that they must practice by hiding under the dining-room table; and perhaps Grandpa, who, poor man, is a warden, might call with a prize.

Presently, (really this is a rather a nice story – and perfectly true) the local warden – they were not in Grandpa's beat – called out, 'Are you all right, Mrs Ferguson?' Betsy, who is quick as lightning, replied, 'Oh do come in,' and rapidly confided in him what she was doing – she knows him.

In comes the warden in his tin hat, while outside the banging and muttering of guns continued; he peeps under the table, sees the two beaming fairies, and says, 'Very good, you are practising very well indeed, and the prize will come tomorrow morning.' (He had apologised for having nothing on him, for the little girls, in the hall.)

The children went off to bed highly pleased, and not a bit alarmed.

And next day, two fresh eggs, each wrapped in red paper arrived, for Miss Ferguson and Miss Mary Rose Ferguson as prizes for good practice!

Kitty, who is brave as a lion, confessed that she was nervous and had determined if a bomb came on the cottage that she 'would throw herself on the babies'. An acquaintance of hers, an ATS, aged forty, sole support of her aged Lancashire parents, not very happily placed in Haslemere, was out with an ambulance and was killed. What will the poor parents do, they are quite old and can't do their own housework.

I hear Exmouth has had a very bad raid again; also Cockington and Torquay. The restaurant in Exmouth where the Brooks used to have lunch has gone, also the newspaper shop. Bit by bit the Hun is ruining the coast towns of England.

Wednesday, 10 March

Met poor Kitty B., who for the first time gave way to tears over the fact that she had not yet heard whether her husband was prisoner of war or not in Singapore. 'And fancy the Japs sending through all the names of the British *officer* prisoners first! Just as if they wanted to upset the lower deck!'

Robin met a mechanic here today who talked about the Beveridge Report. 'We *must* have it: or there will be a revolution in this country.' Robin mildly said that life in this country after the war will not be Paradise. 'Oh, it must be Paradise,' was the rejoinder.

I do pray that our leading statesmen may not promise the people all sorts of impossible things after the war.

Monday, 22 March

I have got hopelessly behind with the journal, but I have had perpetual callers. Our thoughts are very much with General Montgomery and the Eighth Army which, as Churchill told us at the end of his speech last night, has begun the battle.*

To Guildford, where Robin and I underwent the severe ordeal of the Lyons lunch, 'What do I do now?' resounding plaintively in my ears. I noticed that the habituées walked along shoving the heavy trays along the slipway easily and giving their orders to the manner born.†

Then to *Desert Victory*, a most wonderful, skilful rendering of the El Alamein battle. The preliminary bombardment, which our Basil must have shared with the Scots Greys, must have been a real inferno.

Even on the screen, with its very modified form of noises, I disliked looking at it. The waste of sand, the arid plains, the

* The battle for the Mareth Line, 20–27 March. The Mareth Line was a line of fortifications between the city of Gabés and the town of Medenine in Tunisia, originally built by the French before the war.

† It seems from Connie's account that Lyons, previously known for their waitresses, or 'Nippies', had introduced the self-service restaurant, a concept which clearly nonplussed Robin.

Guildford's cobbled High Street looks much the same as it does today, except that here the famous Guildhall clock has been taken down and in its place is the round plaque announcing 'Salute the Soldiers Week'.
Photograph © IWM D25183

now crouching, now rushing soldiery with their rifles, the huge tanks, the smoke and shells and planes and bombs, made one feel that it was hell. We saw the flash of the German guns' deadly aim – a splinter from one of them caught Basil in the right side and nearly ended his life. I would never go myself to such a film again, unless it was directly concerned with my son. I was very, very glad when the film was over.

Monday, 29 March

In the evening we heard the marvellous news that the Mareth Line had been breached. The whole nation is rejoicing. We were all dismayed to hear that we had lost the initial bridgehead gained; and hated to read of the rain which made the dreadful marsh more awful still for our sappers to cope with. It sucked under its black waters all the brushwood and girders thrown on it for hours while the sappers worked on in withering fire.

I am listening to the wireless, hearing how our patrols have entered Gabés. More good news. Robin is very pleased, and so am I.

I have just read in the *Evening Standard* that the Church of England is short of 1,000 parsons. 'There are too many already,' gloomily replies Robin.

Sunday, 4 April

Found a shady spot by the hedge and read again the first of the *Winter Tales* by Karen Blixen,* that were smuggled out of Denmark through the Red Cross. Why does she write in English? She does it beautifully. I love the first tale about the Lapp people, who travelled disguised as birds, often as falcons.

The war seems to be going a little faster. Montgomery is preparing for his next spring.

* Danish author who also wrote under the name Isak Dinesen, best known for her memoir *Out of Africa*.

It is said that a group of Japanese captured at some Pacific isle sang to their British captors the song 'Auld Lang Syne', bowing at the end. Could they really have learned this especially hard dialect song? If so, it is one of the funniest episodes of the war.

Joy came yesterday, looking very pale, and to my great delight she told me she had acquired an allotment with the friend who lives with her, and there they will toil at the weekends. Both girls are at the BBC, and Joy says she must now work every other Saturday as an ordinary day.

There is a huge amount of war work going on in Britain.

Monday, 5 April

From Rosemary, working in the great factory at Derby, about a friend of hers, very young, killed in the air: 'The plane crashed in Somerset after operations and all the crew were killed. The casualties in the RAF are very high, specially for air gunners, who aren't reckoned to last more than about eight flights.

'I am an analytical assistant in the research lab now. We analyse alum castings. The atmosphere is hot and stifling, the window doesn't open because of the dirt from the foundry, and there is usually a colossal row going on. We have to listen to 'Music While You Work' twice a day, till we are all browned off with it.'*

Poor Rose. How will she settle down after the war?

* *Music While You Work* was a radio programme broadcast for the first time in 1940 and devised specifically to make factory workers more productive in wartime by giving them light music to listen to. The show lasted until 1967, when the BBC Light Programme became BBC Radio 2.

Went to luncheon at the hall. A lady informed me that in a recent raid in Brighton, a young couple she knew were killed, but their baby who was out in the garden at the time was blown up into a tree and alive.

Basil asks if the war is not to be long? I fear it is: and all this long struggle to secure North Africa means that Europe will plunge into blacker chaos, while waiting to hear the sound of British boots coming along the roads.

Tuesday, 6 April

Audrey A. on the telephone told me that her nephew had been killed in the RAF.

Poor Clive. He apparently made what observers say was 'a perfect landing' in mid-Channel but the machine sank in the water and Clive never reappeared.

I asked Audrey whether her sister, Clive's mother, was coming south from Berwick to see her, but she answered no, that the affair had made the poor father ill and his wife, herself broken-hearted, is looking after him.

Wednesday, 7 April

Peter writes from Tunisia, 25 March: 'All my old friends are gone – Norman, Tony and Ronald were killed the other day . . . We are all in very good heart and our spirits rise every day. We have seen the Germans running and glad to be captured, and we have enjoyed it. The Surreys have accounted for many a German. They know their hour has come, they have seen the writing on the wall.'

Thursday, 8 April

What do Women's Institutes amuse themselves with these days? There had been a speaker on 'Stretching Your Rations', which meant literally pulling one's rashers of bacon so as to make them longer. Heaven knows what will have to be done with the rinds of bacon! They ought to work hard to flop in and out of soup. To hang in and out of basins, and to appear in the middle of suet puddings, etc.

Thankful I missed all this, as I have not the capacity.

The news is absolutely marvellous. Montgomery pressing on and the meeting of the Americans and ourselves accomplished at last.

Friday, 9 April

Into Guildford. Just as I was looking across at the entrance of the British Restaurant, suddenly a cloud of cyclists, obviously a club out on a spree, arrived at the door, rapidly dismounted, and streamed in.

The WVS were coping valiantly with scores and scores of customers. I was much struck by the number of helpers with snow-white hair: doctors' wives and the rest who were slaving away, clearing dirty trays and dishes, and serving out fine hot beef and potatoes and soup.

They go unthanked, I'm sure their old feet ache; their class is out of popularity altogether, but they do deserve gratitude. Such masses of large schoolboys, for instance, were eating the meal and getting enough for tenpence, or one shilling. Worth doing.

Saturday, 10 April

May Sinclair came for tea, like a great beam of sunshine. She says Evans and Lewis and other big shops are selling off old-fashioned stuff people have found pushed away on their cupboard shelves – and the public, mad to buy, go in to purchase. She was able to buy £100 worth of wooden trays for her shop by a miracle recently, 'and the seller kindly gave me a cup of coffee and some delicious jam tarts.'

Wednesday, 14 April

How thrilling the papers are! With what joy do the inhabitants of the Tunisian cities greet the British! Says one correspondent, 'The people of Kairouan were dancing for joy as I drove through the shimmering heat haze into the city yesterday morning.

'I saw the yellow Star of David which the Germans had forced the Jews to wear as soon as they occupied the city. They were told to take them off, and I saw dozens of the yellow stars being trampled in the streets as the Jews replaced them with V for Victory signs, which they improvised from anything they could find.'

Thursday, 15 April

Suddenly resolved, as I want to be out of doors a good deal this summer, to close the journal, at any rate for the moment. I simply hate to stay in and write it when the sun shines.

It closes when the Eighth Army is forging boldly on; as are the 1st Army and the Americans. Thus the curtain will go up on another and strange scene.

Editor's note: Thursday, 15 April 1943 is the last entry in the journal. In March, 1944, Connie added this typed comment to the final page:

The reason why I stopped writing was partly because there was so much that came my way (quiet though I am in a country village and cut off like all others from visiting London and my friends) that I thought my work would become too long and tiresome to wade through in time to come. I guess that I have done enough and said enough to show what war days were in 1939, 40, 41, 42, 43.

Connie in later years with her granddaughter Mary.
Photograph courtesy of Mary Wetherell

Postscript

Basil recovered fully from the injuries he received at El Alamein, and was posted to Italy, where he spent the remainder of the war. In Naples he met and married his wife, Sadie, who was working as a nurse. After the war he returned to St Thomas's Hospital to complete his medical training, and in 1954 he left London for the Welsh border country of Hereford and Radnor, where he embarked on a long and distinguished career as a consultant physician to the Hereford Group of Hospitals.

Harry remained in Rhodesia, where he joined the civil service. He and Jennie were later divorced.

Connie and Elystan lived in Shere until 1954, when they sold Springfield and moved to Herefordshire to be closer to Basil. Elystan died aged seventy-eight in 1956 and Connie six years later in 1962, aged eighty.

The War Diaries series, produced in association with Imperial War Museums, brings fascinating new perspectives to famous conflicts as experienced by ordinary people thrown into extraordinary circumstances. Read on for details of three further titles published by Simon and Schuster . . .

'An absorbingly good read'
Michael Hickey, author of *Gallipoli, A Study in Failure*

EDITED BY **GAVIN ROYNON**

A PRAYER FOR GALLIPOLI

THE GREAT WAR DIARIES OF CHAPLAIN KENNETH BEST

IN ASSOCIATION WITH IMPERIAL WAR MUSEUMS

A PRAYER FOR GALLIPOLI

The Great War Diaries of Chaplain Kenneth Best

Edited by Gavin Roynon

'Our poor boys behaved like heroes, but are sadly cut up. No clear orders . . .'

Padre Kenneth Best accompanied his troops into the maelstrom of Gallipoli to maintain morale, tend the wounded and bury the dead. As the toll of casualties mounted, Best became increasingly critical of the British Higher Command, few of whom shared his insight into the horrors of trench warfare. The gallantry and indomitable spirit of the men shines through the pages of these extraordinary diaries, and makes for a candid and compelling account of this notoriously flawed and tragic campaign.

ISBN 978-1-84983-367-7

Paperback £7.99

IN ASSOCIATION WITH IMPERIAL WAR MUSEUMS

A NURSE AT THE FRONT

The First World War Diaries of Sister Edith Appleton

FOREWORD BY MICHAEL MORPURGO, AUTHOR OF WAR HORSE

EDITED BY RUTH COWEN

A NURSE AT THE FRONT

The First World War Diaries of Sister Edith Appleton

Edited by Ruth Cowan

'Calm day yesterday. My ill boy is holding his own, but that is all. If there is a bit of lead near his heart, has he a chance?'

With limited resources and a shortage of trained staff, Edith Appleton worked tirelessly to care for convoys of wounded in France and Belgium throughout the First World War. Her diaries record with unflinching clarity the appalling injuries suffered by her patients, as well as their fortitude and courage. Surrounded by death, she never lost her enjoyment of life, writing vividly of small pleasures snatched from rare moments that helped her to keep going. Acutely observant, hers is an unparalleled account of nursing behind the lines in this most devastating of human conflicts.

ISBN 978-1-84983-366-0

Paperback £7.99

IN ASSOCIATION WITH IMPERIAL WAR MUSEUMS

D-DAY TO VICTORY

The Diaries of a British Tank Commander

SGT TREVOR GREENWOOD

Edited by S. V. Partington

D-DAY TO VICTORY

The Diaries of a British Tank Commander

Sgt Trevor Greenwood

Edited by S. V. Partington

'We are being fired at in the tanks . . . machine-gunned from the air, shelled by artillery, mortared, sniped at, machine-gunned by ground forces . . .'

Sergeant Trevor Greenwood of C Squadron, the 9th Royal Tank Regiment sailed for France in June 1944 as part of the Allied invasion of Normandy. From D-Day until April 1945, he kept a daily diary of the final push through France and into Germany, often writing in secret and in terrible conditions. Under fire, often outgunned and facing a bitter winter, he never loses his moral compass or his sense of humour. His astonishing diary has left us a unique record of the war in Europe from the rarely-seen perspective of an ordinary soldier.

ISBN 978-1-47111-068-9

Paperback £8.99